A Certain Kind of Love

The Flower

Listen to me and you will learn
There is much more for you to discern,
For while I'm a puzzle or maybe
A riddle
I'll play no second fiddle.
To those without hope or love in
their heart,
It is with their acquaintance
I must part.
For life is a test I can surely see,
And to those who can wait to
Understand me,
I give them hope that someday
I will in some way
Do all the things you do
Anyway
And once I give them what they need,
Some determination, hope, a tiny seed,
It will grow in their hearts
from a spiritual shower,
And someday that seed will
Become a flower.

By,
Anne Darling Grills
(With help from Dad)

Annie

This book is dedicated

to all who can rejoice and celebrate

in the sharing of their lives

with individuals living with special needs.

A Certain Kind of Love

E. Deborah Wright and Jean Joy Crowley

Versa Press
East Peoria, Illinois

A Certain Kind of Love

Copyright ©1999 by E. Deborah Wright and Jean Joy Crowley

ISBN 0-9673682-0-0
Versa Press; East Peoria, Illinois
Printed in the U.S.A.

A Certain Kind of Love

Contents

Special Acknowledgments

Robert Blumenthal

Carol Brough

Tim Cleary

Monica DiGangi

Alan Shawn Feinstein

Katherine Gibson

Beth Ann Girouard

Barrie Grossi

Mark Hawk

Mary Carol Kendzia

Diane Klotz

Wally Lamb

Carol and John Leach

David Osha

Robert and Ethel Perreault

Beth Pinto

Joanna Pulcini

Mary Quinn

Hamilton Salsich

Dan Smart

Kathy Stelik

Heather Lofkin Wright

Twenty-Third Publications

*and all of our friends and colleagues who gave us continued support
and encouragement during this project.*

Special Tributes

During the process of completing this book I was constantly aware that Jean and I were not in this alone. The idea for the book came to me as I awoke early one morning and from that moment on I have felt compelled to make sure this book would come to fruition.

Many earth angels helped me along the way. My husband, Charlie, gave enormous attention to our family—nurturing all of us, cooking, doing laundry, and being the taxi driver—during the moments, days, and months that this book needed my undivided attention. He always had my cup of tea ready for those late nights of typing, after my teaching day was done. I am so grateful for his constant, loving support. I was propelled by his belief in the beauty and importance of this book, along with the need to help others appreciate the precious souls of the children between its covers. Our own four children have added immeasurable joy to our lives. Our son, Matthew, truly a gift to us, keeps me young at heart, and I am thankful that he helped me see what really matters in life. Our three daughters, Heather, Julie, and Erin, grew into lovely, independent young women during this time. Julie's husband, Juan DelPrado, joined my support staff, along with Jeff Tucker. They all came to my aide in many ways including—editing, producing the web page, taking photographs, researching printers, and creating the layout for the book, along with providing daily e-mail support at just the time I needed fresh ideas, and strong shoulders to lean on. My parents, Bob and Ethel Perreault, always told me I could do anything if I worked hard enough and now I believe them. They taught me to value every life and to strive to make a difference, to which I hope I have found some success through *A Certain Kind of Love*. My very special mother-in-law, Helen Wright, had faith in the book from the very beginning and was always there to listen and give encouragement. My sisters, Lynette Walker and Christine Kenyon, along with my sister-in-law, Heidi Perreault, never tired of hearing about the book and always motivated me to continue the work. I could not have completed this book without the support of my extended family and friends—too many to mention here—but who hopefully know that I am forever grateful to each and every one of them for their kind words, faith, and endless encouragement.

Debbie Wright

Debbie Wright

Special Tributes

To daughter, **Joy:** for teaching me the true meaning of life and happiness through your love.

To my mother, **Jean**, who passed away before Joy's birth, And my father, **Dick**, who died when Joy was four: for opening my heart to love by giving me so much of their own.

To Joy's grandparents, **Helen** and **Maurice**: who have been the most constant contributors of love, guidance, and never-ending support throughout all of Joy's life and mine.

To Joy's dad, **Bob**: for the unconditional love given through good times and bad.

To daughter, **Deirdre**, and her husband, **Mike**: for their continued encouragement and support.

To son, **Jimmy**: for co-designing the cover and for making Joy laugh during the most adverse moments.

To daughter, **Amy**: for being my "best friend" forever.

To my husband, **Jim**: for believing in me when I didn't believe in myself.

Thanks to all of my **family** and **friends**: for enriching the life of our "special angel," Joy, by giving her your "certain kind of love."

Jean Joy Crowley

Introduction

As we travel through life it is probable that within our journey we experience some sort of love. Whether that love is shared with a parent, sibling, friend, mate, or child, it is certain. Our true stories enable you to share "a certain kind of love" first hand through the experiences and lessons that have challenged our families. You will feel the deep love, cry at the heartache, laugh with the children, and learn from the hard truths of living in the world of special needs.

At first, many of our families felt that the reality of raising a child with special needs would destroy their promises of tomorrow. The anger, sadness, fear, and disbelief had to be tempered through patience, perseverance, faith, courage, and unconditional love. The most powerful teachers in our stories are the children. The challenges, heartaches, pain, frustrations, and confusion caused by their special needs were the incentives that forged our writers into facing their responsibilities. The lessons learned have inspired these parents to open their minds and hearts to feel the joy and grow mentally, spiritually, and emotionally. There were times that our writers felt the challenge was theirs alone but there were also times when they had to face the fact that they needed help, be it through friends, family, professionals, or spiritual guidance. Reaching out is not saying, "I'm failing," it is just saying, "My hands are full and tired; I need help."

We have seen children who were born perfectly healthy begin to wither from being unwanted, neglected, or abused. The parents in our book nurture children who were born unhealthy. Through their love, devotion, and positive attitude, they encourage these children to be the very best they can be.

We hope you will learn from, feel the passion, and embrace these true stories. We encourage you to hear their voices and listen with your heart. We are certain that you will be touched. Perhaps your thoughts about how these children and families fit into our lives will change.

If you would like to have the wonderful opportunity to feel part of the life of an individual with special needs, this book is for you. It's just possible that after reading these precious stories you will rejoice and celebrate the experience of feeling *A Certain Kind of Love*.

Free to Go Home By Nancy Rao

Zachary and Eliza

date of birth:
Zachary—February 18, 1981
Eliza—March 26, 1984

Unlabeled Genetic Disorder

The morning that the phone rang and a voice on the other end was explaining to me the concept, desires, and ideas for this book, I felt strangely moved. I heard the words asking me if I would be interested in contributing to this project with my story, and I found myself biting my lips slightly so that I wouldn't begin to cry. Sometimes, even after eighteen years of being in this territory called special needs, I still find myself caught with unexpected emotion.

In retrospect, I believe my reaction was a mixture of being honored that my perspective and insights were being sought after in the first place, while simultaneously grieving that my life has unfolded in such a way that my circumstances would even allow me to fit into the framework of this book. I could imagine myself perusing a book such as this if I saw it on a bookstore shelf, but to open it up and actually see in black and white how your life fits neatly inside the parameters of special families is still somehow astounding.

It wasn't until my children were diagnosed that I realized I had never actually known or interacted with any challenged individuals. And, if I heard the "special" label, it seemed to be applied to the needs, or the individual, but not to the parents. I, someone "ordinary," was about to be faced with an "extraordinary" challenge. It was a sobering onset.

I felt like a seed that got carried on the wind and landed upon unfamiliar ground. Yet, although I knew nothing about special needs, I knew instinctively how to survive. Therefore, I wasted no time sending down my roots, only hoping that the wind that carried me was really the breath of God.

Initially, my new soil felt rocky, and lacking. It was as though I wanted to send myself out to Agway to get a pH test to see what this new ground needed. If only someone could just tell me what ingredients I should add to insure we all would thrive, then this endeavor would be doable. But instead, this foreign terrain seemed somewhat rough and taxing, without a green pasture to lay my head and give me respite. I knew early on I was not dealing with small potatoes, (as my father would say), and I had better rise to this challenge.

Sometimes I've thought of myself as a salient, low-probability mother of two. This situation was not always the case, but instead it unfolded with the passage of time. I describe myself like this because even though you may have to stop a minute and think of the implications of what the words salient and low-probability mean in relation to a mother, I have had enough experience from the looks on strangers faces to know it is an appropriate description.

When I am out and about with my children, we do not blend into the crowd like other moms and kids. It seems impossible not to draw attention to ourselves when we look like a March of Dimes poster that has sprung to life. A florescent pink wheelchair affords my daughter both independence as well as satisfaction, of her (at that time) ten-year-old craving for her favorite color. And, when we are feeling up to it, my

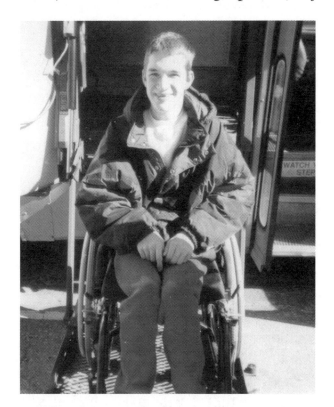

son will leave his green wheelchair at home and support himself with his shiny walker that rattles over terrain with a deafening noise that makes me want to reach for an aspirin bottle. These maladies that accompany our lives however, are not readily camouflaged while we maneuver around the town.

When we are on the go, our appearance will elicit and trigger emotional reactions, especially when we are in new territory. I've been offered words of advice, consolation, physical help, prayers, and even money to buy the kids something special. The most original response came from a little silver-haired lady when I was coming out of the movies with my children and their friend, who also used a walker and wore braces. She inquired "what home they were from" and told me "how good I was

to volunteer my time." I enjoyed a good laugh while considering her comment as I piled kids and wheelchairs into the van. But, other times, I've felt unsettled as I've seen looks of pity, witnessed wonder and amazement, and I believe, even waves of relief that what they are seeing has not happened to them. To this day, I am confident that my children have not registered this phenomenon, a small bonus that goes hand in hand with deficits in cognition.

All these reactions are nothing more than facts that accompany the reality of having two special needs children, coupled with the passage of time which allowed me to adjust to this phenomenon. My mothering career began eighteen years ago, with the birth of my son, and then again three years later, with the birth of my daughter.

We named our son Zachary, which means "God Remembered" and named our daughter Eliza, meaning "Consecrated One." Both of my children's names were already chosen before I came to know their meanings shortly after deciding upon them. Over the years, as the uniqueness of all of our lives unfolded, I found myself thinking a lot about the meanings, reflecting on the significance of what it means to be set apart and called sacred, as in Eliza's name, and in Zachary's case, have God remember. Sometimes, I would find myself wondering, apart from birthing and naming them, (which is obviously monumental) where, how, and why I actually fit into this lofty scenario. But for the grace of God... By the way, Grace, which means "a state of being protected by the favor of God," happens to be my middle name.

Zachary was born under a full moon during a February thaw, at our planned home birth, attended by a nurse midwife and our home birth doctor. It was a quiet, peaceful, uncomplicated delivery, (not to be confused with painless), after a seven hour labor. He passed his apgar scores with flying colors, began to nurse effortlessly, and was cradled in loving arms from the start. We began what I thought was the continuation of "and they lived happily ever after," which I realize now was a naïve but appropriate sentiment.

The first year was basically uneventful in terms of medical complications or significance. Zachary crossed all the milestone thresholds in a timely fashion. He rolled over, sat up, began to crawl, said Mama, and pulled up to stand and cruise along the furniture. Yet it seemed the further he got away from the ground the more unbalanced he became. He wanted and tried to walk, to take those first shaky and determined steps, but something was amiss.

People thought that he was perhaps a slow walker. We decided (along with the physician) there was no need for alarm, but if he wasn't walking by fifteen months we could have some tests to shed some light on this dilemma. Well, since I am in this book, it's no surprise that fifteen months came and went, along with a week's worth of testing at the Children's Hospital in Chicago, and we ended up with the incorrect diagnosis of Cerebral Palsy. We were then told we were free to go home, where we should enter into the world of age zero to three programs, and continue to live our lives as usual. Hmmm…

Since the chances of this happening again were infinitesimally small due to ruled out genetic factors, and because I always wanted more children, we went on to have Eliza three years later. After, once again, a wonderfully healthy pregnancy, we decided to have Eliza in a birthing room, (to allow for, the just-in-case syndrome), with our same home birth doctor. Eliza, too, was perfectly sweet and beautiful, born after a normal and uncomplicated delivery, and this time we were all home in an hour and a half.

I am convinced that most of us would faint if we knew the obstacles and challenges that lie ahead of us. The Bible says in Matthew 6:34, "Do not worry about tomorrow… For each day has enough trouble of its own."

Before I could truly grasp that verse, which was long after I knew that Eliza would also be challenged, I wasted precious energy worrying about Zachary's self-esteem. You see, I was concerned that he would be devastated by the realization that his baby sister would walk before him, because we had been told that Zachary would probably walk about age three. Little did I know that neither child would be an independent walker, and that first statement made by the neurologist regarding when Zachary would walk was only a guess and incorrect at that. But, for us, one doctor's guess became our first introduction to a false hope which would later undergo a metamorphosis. It first became the classic shattered dream, and then mellowed into becoming a resigned part of reality. Today when I read Matthew 6:34, I've learned to say "Amen."

It wasn't until Eliza's development unfolded that I realized Cerebral Palsy was not the culprit of my dismay, but only an impostor standing in for an unlabeled genetic disorder. This realization came about when Eliza followed Zachary's lack of footsteps. I thought to myself—Two Children that could not stand and walk?? (And, of course I had not even considered there would be any cognitive deficits to deal with as well.)

The extent to which that fact really registers is as improbable as what exactly will come up if you scatter seeds on the still frozen ground of March. Even though I felt the need to know what this would mean and how things would manifest, I realize now that having my life as a mother of two special needs children unfold in increments, just like a winter landscape camouflages what lies in wait, saved me from my inability to save myself.

It was at this time that I began to feel the weight of the challenge. As one zero to three year program was just ending I found myself standing on the verge of another. And as time went on, delays, which more appropriately became labeled "deficits" in speech, cognitive

abilities, as well as fine and gross motor functioning were all part of this scenario. And of course, a marriage that was being subjected to its own special challenges.

When I think back I can easily see myself as I took the children out for walks, pushing an unevenly balanced double stroller actually designed for twins. Four year old Zachary on one side, little Eliza on the other, who was constantly getting poked and prodded by a brother who was too close for comfort because of his inability to walk. I felt uncertain about how the weight of another disabled child would bear on my children's father and I, since we seemed to have very different methods of coping with our personal challenges. Months passed, and we continued to drift in and out of parent support groups and counseling, depending upon how rocky our terrain felt.

My marriage of eleven years to my children's father did not survive. Classic psychological research would say, "See, just what we predict; special kids are a heavier weight, making it easier for a marriage to crumble." I say marriage is

In the midst of everything, I realized that the ingredient that I needed for this special ground was a big dose of God. I began to let Him be my spiritual gardener, and realized He has the greenest thumb of all. When I am awake to glimpses of the Divine, I find I am supplied with both always enough and never enough. This remarkable phenomenon does two things. It makes me hunger for more while I am simultaneously fine tuning my responses to the ways the disabilities continue to manifest. I find that my attitude either hinders or fosters my spiritual growth.

much like a garden. Sometimes ground that is simply inhospitable to one plant is sufficient to allow another plant to survive. The trick is finding compatible plantings that will thrive in one common piece of ground, regardless of the rocks that lie under the surface, or lack of sunshine from above. Sometimes, when constant weeding and diligent maintenance does not yield the desired results, one may find themselves transplanted into a new spot entirely. Say "Amen" somebody.

Also, I trusted God for my continued sense of humor. I believed that with this gift I could rise to this challenge. And later, another thing that aided in my ability to not crumble in the face of adversity was to believe, (not to be confused with understand mind you), that everything works together for the good.

When things looked particularly bleak, I tried (and continue to try) to remember that when you focus on one small part of something, you lose sight of the grander plan. Staring at a bleak cold patch of earth in the raw of March is not as grand as picking a bouquet in June. But every New England gardener knows that you won't get much for your efforts without the necessary dormant cold that comes first. This garden of life was going to require patience.

I knew that being able to laugh as I went would help sustain me, since laughter rises from the well of joy. What I didn't know was how easily a well can run dry, and how excruciatingly painful it would be when I couldn't laugh—when I was witnessing my child's suffering and couldn't fix it.

Isn't that what mothers do? Fix things? Kiss it and make it better? As the handicaps began to manifest themselves in our day to day living, I became acutely aware of the magnitude of this affliction. The most sobering part was that this appeared to be a wound that would never heal. Each week, each month, each year, there would be novel challenges to confront, to grieve over, and eventually come to terms with.

New energy, and more love was needed to move on and face the next heartache, which inevitably would be around the next bend.

The realization that my children would be trapped inside bodies that would never respond the way they intended them to was initially devastating. Sometimes it was a word or a sound that they could not articulate, and I would see their frustration in not being

a certain kind of love | Free to Go Home

understood. Other times it would be endless tries of therapy trying to maintain a posture, or searching for a center of balance that would elude them, leaving them on the sidelines watching other children run after balls, or listening to the endless snap of a jump rope on the inviting summer pavement. As they got older, I would grieve over other robbed accomplishments, like the inability to get a driver's license or the resignation of being merely a spectator at a best friend's gymnastics class or dance recital. They would struggle with being prisoners inside those bodies, and I would be forced to witness the lifetime sentence of this affliction. I was guard of this cruel prison, and try as I might, I would never be able to release them or myself from this anguish.

Ah, but I read "the truth would make me free." It took what seemed to be forever for me to begin to grasp what that means. I learned I needed to tackle that promise in the spiritual realm as opposed to using my natural reasoning. When I stepped over to the spiritual path, my heart became much more discerning.

Over the years I got glimpses of revelation. The more I trusted God rather than myself, the more alive that wonderful promise became. One payoff was reaching a place in which I could more quickly catch myself staring at the bleak ground of the disabilities, and acting on the fact that I had the ability to simply change my vision, and at times, even be rid of the desire to look in that direction at all. A gift of grace I'd say.

Sometimes I just needed to be good to myself. Pour a glass of wine and sit by the fire, reading the promises of both seed catalogs and the Bible. I knew that taking the time to soften my heart's ground would never be in vain. I took time to pray.

I am convinced that every parent of a special child will require prayers to aid them with being rescued from the land of self-pity at least once. This is an especially dangerous ground. It is full of the shattered dreams that end up like shards of glass lurking in your perennial bed after someone with no regard has tossed a bottle over your beautiful garden wall. It is like walking barefoot on that patch of ground before you realize what even happened. If anyone opened this book seeking advice, this is where I would say pay attention, because it is too draining to learn from first hand experience.

My children's father got seriously lost here very early on, and I was lost for an entire season fifteen years later. I wept often, and when I wasn't weeping I was licking my wounds. I felt sorry for all the things we were robbed of, and would be robbed of. The list was endless, filled with things such as not being able to say the words "Go out and play," like every other mom that needs a break, to grieving over the fact that I cannot have a conversation with my kids that includes abstract thoughts and ideas, transcending all repetitions and perse-verances, and labored speech. I wanted to have these longed for heart-to-hearts while walking through the woods, admiring the beautiful birds! Well they simply can't walk in the woods. They cannot easily focus on that allusive bird in the tree, and speech is often repetitive,

strained and difficult. And no, even when I've had enough as every mother can attest, I don't even get to say "Go outside," because if anybody goes anywhere they need help to get there.

Well, if you want trouble, just think like that. If you find yourself acting pitiful as you peer down into the well that no longer bubbles up with laughter or joy you just might have confused the need for pity with mercy. A self-absorbed, poor me attitude will dry up that well faster than any drought ever could.

I know that God allowed me to indulge myself in a parched season so I could get it through my head that it was futile to rely on my own strength or natural reasoning. A good hard look at the disabilities in the natural left me feeling overwhelmed and sad. My frantic efforts to keep up on the unwanted weeds that constantly spring up in this land of special needs were in vain. I needed, once again, to be reminded that I had a spiritual gardener, whose Spirit would be my living water for my well.

Over the years God has attentively pruned me (in spite of my objections), so I could thrive in the conditions that I found myself planted in. I found I needed to let go of many things I wanted, and learned to trust that I would always have supplied to me the things I truly needed. Each painful pruning was covered with mercy. God indeed remembers all of us that He has set apart.

Since the phone call, while in the midst of my everyday affairs, I would sometimes think about how different my contribution to this book would have been if I had been asked to write about this journey into the "land of special needs" when my children had just been diagnosed, or before I had time to digest and accommodate my life to (what was then) new and foreboding territory.

What would I have brought to these pages if I had been asked when I first was testing these waters? I am fully persuaded that, as according to the book of Ecclesiastes, "To everything there is a season, and a time to every purpose under the heaven." After eighteen years of being exposed to the elements of special needs, I feel ripe to share this story.

I have remarried, and I believe that my husband is the only one who truly understands my walk as I mother two special needs children. My soul has undergone an alchemy that perhaps only he alone can fully grasp. He has loved and supported me through this often bittersweet journey. I know I am simply not the same person I was eighteen years ago. Instead, my life has been made stronger, richer, and more fruitful because I have been faithful and at times transcended the sorrow in it.

A Gift to Me By Kimberly Brophy

Shaun

date of birth:
September 1, 1986
Pervasive Developmental Disorder

I started to notice that something was different about Shaun when he was around four or five months old. He was born healthy after a traumatic birth. I had walked into the hospital on August 31, 1986, around 11:00 p.m. and gave birth to Shaun on September 1, 1986, at 12:22 a.m.—Labor Day! I had less than one and one-half hours of intense labor, with him being in fetal distress. Despite this, he looked and appeared to be quite healthy with Apgar scores close to ten. He had light skin and hair. He was beautiful! I was thrilled!

In the beginning of his young life, he was a quiet baby. He didn't sleep much at night, being up almost every two hours. But during the day he was content to lie on his back in his playpen, looking around or swinging in his baby swing. It wasn't until he was around four or five months old that it appeared that something wasn't right. He was just too quiet and seemed to lack any desire to try to roll over or even make attempts to move around much. He had an older brother who is three and one-half years older than he, so I knew from experience that

Shaun wasn't just slow, something was wrong.

Family and friends tried to reassure me that it was probably nothing, that Shaun was just behind the normal anticipation of babies developing. But, I had a gut feeling that something was wrong.

I had an appointment to go to Boston Children's Hospital when Shaun was around seven months old. He was evaluated by a team of doctors whose diagnosis was that Shaun was probably retarded, and would probably not speak or walk. It was as if someone was standing in front of me stabbing my heart until the pain was unbearable. I then was in disbelief and numb; how could this be happening to my little baby?

I went shortly afterwards for another opinion at Rhode Island Hospital. Again, almost the same diagnosis, Shaun had a degree of retardation, he probably wouldn't speak, perhaps not walk. I left in tears, my beautiful child, *WHY?! WHY did this happen to him? WHY did this happen to ME?!*

My family and friends tried to be supportive. But still, nobody knew how I really felt or how I coped. I don't even know sometimes how I got through all this. I sometimes felt guilty at my feelings of anger and self-pity, especially when I would look at other families with problems far worse than my own. But it didn't take away the frustration or helplessness that I felt many times. To cope, sometimes I think I just didn't deal with it, I just wanted it to go away.

Shaun learned to walk at three years old. He was toilet trained at six years old. He can speak, not always very clearly, but boy, well enough! I only wish those doctors, who said that my child would probably never speak, could have heard him a few years ago when his older brother taught him a few swear words and unfortunately he was swearing like he was born with Tourette's Syndrome. He was swearing to his teachers, classmates and family. I would have loved to see the expression on those doctors' faces to hear Shaun tell them a few words! But, thank goodness, it was a passing phase and he eventually stopped.

Shaun is eleven years old. After all the hospital visits, doctors' visits, and therapies, Shaun has only been diagnosed as being pervasive developmentally delayed. I have no answers as to what happened to him or why he was born the way he is. But, he has come so far. He has been in childcare services since he was diagnosed at those early months of his life. The days and weeks of therapy and schooling have helped tremendously. He has had some wonderful teachers and therapists.

For Shaun, life is great! For me, some days are totally exasperating! He is very much like the guy from the movie, "Rainman." He's sort of autistic, but yet he's not. He's very repetitious and loves to keep to a regular schedule. He knows when there's a change to his schedule and if he doesn't like it, he'll be sure to let you know that! He is a very happy soul who loves people, movies, and just having a good time. He is just Shaun. He isn't aware that there is something different about him. He lives for the moment. Just don't change his schedule unless it's for something good, like a weekend at Gramma Geri's and Grampa Walt's house. He adores them and they love him unconditionally.

My hopes and dreams for Shaun are that he will always feel happy and not worry about his life. He will never be a rocket scientist, but that's irrelevant. I only hope eventually, that he will learn to be more self-sufficient and not rely so much on others to help him. Maybe someday he can help others to learn to relax and take time to smell the roses, or sit back and drink an orange soda (his favorite drink), or just be silly and giggle over something humorous, because these are the things that make him happy and put a smile on his face and those around him. If he can someday accomplish these wonderful, simple things, then he will have accomplished more than some people ever will in their lifetime, and that is something to be extremely proud about. It is the simple little pleasures in life that we forget to see—the joy, or to appreciate how lucky we are to be who we are!

When I realized that Shaun was different, it was very difficult and sad for me. But as the years have gone by, I have learned to accept that I can not change the way he is. My son has been a gift to me. I believe now that there is a reason for everything. There is a reason why he was born this way, I may not understand why, but it doesn't matter. He is always learning and growing, and by having him in my life, I too am learning and growing with him.

My son is very special. He has enlightened me with his simple wisdom and love. He makes me smile at his innocent humor and honesty. Though it is not always easy, I know that I have been blessed by having Shaun in my life.🌳

Perfectly Ours By Cyndy and Elwood Johnson

Jennifer

June 2, 1970 - October 7, 1995

Partial Trisomy 6

There is in every parent the wish for a perfectly healthy, perfectly normal, perfectly happy little baby. What is the first thing parents do when their child is brought from the womb? They count the fingers, check the nose, look the baby over from tiny head to little toes.

El and I were no different. And till now we'd been blessed. First in 1966 a gorgeous baby boy, El J. Then in 1967 beautiful Heather was born. Happy, healthy, fun! What happened in 1970 shook our world apart and turned life, as we knew it, upside down.

Following an uncomplicated pregnancy, I went to the hospital to deliver our third child with no reason for concern. The obstetrician had noticed nothing out of the ordinary for nine months of gestation. It was the delivery room nurse who first gave a hint of trouble. "This is a funny shape," she said as she examined my distended belly, "looks like you have a banana in there." Still the delivery proceeded smoothly, and fully conscious I expected them to place the baby in my arms, as in the past. Instead, a rush of motion ensued and the baby, a girl I was told, was whisked to the nursery! Wheeled to the maternity ward, I was terrified by unanswered questions. Alone, as El had been on late patrol in Portsmouth when labor began and had not yet arrived, I couldn't begin to imagine what had happened.

Finally the obstetrician came to the room. Grim faced, he was obviously not there to share the usual post delivery announcement. As gently as possible, he said he was sorry but that something was very wrong with the child. She weighed only two pounds eleven ounces and seemed very ill. At that point he was unable to explain it but assured me that the pediatrician would run tests and see me later.

Waiting for El, I placed calls to my mom, my sister-in-law, and my friend. To each I repeated, "Something is wrong with the baby." Hoping for some kind of reassurance that life was still on track, I listened to their words of encouragement. Still, something inside gnawed on my heart and I was afraid.

When I went home the next day, the baby, whom we named Jennifer, remained behind in the incubator attended to by the caring nurses. Failure to thrive, possible heart, kidney, thyroid, genetic problems were all posed by the pediatrician as possible culprits. She was so small, so thin. She had no instinctive sucking reflex. Feeding was laborious and around the clock. Unfortunately, she also got sick after eating, so ground was constantly lost. The hospital had a rule that babies weigh five pounds before going home, but after one month, Jen was released at four pounds plus!

Trying to get a diagnosis took a very long time. All we could do was do our best to feed her, protect her, and help her to grow stronger. Finally at eight months her tiny veins were able to be probed for blood to test. The results were worse than ever imagined.

Not only had doctors found a malfunctioning thyroid and a hole in her heart (which later healed itself), but they identified the more serious problem. Jennifer, through some anomaly of nature, possessed a faulty genetic structure. At the time, we were told that she had partial trisomy 6. Doctors had no good news. This genetic condition was extremely rare. They knew of only six reported cases worldwide and the prognosis was for complete mental retardation with death by four. We were overwhelmed with grief. What now for our growing family? What now for our plans to travel, to play, to live fully? Advice was given to institutionalize her. This we could not do. We loved her; her sister and brother adored her; and she needed us, of that we were certain. In that case, one doctor responded, "Save your money, stop trying to find a miracle or a cure. Just take her home and love her." And that we did.

Loving Jen was always easy. Caring for Jen was never easy. Jen's life I can only describe as a constant struggle for survival! Everything that could go wrong with a child seemed to go wrong with her.

There was the great difficulty with feeding and with holding food down. She got sick a lot in the first several years of her life and then again after her surgery at age eighteen. When she was

just a baby, we'd go out with our family for dinner and part way through the meal Jen would start to cough or choke and then get sick. Of course it was difficult in a public place where people were trying to relax and enjoy their time. So we went out a lot less to places from which there was no chance for a hasty escape!

And she was prone to croup, to wracking coughs, to seizures. So many weeks would be spent battling one illness only to have another take its place. So often her body would droop, as limp as a rag doll, just exhausted after one of those battles.

Jen was also unable to speak, so there was great frustration. It is so hard, as every parent knows, to be unable to understand and thereby help a little baby crying for an unidentifiable reason. Most babies soon learn to communicate but for Jen the problem lasted for years. Eventually signing and gesturing filled the need and in spite of the doctors' predictions, Jen was beginning to learn, to function, to interact in her environment.

There were also her physical handicaps. She never learned to walk independently, though she was strong for her size. Perhaps from the beginning there was some pressure on her brain that prevented the balance she so desperately needed. It took years for Jen to sit unsupported and to scoot about on her butt thereby gaining a measure of independence.

In addition to these difficulties, there was the doctors' prognosis for complete retardation. They said Jen would never know anything. But she was not typical in the definition of retardation. She had energy and brightness. She looked at you with eyes that understood. You felt communion with her. She had intellect. It was obvious to us early on that she did. She felt pain. She felt joy. She felt love. She felt fear. Could one experience these human emotions as fully as she did with no intellect?

She possessed a concept of numbers and would know when something was missing from her group of toys. If a bead from her set was lost, she'd get our attention, point to the beads, and engage our efforts in the hunt.

But while we didn't agree with the label of retardation, there was no doubt that her thoughts were somehow locked inside her mind. Something was missing which might have allowed complete interaction with the world. There's no question about it. Whether it was a chemical imbalance or pressure in her brain, we'll never know.

The description given by doctors and educators, who had to label for placement in appropriate settings, was severely and profoundly retarded. It's about as extreme a label as you can get. It pointed out to others that she was in dire need. And the truth is that Jen needed complete care always, much like a baby. She couldn't get up and get her own food, get herself to the bathroom, or go to a closet to get a coat and run out to play the way another child might. Jennifer could manage to get herself out of bed at one point and scoot about the house on her bottom. She'd wake us if she wanted us to get going or she'd get into her drawers and pull out some clothes or she would go to her toys to play. She'd investigate her surroundings to see what was happening in the house, who was there, who was not. For that I'm glad.

Jen was, by description, severely and profoundly retarded, but it was a term that, once we got to know Jen, we never used for her. We would just say that we had a handicapped child. That was the way we felt about her—that she had some handicapping conditions that made her life difficult.

Whether it was playing, eating, going somewhere, or trying to become part of the larger group, Jen had to work harder and longer than anyone else did. Perhaps that's why she learned to persevere. Then again, maybe she came with perseverance that allowed her to endure! But in any case, she did as much as she could do.

I remember especially the enormous number of visits, impossible to count, to doctors, to Rhode Island Hospital, to Meeting Street School in an effort to help Jenny be all that she could be. For a long time, we went at least monthly to be weighed, measured, analyzed. We'd put Jen in the car and off we'd go. She was trained in physical skills and fitted with adaptive equipment that might make her stronger and more able to function.

We were blessed to live in an era that saw value in educating the handicapped and disabled. When Jen was about two, a small program was started locally. She was invited to attend for a few hours each day, to play with other children, and to explore new settings. Later, she attended a program at the local public school, which closed after a few years. Jenny, at seven years old, began to attend the Arthur Trudeau Center in Warwick, RI, where she stayed for fourteen years. While there she made friends and developed a routine that was more like that of other children. At twenty-one her public school education, in effect, ended and she was transferred to the Frank Olean Center in Westerly, RI, for

another day program. Because this followed so closely on the heels of major surgery, it was a scary transition.

In 1988 we realized that Jen was losing her sight. A craniotomy was not able to reverse the loss. It did, however, leave her incapacitated for a long time and the road to moderate recovery was grueling. By the time she entered the Olean Center, she was blind and much weaker than she had been for years. I know it was because of the great compassion of the staff that Jen was able to resume a semi-normal kind of existence there, in spite of the great physical demands and strain. In spite of the blindness, she went on trips at the center, did little jobs and activities, and loved it there.

Other than her schooling over the years, Jenny, of course, stayed mainly with us at home. We had a pretty good arrangement, I think. All of us were living our own lives and coming together as a family, as families do, and having Jen did not change that. We each had our separate circle and we had our family circle, which was so incredibly important to all of us. I think Jenny flourished there. We had a supportive extended family, as well. Jen had grandmothers she loved, aunts and uncles, and dozens of cousins all living fairly nearby. All were part of her growing and changing, and with them she developed very deep and loving relationships. Jen was special, and all but the oldest cousins went through that discovery of being the same size as Jen then growing bigger and becoming more capable and seeing Jen stay as she was. They realized early on that Jen was unique and very special. We were indeed blessed by a great and loving support system of family and friends.

In spite of her great struggle for health, for independence, for joy, for her very survival, Jen's life was fully lived. She knew the great blessing of being loved. She laughed and loved to play. She triumphed time and again over adversity. She had courage and stood up for what she wanted against all detractors. She found in music a special joy and peace.

Was her life perfect? No, it was far from perfection. And there are episodes that I would so like to erase from her list of traumas and sufferings. But to have Jen with us for twenty-five years is something I would never change. She was such a gift to all who knew her. She was so perfectly ours!

In his eulogy to Jen, my husband referred to one of the few phrases Jen was ever able to enunciate. "Good girl, good girl," she would croon to herself when in a particularly happy mood. In this farewell he was able to share with others some of Jen's gifts to us. I share it now with you.

Jennifer loved to hear the words "good girl, good girl." She'd beam with joy each time anyone expressed that to her.

*Well, "**Good Girl, Jen.**" Good girl for teaching mom and dad about true and unconditional love, that love we saw in your face every day that so filled us with peace.*

*"**Good Girl, Jen.**" Good girl for teaching so many about strength and courage. None of us have ever known a person who fought so long against so many enemies as you in your battle with illness and bodily hurt. You conquered so many hurdles that seemed so insurmountable to us.*

*"**Good Girl, Jen.**" Good girl for teaching us about faith. It never ceased to amaze us, that you could have a seizure, a croupy cough, or some other physical insult and at the next moment give us a smile or take our hand to give us orders about something you wanted, like to play with beads or to eat a pancake. You had the faith to go on and get through the crisis. You also had faith that those around you loved you and wanted what you wanted.*

*"**Good Girl, Jen.**" Good girl for teaching us about perseverance. It took you a long time to get your point across, and an even longer time for us to understand how much you had to say. But we are so thankful that you found expression through signs and body language and sounds to speak to us. One of the happiest days of our lives was when you first signed "I Love You" back to us.*

*"**Good Girl, Jen.**" Good girl for teaching us about determination. Few were ever more firm in their decisions. You have a grand and feisty spirit, undaunted by the physical restrictions life placed on you. All of us felt that determined spirit every day. There was no making you eat what you didn't want (unless a little syrup was sprinkled on), and you did manage to dissuade us from using your walker.*

*"**Good Girl, Jen.**" Good girl for helping us to know that God knows more than we do. And for teaching us what a privilege and a blessing it is to care for and take care of someone you truly love, no matter the severity of their need.*

*"**Good Girl, Jen.**" Good girl for teaching us about the joy to be found in music. Whether the notes were rock or opera they made you smile and you moved your hand along with the pulse of the music as though you were conducting.*

*"**Good Girl, Jen.**" Good girl for teaching Daddy that simple pleasures truly are the best.*

Jennifer we love you. You will always be with us. We miss you so much.

"Jenny, you are a good girl!" ♔

Bright Promise By Heather Johnson LaFreniere

(sister of Jennifer, *Perfectly Ours*)

Cameron

date of birth:
September 11, 1996

Cystic Fibrosis

When Cameron was born, my first thought upon seeing his face was "he is not going to be with me very long." I don't know wherefrom this thought came. I wanted it to go away and felt as though I had somehow hurt him by thinking it. But then my son looked at me with such peace and dignity, I felt humbled by him and soothed by him in the same moment. He was a very old soul indeed, and he had a lot more to teach me.

Having come home from the hospital two days later, I was so tired and sore from delivery that my mind could only function to care for my newborn and in between soothe my body with sitz baths.

The next day we had visitors till 6:00 p.m. I barely had the chance to hold my son all day. Nor was I able to rest, so when my sister-in-law offered to stay an extra hour with Cameron to allow me some time alone, I eagerly accepted. Woken up every hour the night before by my hungry baby had left me fantasizing about being in a big island bed alone for days.

Yet, when I laid my head on the pillow, my body collapsing in line like a demolished building, I began to cry. Not since my sister died the year before, had I cried so hard. Hormones were a part of my cacophony of sorrow, but it was old grief revisited, which drove my tears. Like a bear woken up too soon before winter's end, my grief consumed me in that moment. My joy in Cameron's birth reminded me of my sorrow in Jen's death. While I felt like my tears were stinging God's own face, I was powerless to stop them.

After an hour of this, I suddenly stopped as if I had awakened from a bad dream. I had not held my newborn in several hours, due to our visitors. I suddenly felt panicked and hurried to get him in my arms.

My husband, John, was rocking him. The baby had been crying most of the day. It seemed unusual for him to be so fussy, since he had been so content for two days prior. All his visitors kept assuring me that newborns had fussy days. Had I been less fatigued, I would have been less easily swayed. I will never again let my own body's pain and fatigue affect my maternal instincts.

When I finally held Cameron in my arms, my alarms sounded. "Cameron has a fever!" I cried out to my husband. Brushing past him with Cameron clasped to my heart, I called the doctor then tried taking his temperature with the doctor on the phone.

Almost as afraid of taking his temperature as calling his doctor, I suddenly grew up when the pediatrician told me to

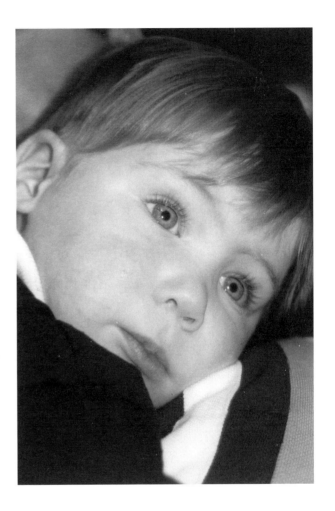

bring him to our local children's hospital's emergency room immediately. Cameron's temperature was 101.8 degrees. I rushed about his bedroom, getting his diaper bag ready, trying to calm his cries along with my own.

Desperation and fear made the fifteen minute ride to the emergency room seem like fifteen hours. All the while, I kept looking at Cameron in his car seat afraid that he would disappear and leave me forever.

He was admitted to the ICU nursery upon the completion of the initial diagnostic tests in the emergency ward. His temperature had risen to 102.4 degrees and his respiratory rate was excessive.

All night, Cameron was on the brink of life and death. None of the doctors could determine what his illness was, even though a battery of tests were done including two aborted spinal taps.

In the emergency ward, while Cameron was being poked by needles of various shape and purpose, my husband and I stood by his gurney. We held onto his hands when permitted by the doctors, talking to him in soothing and upbeat voices even though our hearts were breaking. We told him over and over how much we loved him and how thankful we were for him, what a great boy he was.

As I stood in that hospital, my mind flashed back to 1988. That year my sister ended up in a different ICU fighting off death. I was not strong enough then to accept the reality of her potential death. All I felt was fear and anger over losing her. I was unable to recognize the precious gift of her presence with me at that time. I wasted precious days and hours, which might have proved to be her last. Lucky for me, she held on and gave me a second chance to say good-bye properly in 1995. I swore never to make that mistake again as I stood near my son, giving him only love and peace. It was not that I was not afraid. Rather, I simply refused to let my fears overtake my love for my son.

Just before Cameron was given the spinal taps, we were ordered to wait out in the hall. As I was leaving, I asked the attending resident if the test was painful. He said, "No." I knew that it was a lie, but I didn't argue with him. I wanted so desperately to believe him. Doctors should not lie to parents or patients, for we are the strongest ones around and deserve the truth always. After all, we have the most at stake in the answer.

Waiting in the halls of the emergency ward, I began to cry. I could hear my son's screams barely filtered through the swinging doors separating us. I wanted to go to him, but all I had been given room to do, was wait. So I prayed and cried in succession, until we were allowed back beside Cameron. There is a tragic irony in the practice of ushering parents away from their children just at the time when the child needs their presence the most.

As I stood in the hall, praying behind a vending machine for privacy in the very busy emergency waiting room, I vowed never to waste time dwelling in past sorrows again. I also made a vow to God in my prayers to be strong for my son, stronger than I had ever imagined I could be. If only God would let him stay with us longer, I would gratefully cherish him every moment for the rest of my life. I believe God was testing me while showing me how to live at the same time in a way that only time would reveal. I was able to see the beauty and His love in the lessons later.

When Cameron was transferred to the ICU, we had to wait again in the halls outside of another set of swinging doors. It seemed to take too long for the doctors and nurses to set him up in his cubicle. During that time, I split into two parts emotionally. One part of me refused to give into fear, sending out love and strength to my son. The other part was crumbling and dying from fear. The stronger part shoved the weak part of me deep down, so I only recognized its existence when I had moments alone. In those moments alone I pushed the fear back down with prayer.

So began a very long night of standing by Cameron, both literally and figuratively. No matter what happened, I would not leave him unless ordered by the doctors. Touching Cameron's body with my fingers, I sent him my energy, my soul's very life force to communicate to him my will for his healing, my commitment to his life. I would not fail him as I had my sister almost ten years before. While dedicating my whole being to his healing, I understood his will may have had a different goal. The greatest thing a parent can do is to be bonded with their child in both joy and pain, to feel their joys and sorrows honestly without fear darkening the beauty of both.

After Cameron had been hooked up to the monitors and placed on a warming bed, he looked alien to me. The warming bed was up so high and tilted so far forward that it seemed as though Cameron was on an easel for display, our little masterpiece.

Still I felt the nagging set of opposite urges fighting within me. These were created out of the true opposites of love and fear. Fear, not hate, is the true opposite of love. A very small voice inside still urged me to disconnect from him, while my soul rang out my burning desire to hold him to my breast and heal him with the sheer force of my will. I did neither. Due to the many monitors, IVs and tubes connected to him, I could only hold his tiny hands, rub his soft forehead, and sing to him gently about how much he was our world. I covered my small fears with my overwhelming

and endless love for him. I made good on my vow and Cameron was transferred to the general infant ward the next afternoon. God had listened to my prayers. What power we had in prayer and faith! For nine more days, Cameron was hospitalized. Every hour, I loved him more, which seemed an impossibility, since I had loved him so completely and unconditionally from his birth.

Sticking to my earlier vows, I focused on the joy and beauty within Cameron and around him. I concentrated on his smile when the oxygen tube started to frighten me. I made myself hoarse by singing over and over to him when the monitors were trying to distract me with their beeps and buzzes. I tuned into the music of his bear toy when the whining of the oxygen tube began to drive me to worrying. I stayed on the road of positive thought and healing by centering my energies on the treasure before me, Cameron's life. During those times when fear was beginning to overtake me, I went to the chapel to pray. How I prayed! Prayer is a powerful source of healing and coming to acceptance of

God's plan. I felt peace from my prayers and the prayers of family and friends. My strength came from my love for my son, but also from the many prayers being recited on his behalf. I had people who loved us, all over the nation, praying for my son. My uncle, who has often doubted the existence of God, found enough faith within his cynical mind to pray for Cameron every night. There was great healing power in those prayers for us all. We felt the energy and healing work of those prayers like the first rays of sunshine breaking through a dark stormy sky.

Finally, when Cameron came home from the hospital thin and weak, but breathing well, I cherished every moment with him, since God had rewarded me so greatly. I foolishly believed that I had passed all the tests and there would be no more. Yet God's plan was barely unfolding. The lesson of acceptance had more parts to it ahead.

So a week later, I did not like the expression on the pediatrician's face, when she was informed about Cameron's weight at his next closely scheduled appointment. First, she questioned me about his feeding habits. Satisfied with my answers, she gave Cameron one more week to gain weight. During that week I practically force-fed Cameron and searched for my own answers to his poor weight gain in-between the hourly feedings. I did not want the answer which I kept finding. Another week later, again at the pediatrician's, I smiled as the nurse said, "Think heavy thoughts, Cameron," when she put him on the scale. Seeing her look of concern at his weight, my smile faded.

Cameron was diagnosed with "failure to thrive" that day. I felt like a failure as well with this diagnosis. Yet this was not a time nor a place for guilt. It was a time to take action, to believe in my ability to care for my son, to be stronger than everything threatening him. So I did and I was.

Cameron had tests done of his blood and stools that day. Waiting in line at the laboratory, located on the ground floor of the pediatrician's building, I felt a small urge to leave with Cameron and deny the possibility of any illness. Yet again my love for him kept me in that line and willing to face whatever lay ahead. My strength was growing.

The pediatrician also made an appointment with a "specialist" (as she described it) in order to determine the source of Cameron's failure to thrive. She didn't explain any further details. I wish that she had. She should have prepared us. I came to understand that often parents must demand the truth. After all, doctors are only human. My reality check was to come from the appointment with the "specialist."

When the stool test showed large fat deposits, Cameron was then scheduled for a sweat test. I began to really hate what my mind and research were telling me. Part of me had already started down the road of acceptance at that point.

The day of the sweat test I was angry with God for breaking our agreement, as I saw it. The sweat test itself was relatively easy, but I found the hospital

surroundings very poor and disheartening. The test was done in the basement of an ancient building in bad need of cleaning and repair. I was disgusted by the whole set-up. How could any compassionate person allow tests of such magnitude to be performed in such dreary and unsightly surroundings? I only felt better once we were back in our car and on our way home.

The rest of the day we waited for a phone call, which never came. Since the lab technician had assured us that if we received no phone call that day, it meant the test had been determined to be negative, I began to believe my concerns would be proven incorrect. We felt elated the next morning, because we had put faith in the technician's declaration. How could we know she had spoken out of the side of her mouth from practice?

Without concern, I called the pediatrician to discuss the next step in determining the cause of the failure to thrive. I hoped it was just a food allergy. My heart came crashing up into my vocal chords, when I heard the doctor say, "I'm so very sorry…" The floor below my feet buckled and I felt dangerously close to falling even though I was sitting down already. "The test results were positive for Cystic Fibrosis," she said.

At that moment, my merry-go-round world of childhood dreams came to a sickeningly lurching halt. I no longer felt like I was in my body. I was a shadow of my former self reeling through space and time screaming out "No!"

In a short time, I would learn the healing and strengthening power of love and compassion once more. I was also to comprehend, with the passage of the days, the powerlessness and uselessness of fear. Cameron's initial hospitalization actually prepared the way for my survival on this uncharted and daunting new journey. I came to understand that hopes have the greatest resiliency when they are founded on the rock of love. But for a while, I floundered like a fish out of water.

So in that moment, I clutched Cameron in a desperate and terrified grip of fear, feeling like someone was trying to take him from me. With time and love, I came to understand that he had made this choice for himself. Otherwise, nothing in life would ever make any sense. I cannot believe in nothing, so I have come to believe in love and the gift of choice from God. But in that moment I felt afraid and alone.

Due to my attack of fear in that second, Cameron seemed like an alien to me. This was not supposed to happen to me, my husband, our child, our families, I thought to myself. Images of the book, *Alex: The Life of a Child,* flashed through my mind. Having read it as a teenager, I had stored in my memory banks images of her thin body and sickly eyes. All the pain in her story ran through my mind rushing out through me and becoming my reality. It was difficult to remember the message of love central to the book with my son just diagnosed. I wondered why this disease was allowed to take root in my son? Hadn't I suffered enough watching my sister's long struggle with genetic problems, illness, and young death at age twenty-five?

The part of me which always functions, no matter the crisis, held Cameron gently yet firmly, willing him to be the exception, laying down a hundred strategies to ward off the hold of the Cystic Fibrosis over him.

My grandmother, already greatly tested by life, seemed to wither before my very eyes as I informed her of the news. I could not help from crying, as I saw her heart break one more time. She, while melting herself into grief, kept her eyes focused on me and reached her hands out to me. Her love strengthened me somehow, while I still felt like the sky was turned upside down.

I next had to phone my husband at work. All I could manage to utter was, "…the test came back positive for Cystic Fibrosis." My heart tore further each time I repeated the diagnosis. The change in John's voice revealed the terror my words had brought to him.

Then I had to tell the news to my parents, my brother, John's parents, John's siblings, and the whole extended family. Being the bearer of bad news had never been relished by me. Yet with each telling of the Cystic Fibrosis diagnosis, new wounds were cut into my fiber, my soul. Each time was a clarification, a verification of the stark cold reality of Cameron's Cystic Fibrosis. I could not make it go away. Tragedy and grief were being force-fed to me and my loved ones, it seemed. I had not even recovered from Cameron's hospitalization yet. I came to understand the way in which the two events fit together just recently.

The next day, we brought Cameron to the appointment with the "specialist." We had no idea it was actually an appointment with our state's only Cystic Fibrosis clinic. Cameron's pediatrician had been vague in her explanation of the appointment's purpose to the point of insensitivity. The Cystic Fibrosis clinic was a part of our state's Child Development Center, which was too familiar to my mother, who accompanied us to the appointment. Nothing could have prepared me or my family present, for the assault on our souls, which was about to take place there.

In the lobby, I saw an omen. Being escorted out by a nurse, a woman sat with a seven-year-old boy on her lap in a wheelchair. The boy's eyes were sad, tired, and sickly. His face and body were thin, pale, and joyless. The mother's face told the tale of her son's illness and her own terror. There was no hope for these two.

Upon seeing these two, I had the strongest urge to take Cameron home that moment. Yet, my logical mind reeled in my instinctive thoughts and feelings. We took the elevator to the sixth floor for the appointment after registering.

Walking out of the elevator at the right floor, my mother gave out a small cry. "This is the Child Development Center where I used to bring your sister." She warned me, "They never did anything helpful here. They would keep us waiting two hours at a time, while she vomited in my lap."

Still I sat down in the middle of a row of chairs in the hallway outside the doors to the center. My mother, grandmother, and husband took up positions along the wall closest to the exit. Cameron was the only peaceful one among us, as he slept in his car seat on my lap. The rest of us felt like we were on death row.

As I was trying to control my tears and my urge to leave, a blonde young woman with eyes of pity and smiles of plastic sat down next to me. She then vomited all over me and my son with her insensitive words.

"Hi, my name is Pam. I'm the Cystic Fibrosis program coordinator. So your son has Cystic Fibrosis, just remember he is still your child." She spurted out as though giving a weather forecast of partly sunny with good chance of rain showers. As she continued to chatter out the facts and figures of attending the clinic, she began to resemble a toy monkey with two loud cymbals clapping and chattering nonsense annoyingly over and over... I stopped listening when she said, "Remember he is still your child."

Still my child? I was hurt and angry at her lack of compassion. Yet, I was most hurt and horrified to recognize a certain amount of truth for me in her words. I had been emotionally removed from my son since the diagnosis. I hated myself for it, too. I felt disconnected from my own body as well. My family and I had already gone through so much. Sometimes it is impossible to put your best face forward when life hits you in the groin. I wanted to scream, "No, this is not my son because my son was supposed to be healthy." Yet my love for him, which has always been so much greater than my fear for him, held me fast by his side that day.

Cameron was next weighed and measured in the center's "growth and nutrition room," which belied its décor. The whole time, as I undressed him, handed him over to be weighed, and redressed him, my tears poured out. Angry at myself for showing my deepest pain before the stone-faced nutritionist, I lashed out at my husband, who could only remain silently loving. (This was a coping mechanism, which I employed to his detriment again and again until recently.)

Then we were brought to one of the examination rooms which ran along the back corridor of the center. I sat in a chair against the wall with Cameron asleep in my arms. My mother and grandmother sat on either side of me. My husband stood against the wall perpendicular to us and opposite the door to the tiny room.

Behind a table to my right and my husband's left sat the doctor who ran the clinic. She spoke to us about Cystic Fibrosis and our son as though she were giving a lecture to her medical staff. Always in charge, she looked at us with disinterest at best, contempt at worst. I found no compassion behind those wire-rimmed glasses and cold expressionless eyes. My initial negative impressions of her body language and speaking manner proved to be accurate reflections of her soul. In response to my statement, "I know enough about Cystic Fibrosis to be terrified," she quickly and haughtily responded, "I don't even know enough about Cystic Fibrosis and I have been the leading specialist in this state for twenty years." She had not really listened to me.

At that moment, I had the urge to hand my son to my mother, peel my heart off the floor where the doctor had so self-righteously stomped on it, and hit her with everything I had inside me. Instead, I bit the bullet and sat there, allowing her insensitivity to burn me and my family like an acid bath. I was rendered speechless. Someday, I will forgive her, but it will take time. For that doctor took away hope's light with her lack of compassion and abundance of self-validation at our expense. I knew my son would never attend this clinic, even if there were none other available. He would only sicken quicker in a place of such cold science, I was sure of that. Without love as a factor in the practice of medicine, there is no hope. My omen had been a picture of the consequences of putting faith in such medicine.

I have become grateful for our experience at this clinic. It taught me how to be strong, empowered by love. When faced with adversity, I now take a stand and trust in my abilities to be the conqueror. There is great potential for healing in the practice of creating your future with the power of choice. This power of choice is based in believing in one's ability to change the course of your life and refusing to give up hope. My faith in God and my faith in my son's right to hope help keep my fears of losing him to the disease in check. My fears do still exist but mostly reside in the small dark recesses of my mind. Every life experience truly is a blessing in disguise.

Finally, we left the clinic never to return. The next day, we took Cameron to his pediatrician for his scheduled follow-up appointment. Having had time to collect my thoughts and my emotions, I realized it was vital to my son's well-being to become an informed and demanding consumer of medical services. I had never before questioned any medical professionals due to my society influenced belief in their unquestionable supremacy. I now understand even doctors are human. No better than, no worse than, the general public.

As soon as his pediatrician exchanged greetings with us, I told her if she ever so ill-prepared us again, it would be our last appointment with her. She apologized, realizing her mistake, and we were able to begin anew. She has since proven worthy of our loyalties. Yet, I never again have trusted any doctor with my son's health nor my heart completely. Those precious valuables are in my hands alone.

Upon our request for referral to another clinic, the pediatrician gave us the number for the Boston Children's Hospital Cystic Fibrosis clinic. She further agreed to coordinate her pediatric care with the Boston Children's clinic staff. Having the clinic's number in my pocket, I began to feel glimmers of hope.

During Cameron's first two months of life before he became a client of Boston Children's clinic, he was very weak and underweight. He would fall asleep after only a few sips of milk every time I fed him. So getting him to eat more than two ounces every two hours was a real struggle. His facial appearance resembled a tired old man and broke my heart. He also was having huge smelly bowel movements with every bottle, which left his skin red and rashy. The real spirit in Cameron did not show until he began to

put on weight through the medication and care he received from Boston Children's.

I called Boston the next morning and made an appointment for two weeks later, which was the next available time. During those two weeks, I fed Cameron a predigested formula, called Pregestimil, which his doctor had prescribed for him. It has the taste of envelope glue but Cameron did gain some weight from it. He went from a three-ounce gain per week on plain breast milk and formula supplementation to a six-ounce gain per week with the Pregestimil. However, he still seemed tired and unhealthy to me.

During that first and only appointment at our state's only Cystic Fibrosis clinic, Cameron was weighed and measured. There was no mention of blood tests nor x-rays to determine the current status of his health, which is an important step in fighting Cystic Fibrosis. Neither were any vitamins nor other common Cystic Fibrosis medications, such as digestive enzymes, prescribed. We were told by that clinic's doctor that such medication was unnecessary due to the existence of Pregestimil. We found out at Boston Children's that the bare minimum had been done for Cameron by the Cystic Fibrosis clinic in our state. The doctors in Boston had bigger and better plans for fighting the Cystic Fibrosis.

What I expected from Boston was to be given some hope, some light in the darkness. I found hope there and much more. I found love and a collective bonding against the common enemy of Cystic Fibrosis.

From the registrar to the social worker to the doctor, we felt an energy and a commitment to our son's cause. They were all on the same team as us. At last, I found a smile on my face, while discussing the disease and my son in the same breath.

The only similarity in procedure between the two clinics, which we had experienced, was the initial weighing and measuring of Cameron.

Within minutes of sitting back in the waiting area, an angel in a white coat seemed to float over to us. The warmth and understanding flowing from her smile and eyes were like being found by one's own mother after getting lost in a maze. She seemed to understand that a need for healing in parents of her clients existed as well.

After introducing herself and shaking our hands with a firm grip, she gazed at Cameron in a caring manner. "Why don't we go see what's going on with this beautiful boy?" she said with a smile. She then escorted us toward her office.

Upon sitting down, this new doctor gave us a very brief synopsis of the program and her role in it. I silently thanked God when she explained she was Cameron's assigned primary CF doctor. "Tell me about you both and Cameron, if you would?" she next asked politely curious.

We spent almost an hour telling her about every event in Cameron's short life, which had led us to her. When we finished, she said confidently, "We are going to do things a little differently here." I already felt they had. They had taken my fear and banished it with the hope offered by their professionalism, compassion, and commitment to my son.

That day, preliminary data was gathered through blood tests and x-rays. Prescriptions for his troubled digestive system were given, including the digestive enzymes and Zantac, whose value had been negated by the first clinic. Fat-soluble vitamins were ordered as well.

My faith in this new doctor and new clinic has been well rewarded. Since that first appointment, Cameron has maintained an amazingly healthy weight gain and truly thrived in every aspect of his life. Giving the digestive enzymes to Cameron has never been an inconvenience, despite the negative spin placed on them by the first clinic. Once Cameron began ingesting the enzymes with every bottle, his weight gain tripled. The most important change in the prescription given by Boston Children's clinic was the

factor of love, which runs through every part of it. Love brings hope and even miracles sometimes.

Cameron has been relatively healthy since that day. I have been able to do some healing of my own as a result. With his healing and my healing, we have been able to live our lives relatively carefree. The beastly CF has been tamed by proper medications, nutrition, closely monitored care, and most especially love.

Now we spend our days laughing, playing peek-a-boo, and crawling together on the floor filled with his toys. We are living in the present moment for there resides joy, light, hope, and peace. None of us know the future. Parents of children with unique challenges are uniquely challenged as well, because we must live life as though we have nothing to fear while having been given forecasts of our children's futures, which seem to be filled with potential hardship as well as joy. Cameron, being an infant, naturally always lives in the present moment. I believe that within our children's abilities to live in the present moments, we have the key to peace and acceptance.

I have learned a lot more from my son. He has shown me that his life is his own. I have no right to waste it with my tears. My one responsibility to him is to love him enough to let him fully experience the life which God gave to him. His life is a great gift to me and my husband, as well as our families. He brings joy and God's pure light into every room which he enters with his zest and love of life emanating from every pore.

He has taught me this great truth through his eyes and his hands slowly over time. Once unable to keep myself from crying, while holding him, he suddenly stopped drinking his bottle, raised his left hand, and cradled my face with its palm. This action combined with the gaze of his suddenly serious eyes stopped my tears and opened my heart. He kept his hand and his eyes fixed on my face as if telling me, "There is no reason to cry. I am your son, who loves you. That is everything, so give thanks." The wisdom revealed to me at that moment by my son's gesture and expression was the next turn in my journey toward peace. I vowed to love

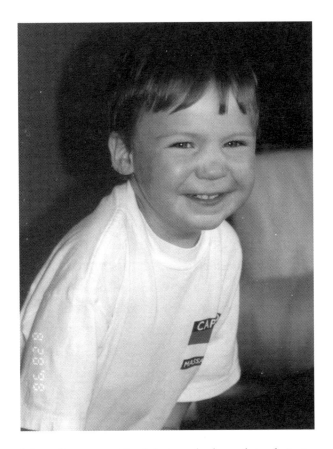

him the way God intended and to let go of my sorrow.

Cameron has also taught me by example to laugh for the pure feeling of it rolling inside your chest, up your throat, and out of your mouth finally tickling your ears. Laughing has become our mantra. It sets everything in proper light. Being able to make Cameron laugh brings me particular joy, because I know the laughter is healing him where medicines cannot reach. He has thrived largely because he knows laughter.

Once when Cameron had been vomiting for about five weeks straight in the fourth month of his life, I had a day in which I barely wanted to get off the couch. Every time I fed Cameron or laid him down, he threw up. Sometimes he would give out a few coughs as warning, sometimes there would be no time. As each day rolled by, I got used to carrying him around the house, never putting him down for fear of him losing his last meal. He lost ground during that month, falling from the seventy-fifth percentile for weight to below the fiftieth. I could tell by the change in his appearance that we were falling back.

Every time Cameron vomited, all I could think was how much he needed the food. All I could do was clean up the mess and try again later with a new bottle. Every time I could only see the negative side.

Yet, Cameron's spirit was not daunted by this problem. He would finish vomiting and then look at me and smile. He was not bothered by such small matters. He even found the clean up afterwards rather entertaining. Once, as I reached for the paper towels, he managed to fingerpaint with the mess on the kitchen floor. Then he looked up at me and laughed, his hands covered like the front of our shirts with his second lunch of the day revisited. I yearned to find it all so amusing.

Only when I stopped being afraid and began laughing again with my son at his antics, adding some of my own, did the potential blessing of this test reveal itself. I began to understand how the vomiting was really only Cameron getting rid of excess mucus, the bane of people with Cystic Fibrosis. My handling of the frequent vomiting became positive in nature. I would hold Cameron out in front of me and gently sing to him, assuring him of my love. Then we would go to our bathroom to clean up and always stop a few moments before the

large vanity mirror to laugh at our reflections. We went through a lot of laundry during those weeks, but we also found a lot of joy as well. The irony here is how Cameron stopped throwing up after I changed my attitude. Even with the benefit of newly prescribed medication, it was not until I stopped feeling sorry for myself that Cameron got over this problem.

Lastly, Cameron has taught me about love. When do we really love another unconditionally? Cameron has shown me that the answer lies in willingness, to give up one's personal hopes and dreams for the other in exchange for being graciously joyful for their simple presence. Loving unconditionally is to allow the loved one to live in the absence of fear, regret, and disappointment. To do any less would be human, but we, as souls of God are called to be much more. My greatest challenge in life also involves my greatest joy. To fail to meet the challenge presented by my son's own challenges would be to fail as a mother. Whatever happens he deserves love, pure and strong, strong enough for him and myself to ride out any storms ahead and to revel in all the bright promise of today.

My love for Cameron has transformed me from a nervous, naïve, and self-righteous new mother to a confident, informed, compassionate, and strong person in my own right. I have been given such gifts in Cameron.

Bobalou's Birth *A Story for Children*

By Heather Johnson LaFreniere

Bobalou was born in the season of the harvest.
So as the other beavers gathered their sticks, their rocks,
And their bits of mud to build their lodges, his mother was
gathering her baby to her breast and giving him her essence,
which contained all her love for him, all the best from every cell of her
body.

There was great joy for Bobalou
in being born
in being loved
in living.
There was great joy for his mother
in giving him life
in loving him with all she had
in being his mother.
Bobalou's father had a love for Bobalou,
which burned to the core of his heart.
Bobalou's father had a dream for Bobalou,
which lifted him in its flight.
Bobalou's father had everything in Bobalou.
Bobalou's father wanted the world for Bobalou.

So these three happy to be alive
with the miracle of Bobalou,
were unaware of unhappy things.
Yet as day melts into night,
their joy had to become greater still, to be stronger than
all that could displace it and these three as well.

Bobalou, the beaver, was soon brought before the great
beaver healer to receive a blessing,
as all new beavers are gifts to be celebrated
with the touch of the most noble to their brow.

As the great beaver healer held Bobalou to bless him
with the great river waters before them, and the great
forest around them, he felt the wind's whisper
telling him to hold Bobalou to his heart and give him the
healer prayer for protection.

The wind swept around the healer as he held Bobalou to his
chest waiting for the rest of the story.

Before the whole story could be revealed to the healer, the
wind circled and swept through these two, with a gentle
embrace, giving them the strength of all the winds to tell it.

The healer bowed and swayed to the wind's embrace, rocking
Bobalou in the rhythm, making him a part of their divine
understanding.

Bobalou looked up to the healer's eyes.
He held out his tiny paw and placed it on the healer's
heart, giving him his understanding,
telling the healer that Bobalou was the first to know
of his life's challenges,
for he had chosen them with the guidance of Mother Earth,
for the greater good of all.

The healer became the student.
The newest student became the healer.

So the healer, once again held his head high,
lifting Bobalou up to the wind, the sky, the river,
welcoming him,
blessing him,
and thanking all there is for him.

Bobalou, from his lofty perch, could see all the beavers
below him and he felt such love for them.

Bobalou's mother knew as the healer had swayed to the wind,
that Bobalou was unique.
She prayed that he wasn't going to leave her too soon.

But when Bobalou looked into his mother's eyes
from high above her,
feeling the love of the universe,
he told her with his eyes that
he loved her
she loved him
and that was all.

So when the healer returned Bobalou to his mother's arms,
she celebrated him in all his glory,
and let go of all her sorrow
for that is all.

"Awoogala," she sang to him.
"Awoogala, awoogala, awoogala, woo."
"You are here with me now
and I am with you.
All I have ever wanted is right
here in my arms.
So, awoogala, I sing,
you'll come to no harm."

Moment by Moment By Anita Greene

Kent

date of birth:
January 8, 1985
Pervasive Developmental Disorder

JOURNAL ENTRY:
DECEMBER 20, 1990

Kent's feet just about hit the floor this morning as he got out of bed and he was crying. Had I saved the four itsy bitsy pieces of waffle he hadn't eaten yesterday for breakfast? I hadn't because we had more in the freezer. He cried and kicked. "I hate you, you're stupid, you never do anything right. I'm not going to get up Christmas morning and eat the coffee cake you made." All I could do was hold him, his back to my front until he calmed down. It took a while. He didn't want to take a bath. He finally did and was happy, singing and splashing. By the time he left for school he seemed happy again. At school there was a substitute teacher. Everyone was singing and he wanted a story. He threw a tantrum, crying so hard he threw up all over his coat. The school nurse called Ed and told him the condition Kent was coming home in. Sometimes I feel my parenting skills are nonexistent.

Kindergarten—what possessed me to think that all we would have to deal with was the usual lessons of sharing, following rules and learning the alphabet? As an only child, it was not always easy to see Kent's differences. And the differences became "normal" as we lived with them daily. Kent was sensitive to heat. (The aforementioned bath was cold at his insistence). He was very rigid about his daily routine. Kent was, and still is, afraid of heights. He also isn't very coordinated. As a child, fine motor skills, like holding a pencil or crayon, were difficult to master.

By November, I had already had several conferences with Kent's kindergarten teacher. I remember leaving one meeting crying and thinking, "It's only kindergarten! What can be so hard about kindergarten!" Being told by a teacher that in her many years of teaching she has never seen a child like yours is discouraging and frightening. Today, I can say "God bless an observant, caring teacher." It was the questions this teacher raised, her willingness to keep a journal of classroom observations, and her honesty with my husband and me, that led us to seek the help Kent needed.

TEACHER'S JOURNAL: DECEMBER 10, 1990
Kent... has been experiencing difficulty adjusting to the ordinary routines of a classroom situation and also socializing with peers. Intellectually he appears very bright.

...Kent fidgets and talks to himself daily. He plays with his fingers when nothing else is on the table. He unravels the carpet squares when sitting on one. He sings during rest time and talks during singing time. He has improved in that he is not constantly talking out loud but mumbles to himself which is at least not distracting to the other children.

Our journey through Newington Children's Hospital's PEDAL Program (Program for Evaluation of Development and Learning) began in the spring of 1991. At the end of the journey we had a diagnosis: Pervasive Developmental Disorder (PDD).

We had questioned some of Kent's behavior as a toddler and preschooler, but were looking in the wrong places for answers. I could walk into a room and talk to Kent and he would sit as though he never heard me. We had his hearing checked. That was fine. He had an EEG done to rule out petit mals. Now we know that it is the autistic behavior that is part of PDD. There are degrees of autism, and though Kent is very verbal, he can happily slip into his own world and "play" inside his head if there is nothing of interest to him in the real world.

PDD is a neuropsychiatric disorder. He is behind developmentally in most areas. At the end of first grade, he was still unable to identify the letters of the alphabet or tie his shoelaces. Socially, Kent does not pick up on body language or unspoken cues. Emotionally, he tends to overreact to injustices, can react inappropriately to circumstances and is often upset with himself. He struggles with self-doubt and low self-esteem. Kent is bright and knows he is different. The only area he is not behind in is his growth. He is very large for his age. His behavior is about two years behind his chronological age, but physically he looks two years older than he really is!

Kent is by no means a textbook case of PDD, if such a thing exists. Children with PDD usually have an IQ of about 80. That Kent has an overall IQ of 111

has helped him immensely. He is also dyslexic and dysgraphic. Dysgraphia is to writing what dyslexia is to reading. It is unusual to see this with PDD. Sometimes I am unsure where PDD leaves off and dyslexia begins. Kent is twelve now and still tends to want to stay close and hold on to my elbow or the grocery cart. Dyslexics tend to do this to stay "connected" to the world.

It is not easy to sit before seven professionals and listen to all that is wrong with your child. The doctors prefaced the meeting with, "Remember, when you leave this conference, your child is the same child as when you came in." I remember coming out of the room thinking, "Who is this child? How are we ever going to get through this?" Within twenty-four hours it finally did sink in that Kent was the same child. The diagnosis was just putting a name on what we had lived with for six years. I was relieved to finally have information about Kent, and to have answers to questions I could never put into words. How do you form a question about a nebulous gut feeling that you don't understand yourself? After the initial feeling of numbness wore off, I realized all this information empowered me. I could now help Kent because I knew what his challenges were and the doctors had given us recommendations for intervention. I could explain Kent's behavior to our families. I could work with the school so Kent would be successful in class.

Over the years, Ed and I have made a good team in advocating for our son. Ed is a man of few words, but he is always thinking. In IEP (Individual Education Plan) meetings with the school, while I am carrying the conversational ball, Ed has time to mull over a point made earlier in the meeting. Often, he has brought up a point again for more in-depth discussion.

Of course, "Why us? Why do we have this child?" are questions we couldn't help but ask. I don't know "why us." But I do know that God had a reason for giving us Kent. And knowing that, I do all that I possibly can to help him grow into a productive adult. This quest has led us to many interesting ideas and places. Kent was involved in a social skills group. While the kids were learning to interact with each other, the moms were having their own unofficial support group in the waiting room. After keeping a food log, I became aware that food dyes turned my normally cheerful son into an angry terror. When food dye disappeared from his diet, the anger also disappeared. Alternative medicine has shown us how to work with Kent's neurological disorder. Through exercise, he can switch on the electrical impulses in his brain to help him think clearly. By not being afraid to try new ideas and not letting criticism of unorthodox practices deter me, we have had wonderful results. I remind myself often, "I'm the mom. I know this child better than anyone." Working with so many professionals and specialists, it is a normal tendency to look to them as the ultimate authority on an issue. What I have tried to do is listen to all their information and recommendations to see what can be applied to our personal experience.

Kent is in sixth grade now and is reading at a fourth or fifth grade level. Because classroom textbooks are at the sixth grade reading level, most evenings I am helping him with his homework. He still spells phonetically though he has recently started asking me to check his spelling. Essay questions are kept to a minimum in his work. Writing the answers takes a great deal of time because of the dysgraphia. He still prints like a second or third grader and has never learned cursive. "Cursive is like a different language, Mom." He has finally learned the printed alphabet and can print it without flipping the letters d and b, p and q, m and w.

Kent has made great strides socially though he still struggles. I don't think that will ever change due to the autistic nature of PDD. In the past I have worried about trying to get him to socialize more outside of school. He was in Cub Scouts for five years and he participates in youth group at church. He doesn't care about having friends over after school or on weekends. He has had to deal with people all day at school and that is all he can handle. As a preschooler and in early elementary school, Kent would go into overdrive when in an unstructured social situation such as recess or birthday parties. Often we would leave family gatherings early because he would become unable to handle the noise and stimulation and he would become disruptive. Kent handles these situations wonderfully now. He will seek out a quiet corner and get away from people, if he needs to, or come to me and ask if we can go because he is tired. Not sleepy tired, but tired of trying to deal with people, read body language he doesn't understand and process all the hubbub going on around him. When Kent talks with someone, he is struggling to understand what comes automatically to the rest of us. *What is Gramma saying to me? Why is her voice that tone? What does that facial expression mean? Now she is moving her hands, is that of special significance? I hear a TV going and have to struggle to block it out. The cat is rubbing against my leg. The birthday candles are being lit on the cake. What did Gramma just say? She has on a big bright necklace.* Kent finds it hard to filter out the insignificant.

We have worked on social skills and conversational skills. Kent prefers to talk about his interests and must be reminded to let others talk about what interests them. He is very focused, almost to the point of obsession, on trains. Model railroading is his hobby. If he joins a group of people, he will immediately try to engage them in a conversation about trains with total disregard to what the group was talking about.

I am fortunate in having extensive support in working with Kent. School administrators and teachers, family and friends have never criticized or discouraged me from pursuing new ideas or putting Kent's best interest ahead of other considerations. When I first started looking into alternative medicine, I was trying something that I did not understand fully and therefore could not explain it very well to family. To hear them say, "Whatever it is, if you think it will help, we're behind you 100 %" was a relief. Even my employer has supported my efforts by letting me cut my hours so I have the time I need to work with Kent and still keep order and sanity in our family life.

For six years, Ed and I have put many of our own goals and dreams on hold because of the time intensive help we have given Kent. But it has paid off. This year, sixth grade, Kent is mainstreamed for Science and Social Studies. He is in resource for Math and Language Arts. Kent has been getting A's and B's and has expressed an interest in going to college. He has a wonderful sense of humor and enjoys making up his own jokes (some are actually very funny) and stories to tell. Kent is helpful and caring. He is no longer rigid about his daily schedule. When he was a young child, I would have to start telling him Wednesday if his Saturday routine were going to change.

And even then, I was not guaranteed a smooth Saturday morning. He now can easily "go with the flow."

Kent is aware of his limitations and challenges. Together we find solutions, and at the same time we find closeness and joy. There is a depth and richness to our lives that we never would have believed possible six years ago. Ed and I show Kent our own silly mistakes and tell him about our "bad days," so he knows he is not the only one experiencing discouragement or confusion. We show him all the areas he is "normal," and bring attention to his achievements, no matter how simple. Kent is now more often feeling good about himself, rather than "stupid" or "different." We will continue to repeat lessons, both school-work and life lessons, as often as needed.

The blessings we have received through all of this can not be measured. Not only has Kent grown and changed for the better, but as a family, we have become closer. My self-assurance and tenacity have grown with each challenge. My faith in God has become stronger. I have learned that in everything I have choices. I can choose to be happy or unhappy. I can let anger be the spur that prods me into action, or be the acid that burns up my energy and disables me.

My greatest challenge is that I live my life every day, moment by moment, as an example for Kent to watch and learn from. My life is Kent's "How To" manual. I still wonder if I am qualified to "write" the manual. I hope so, and I hope he is "reading" it!

Falling in Love with Sarah By Paula Agins

Sarah

date of birth:
August 19, 1985

Rett Syndrome

On August 19, 1985, I gave birth to my last child, and only daughter, Sarah. She was a beautiful baby who brought joy and life into a family that had buried her grandfather eleven days before her birth. My Dad's goal was to live to see his grandchild born. He hoped this time it would be a granddaughter.

A few weeks after her arrival I sensed a chill going through me as I sat nursing her. In the crevices of my mind I began to acknowledge that something was different about Sarah. But then, she would respond to me and I would push that thought further back into those dark crevices and quickly bury them. Life would be good, a mother of three beautiful children.

As Sarah approached a year, I found myself conducting secret tests, assessing her response to noise, motion and all her world offered her. Those crevices began to overflow with the realization of the differences in Sarah's interaction with her world.

A pit of fear, anguish and feelings of loss overwhelmed me. I felt this need to "fix." Out of an uncertainty on how to deal with these feelings, I focused my energies and love into a quest to seek and cure.

Sarah was my baby but I somehow had moved her into a segment of my heart that was a safer place, a place that I could protect myself from the pain of losing my daughter. With Rett Syndrome her life would be marked by the losses of skills and the gradual movement into the world of profound retardation. I would no longer see her crawl or hear her say her limited words. I was losing my dream of seeing her attend the local nursery school, take dance lessons, or play on the street with all the other girls in the neighborhood.

It was with endless energy that I pushed, persevered and obtained only the best for her. In each step of this journey I was able to distance myself from her gaze, her smile and her being.

But, for three years Sarah, too, had persevered. She continued to look intently into my eyes, she continued to laugh with a pure joy that hung in your ears, and she continued to touch with an intense feeling of love and trust.

Finally Sarah succeeded in her journey, for she made me stop and feel her presence. She made me stop and feel that she could touch me as her brothers did. She could make me laugh and enjoy her for who she was. In doing so I came to a peace that Sarah was, in all her glory, Sarah. I couldn't fix her nor support her until I was able to recognize and respect her for herself. In doing so, my commitment changed from one of "fix" to one of unconditional love.

I would continue to persevere for Sarah, but out of her needs, not my own. I would open my heart to feel her pain and her frustration. In doing so, I opened my heart to her joy, her laughter, and her dreams.

I opened my heart to loving her and being loved. 🌳

Light at the End of the Tunnel By Stephen J. Scibilio

Brandon and Stephen

date of birth:
Brandon—August 27, 1985
Stephen P.—May 4, 1987

Brandon—Behavior Disorder and Pervasive Developmental Disorder
Stephen P.—Attention Deficit Hyperactivity Disorder

On August 27, 1985, Brandon was delivered by emergency C-section at 7:40 p.m. at a hospital in Rhode Island. Brandon is the son of Stephen Scibilio. He has a younger brother named Stephen Paul.

Prior to that day, my wife had a normal pregnancy and regular doctor checkups. One day during a scheduled checkup the doctor noticed something was wrong. He was concerned that the baby was not heading in the right direction. So he had my wife go to the hospital to have a sonogram. The test showed that the baby had turned himself around and was breached. The doctor was not concerned at the time because everything else seemed to be normal with the baby. As the following months passed and the baby was nearing the final month of the pregnancy, the doctor scheduled a C-section to be performed on July 29th, which was just a little before the due date of the second week in August.

About two weeks before the operation was to be performed my wife went to have her final checkup at the doctor's office. At that checkup the doctor thought the head of the baby appeared to be back in the proper position but still sent my wife directly to the hospital to have another sonogram. That test showed that the baby had turned himself back around and was now in the correct position. Even though the doctor thought it was a little odd that the baby was able to turn around so late into the pregnancy, he felt that everything appeared to be normal with the baby and therefore cancelled the C-section so the baby would have more time to reach full term.

On the afternoon of August 27th, I went to the doctor's office with my wife for her regular checkup. He felt the baby was still doing well but I told him I wanted to speak to him about the concerns I had because the baby was past the due date and nothing was happening. The doctor took us in his office to sit and talk to him. After we talked for a while he said he felt that there was no need to worry because everything seemed to be normal. The baby was still high and he wanted to wait a little while longer to see if the baby would drop lower. However, due to our concerns, he chose to send my wife to the hospital to have a stress test. We arrived at the hospital around 3:00 p.m. and the heart monitor was connected. Before the test even started the monitor showed the baby was in fetal distress. The doctor arrived in less than five minutes and felt it was necessary to schedule an emergency C-section for 7:00 p.m. that night.

Brandon was delivered at 7:40 p.m. on August 27, 1985. Everything appeared to be normal except he had a lot of mucus and had to be suctioned frequently. I was able to attend the delivery in the operating room and how relieved I felt knowing that Brandon was alright! He had a normal weight of seven pounds.

While the nurses were taking care of Brandon's needs they asked if I wanted to come over to watch. I can remember how cute he was and how good I felt the first time I saw him. Before they brought him to the nursery they took him over to my wife so she could see him and touch him. Then I kissed my wife and told her that I loved her and went up to the nursery while the doctor completed the operation on my wife. Brandon had a normal hospital stay. My wife and baby were able to go home five days later.

During Brandon's first month at home his severe nasal congestion continued which required frequent care throughout the night. The head of his crib was raised to help him breathe. Also during the month, he had episodes of stiffening of the whole body. These episodes occurred at any time, but subsided by the time he was a year old. Brandon also did not eat very much. When we tried to feed him solid food he would take two or three little bites and then stop. Brandon didn't sit up until he was nine months old. He didn't crawl until around fifteen months and stood at seventeen months.

Brandon started to walk at eighteen months. He said his first word at approximately two years of age.

On May 4, 1987 our second child, Stephen, was born. I was also able to attend Stephen's delivery. His delivery went smoothly and Stephen showed no problems at birth. I had such a good feeling as I watched the nurses care for my baby. Stephen was also very cute. The nurse brought Stephen to my wife so she could see him before they brought him to the nursery. I gave my wife a kiss before I went to the nursery with my youngest son. My wife and Stephen were able to go home in five days.

In February 1988, my wife and I separated. We went to court on August 1, 1988 for a divorce. When we went to court that day she surprised me before going into the courtroom, saying that we would still have joint custody but she wanted me to have physical custody of the boys starting the first week of September. I agreed and the judge approved our agreement in the courtroom. I didn't know how much my life would change that day.

When I got home from court my wife called to say that I could keep the boys starting that very day. At the time I was living at my parents' home and only had one crib. My wife would not let me back into our apartment to get cribs or clothing for the boys. I had to make some fast decisions that day.

From that day on my whole life changed. Now I know how women feel when they go into the courtroom and come out as a single parent. It is a scary feeling. The kids and I stayed with my parents for one month and then we moved into our own apartment.

Grandma Scibilio's Story

During the years that my two grandsons were born I was still employed as a secretary. The day Stephen was born I came home early to see him at the hospital. I couldn't believe what a beautiful baby he was. He looked like a little china doll. My heart just melted.

When my son became sole custodian of the two boys I decided to retire from my job, even though I liked working and enjoyed the people I worked with. I had two cribs and a twin bed in one small bedroom.

Brandon was almost three, Stephen was fourteen months old and the two were still in diapers. Stephen was still on a bottle and both had trouble eating solid foods. My wonderful sister-in-law saw me struggling and said she would help. That's when she started taking care of Brandon. With only Stephen to take care of during the day I found it much easier, but my son decided Stephen should be in daycare. He started out going mornings. I would take him to daycare and pick him up at noon. For the longest time all he wanted for lunch was a hotdog, rice and beets. Whenever I tried something different he wouldn't eat. It seemed like he became a creature of habit and whenever his routine changed he would get very upset and give me a hard time for the rest of the day.

At age four Stephen started preschool and we walked to the school which was just up the hill from where I live. He liked it there but didn't get along too well with the other children. I think it was because he couldn't speak clearly and the other children couldn't understand him. That's when he started on speech therapy. Because of his problem he wouldn't talk too much. Now after all the help with his therapists we can't shut him up. He loves to argue and wants to have the last word. However his father has punished him for it and has had long talks with him about it, so he is doing very much better at it.

When Stephen started kindergarten I would put him on the bus. He liked going to school and loved riding the bus but he had a hard time in school. He couldn't sit still and hated homework. Because of his short attention span he had some bad days and didn't do too well.

After all the work and all that his father has gone through, trying to straighten him out, I think he has finally gotten on the right road. Now in middle school he is doing much better in his group and has even made the honor roll. He is so proud of himself that he tries even harder to get his homework done every day.

We take Stephen overnight one or two nights a week. He loves it here and now that he is older we have long talks and get along good. Now he walks to middle school every day. He calls me in the morning and when he gets home after 2:00 p.m. I like it when he calls because I know he got home okay and is doing his homework.

We take Stephen out to eat almost every Saturday night. He likes to order his own prime rib dinner and even tells the waitress how he wants it cooked. Later that night we go to church together. He had a real hard time sitting still and paying attention for the longest time but even that has changed. He sits real good now and is proud of himself when I tell him how good he did during mass.

I really loved having Stephen all these years and I think he has kept me feeling young. It breaks my heart when every once in a while he asks about his mother whom he has never known. He compares himself to some of his friends, who have mothers, but I just tell him he is special to have a Grandma and Grandpa who love him double. He is happy about that.

Stephen is a very lovable child who likes to hug and be hugged and of course Grandma just loves every minute of it.

Dad's Story Continued

After I got physical custody of Brandon and Stephen I contacted people from the Special Education Department in our local school system in Westerly, RI. Brandon was two and one-half years old at the time. They met with us and did some educational testing on Brandon. They suggested I take him to a child development center in Providence, RI, to be evaluated.

The center conducted a full educational and physical evaluation on him. Brandon had all types of physical testing ranging from a CT scan to blood work, in order to find the cause of his condition. All tests came back negative. I remember how I felt when they couldn't find a cause or a name for his condition. How frustrating it was! Brandon was very small at three years old, weighing only around twenty pounds. He was so little. After about two days of testing the team from the center

made some recommendations. They recommended that Brandon attend a special education preschool program in our local school district.

The center also was concerned about his nutritional intake because of his poor eating behaviors. They recommended that I take him to a special feeding program at the hospital. My Aunt Julia and I took him there for nine months. This was very hard on my aunt and it was also hard for me to watch Brandon through a one-way window as people tried to teach him how to chew the solid food and swallow it. The food that they would feed Brandon was food that we brought from home. They asked us to bring a whole meal that we would normally eat at home so that the food would be familiar to him. After about two weeks of watching the specialists feed Brandon, I was asked to sit in on one of the sessions to learn the technique to get Brandon to eat more at home. I did this for a few weeks and then my aunt was asked to sit in on the sessions so that she could learn the technique also.

These sessions went on twice a week for nine months until they felt that Brandon was eating well and they were confident that we would be able to continue to use this technique at home without their assistance. This was a wonderful program and it worked very well. Brandon was able to eat on his own after a while and he finally started to gain weight.

When I first had Brandon evaluated at the child development center, I was hoping that they would find a cause for his difficulties or at least be able to tell me what kind of disability Brandon had. When the tests came back negative I was both relieved and disappointed. The doctors were also a little disappointed because they said that I might never know what caused him to be this way. Sometimes with the CT scan they are able to pinpoint the cause of children's developmental difficulties, but not this time. The doctors were also hoping to put a label on Brandon's disability. I can remember all the emotional feelings that I was going through at the time. First the disappointment—and then the anger

because he was like this. But after a while all these feelings subsided and I was able to accept the fact that he had a disability and I learned to deal with it.

After Brandon was evaluated at the child development center they made some recommendations to the school department. He was placed in a special education preschool program at the age of three. During the next few years Brandon made slow but steady progress. I can remember at the beginning I was always hoping that he would catch up to the other kids. It took me many years before

I realized that he would never catch up. Therefore, I just proceeded to get him as much help as I could. Even though it has been frustrating at times, it has also been very rewarding. We have helped Brandon become very good at taking care of himself and I have to do very little for him.

My Aunt Julia and Uncle Ernie have spent a great deal of time caring for Brandon. The following section contains their stories and what they have to say about him. They have a lot of patience with Brandon and they have taught him a lot. Aunt Julia has much more patience with him than I do and she has brought him a long way. Without the help of my aunt and uncle, I know Brandon would not have come as far along as he has.

Aunt Julia's Story

The first dealings I had with Brandon were when he was three years old. He was a small, petite child who did not like to be cuddled. His vocabulary consisted of three words: cookie, juice, and bye-bye. We also found out he didn't know how to chew. That started a long session of going to a hospital twice a week for the doctor to feed him by actually moving his jaws up and down after every bite. We watched him behind a one-way mirrored glass. After a few weeks of watching we tried feeding him ourselves while the doctor watched us and gave us pointers.

Brandon tried really hard to talk. He would watch our lips and make some sort of noise along with us. His speech started slowly but now we can't shut him up.

He really didn't know how to play. He had no interest in anything. The only thing I know he played with was a play stove. He would watch me cook on Saturdays and he would pretend to cook right along with me. When he went to school the kitchen set was the only thing he would play with. The teacher tried to get him to play with trucks or puzzles but he always went back to the play kitchen.

Noise was Brandon's biggest problem. If a truck came by while we waited outside for the bus, Brandon would run right back into the house. If he saw a balloon he would pull away from you and scream. I think he was afraid because he heard a balloon pop one time. At parades he was afraid of the guns even if they weren't shooting.

Brandon did make his First Communion. He had his own teacher and learned all his prayers which he still says every night. At Christmas time they selected Brandon to bring down Baby Jesus to place in the manger. He did an excellent job.

We thought Brandon would have no problem reading because I started him learning phonics at the age of four. It was a great program with a tape and a book that you used to sound out your

letters. He really enjoyed doing this. Maybe this is why he is a good speller. But I don't know why he doesn't read that well.

I have noticed now he will play more. He has two play buses. One has a wheelchair. He names the little people. He picks them up, then brings them home making them bounce along. He has every truck available. If he sees any construction on the way home, out come all the backhoes and trucks. If I iron, out comes his ironing board and iron. He will take his clean clothes that are hanging up and iron each one and put them back on the hanger and put them away. If I dust, he dusts. He is still afraid of the vacuum. I guess it's the noise again.

Sometimes Brandon's span of attention and understanding is better than at other times. He thinks everything is funny. If you bump your head, Brandon will laugh. If you trip and fall, he laughs. If you cry, he still laughs.

We are still dealing with him talking to himself and hurting himself. Brandon will dig his nails into his arm and keep looking at it and then do it again. Now that Brandon is getting older he is getting a mind of his own. He has his good days and some bad days.

Brandon has to have a routine. Everything has to be in its place with chairs pushed in, doors closed, and all drawers shut tight. Sometimes it really gets on your nerves. You could be reading him a story and he will get up to straighten out a picture or a book. We call him, "Mr. Perfect."

Brandon has a great personality. You can take him anywhere and people go out of their way to come up and talk to him. He also has excellent manners. He likes going to a restaurant to eat. When the meal is over and you start to leave he will go up to the waitress and say, "Thank you very much." They look forward to seeing him again.

The new program that Brandon is in now, from Bradley Hospital, is terrific. The home service counselor, Roy, is one in a million. He has taught me many different ways to handle Brandon. Now that he is getting older, you have to change your ways. You also learn you have more patience than you can imagine.

Brandon loves to go to the Mystic Aquarium in Connecticut, to see all of the different kinds of fish. Now he can really understand the shows the whales put on, and he claps away like everyone else. The best part for him is going out to eat after the show.

We enjoy taking Brandon shopping. He has never asked for anything! If he starts to touch things all you have to do is look at him and those little hands go behind his back.

Brandon has really brightened our lives. God has sent us this special child and we love him very much.

Uncle Ernie's Story

Brandon loves to sing. I sing with the "Senior Songbirds" so I teach Brandon some of these old songs, while we wait for the bus in the morning. The teachers love to hear Brandon sing all these songs: "Bicycle Built for Two," "Down By the Old Mill Stream," "Yankee Doodle Dandy," and "You Are My Sunshine." The bus driver's name is Mary, so he gets on the bus singing, "Mary, Mary, That's a Grand Old Name."

If it snows, Brandon will take his little shovel and come out to help me. His job is shoveling off the porch. In the summer he will help me cut the lawn. I let him stand in front of me and we both cut the lawn. If I am painting outside, I will put water in a pail for him, and let him "paint" all he wants.

Aunt Julia's Response: "There are times I have to play referee. These two argue quite a bit. I can't leave them alone for a minute. Sometimes I wonder, 'Who is the kid?'"

Dad's Story Continued

In February 1995, I met with the Assistant Special Education Director from our local school department. I asked her to recommend a doctor who could evaluate Brandon to see if medication would help him with his hyperactivity and his inability to focus. The assistant director recommended a doctor at a hospital in Providence, RI. On March 22, 1995, we had our first visit.

Brandon is still under the doctor's care there. We tried all kinds of medications to see if they would help. Instead of these medicines helping, they did just the opposite. This was very frustrating because I was really hoping that medicine would help him. This went on for almost two years before we decided to take him off all medication and try a behavior management plan. The hospital has a program that we waited a long time to get into, where they have a counselor who comes into the home. He would work with Brandon in setting up a structured plan after Brandon gets home from school. This counselor would also work with me and my son Stephen, in dealing with Brandon and his behavior. This program started at the end of April in 1997.

My younger son Stephen started having problems, which we noticed by the time he was four years old. His speech was not improving. He had a speech teacher work with him starting in the first grade.

His speech has improved a lot, but he still has a way to go. He will continue to work with the speech teacher as long as he needs it. He also had trouble with his attention span and being able to sit still at his desk in class. When he was in the second grade the teachers and the school psychologist tested Stephen for hyperactivity. He was on the borderline but they didn't feel that he should be on medication at that time.

When Stephen was in the third grade the teacher came to me and stated he was still having problems with his attention span and being able to sit still in class. He was also having some behavior problems. I spoke to Brandon's doctor at the hospital prior to taking Brandon to see him. The doctor said he would be glad to see Stephen when I took Brandon up for his appointment. On February 2, 1996, I took Stephen with me for Brandon's appointment. The doctor observed Stephen and reviewed the letter that the teacher had sent explaining what she saw in class. Stephen exhibited signs of having Attention-Deficit Hyperactivity Disorder, (ADHD), and the doctor felt that medication would help him. He started taking the medication that day and we saw an immediate improvement. His attention span improved and he was able to sit still. His behavior problems also stopped. Stephen was able to study better and do his homework without asking a lot of questions. His grades also improved.

Stephen was on this medication for about a year when all of a sudden he started having problems in school and at home once again. This was very disturbing to his teachers and me because he was doing so well prior to that. He started to become very compulsive about getting everything done just right with his work and he would be constantly erasing, which was putting him behind. He started to have behavior problems again and he wasn't able to sit still in his seat in class. This went on for about two months, which was a very frustrating time for me.

After about the second month of trying different things, his teachers called up Stephen's doctor at the hospital to set up a meeting with them at his school. I also attended the meeting and after a lot of discussion we decided to try to take him off all of his medication. He didn't improve at all after stopping the medication so the doctor decided to try a different one. This medication seemed to work better than the last one. Stephen's compulsive behavior stopped, his work improved, and his grades started to go up again. He was able to sit still better and the behavior problems disappeared. He also seemed to be much happier on this medication.

Once again, this only worked for a short time. I had the doctor stop all medication for Stephen. At the same time I also stopped Brandon's around May, 1997. This was another disappointing and stressful time for me. It was at this time that I called the people who are in charge of the behavior management program at the hospital to see if they could help me with Stephen. They said that they could include him in the program and have Roy, the counselor working with Brandon, spend some of his time working with Stephen. Roy worked with Stephen to see what areas he was having trouble with. Roy also went to his school to talk to his teachers and to observe Stephen to see where he was having difficulties. Stephen was two months into the fifth grade and having a real hard time doing the work because of his behavior. He was having difficulty in many areas. His attention span was short, he was not able to focus in class, he was unable to sit still while at his desk, and he was not able to sit at his desk for a long period of time. Stephen was talking to the children around him and he would also call out and disrupt the class. He had a negative attitude about the schoolwork to be done, and he was argumentative about how it would be done. Stephen would also have this negative attitude at home when working on his homework. It was just the beginning of the school year when he felt he wasn't able to do the homework because he was "dumb" and the work was too hard for him.

Stephen was very argumentative with all of us at home and was generally negative about everything. We knew he was able to do the work in school and at home, but his behavior was getting in the way.

This was a very stressful time for me because I didn't expect him to have this behavior or to struggle in school this year because things had gone well for awhile. The timing was also bad because Brandon was having some difficulty adjusting to his new program at the middle school and he also had some behavior problems in school. These behaviors needed to be addressed now. We couldn't go on like this.

I became involved with the Bradley Hospital's Behavior Management Program because I was becoming more and more depressed and frustrated with what was happening with both my sons. I was putting great effort into helping my boys but not seeing positive results. I was feeling very inadequate as a parent. I kept hoping that the medication that Brandon was on would help his behavior improve, and help him function better, but it didn't.

I was also becoming concerned for Brandon's health because of trying so many different kinds of medication. What would it do to him in the future?

Then putting Stephen on medication for the disorders that he had, and having these medications work for awhile, only to have his behavior problems return, was more than I could handle. I was finding myself yelling at both boys more often and hitting more. Because the behaviors of Brandon and Stephen were getting in their way academically, they were both suffering in school. Around February of 1997, I mentioned to our doctor at the hospital that I was at my wits end and didn't know how much more I could take. I was very frustrated with the results of the medication and what was going on at home. My family needed help.

At this time the doctor mentioned an in-home behavior program that they offer at Bradley Hospital. He explained the program to me and said he would look into it to see if I met the criteria for the program. He asked if I would be interested in this program if I qualified, at which time I said I would try anything for help. A short time later, the hospital notified me that I was accepted into the Early Preventative Screening and Diagnostic Testing program (E.P.S.D.T.).

The E.P.S.D.T. home-based treatment program started at the end of April in 1997. Since we lived so far from the hospital, it took a while for them to hire and train a therapist before he could begin the program at my home. In the meantime, I did meet with a Clinical Social Worker at the hospital. He explained the in-home treatment program to me. He also kept me updated on what was happening until the program started.

Around March, I was contacted and told that they hired a therapist and the program would start soon. The therapist's name was Roy. He started at the end of April in 1997 and he spent about three weeks at Brandon's school getting to know him before starting in our home.

The purpose of this program is for a therapist to come into your home and evaluate the behaviors he sees taking place and see how the adult handles them. Then he recommends solutions in handling the inappropriate behaviors. He also works with the children on their own behaviors. This program also works with the school system. The therapist would make periodic visits to Brandon and Stephen's schools to meet with their teachers to see how they were doing and to observe them in class. This was very helpful.

Roy has been doing a lot of community integration with Brandon. He has been taking him to different stores to look at woodworking tools. Brandon has a special interest in all aspects of construction. Roy worked with him doing woodworking projects and Brandon enjoyed this.

The therapist also spent a lot of time in the Westerly Park talking to Brandon about the different types of trees. He spent a lot of time talking to both children about their behavior and how he was there to help them stop inappropriate behavior and learn to function better.

The strategies that Roy and I came up with had good results. At one point I thought I was going to have to put my son Stephen back on medication because of the problems he was having in school, yet I was determined not to do this at this time. One idea I came up with and

wanted to try was a point system. I ran this idea by Roy and he thought it was a good one. I met with all of Stephen's teachers and talked about this point system and asked if it would be possible for them to set it up at school. After a while they developed a system where Stephen had to meet certain goals during the day to earn points. He could earn one to twelve points each day. The teachers would write the amount of points he earned in his assignment book at the end of each day. I also had a separate calendar where I kept track of one or two points Stephen could earn at home each day. He could earn points both for the kind of day he had in school and for the grades that he received on tests. After he earned so many points at the end of each week and each month, he was rewarded.

Stephen had great results from this program. His behavior problems have decreased and his grades on tests have improved. He is doing much better getting his homework done and studying for tests. His teachers have seen a big improvement in him and he seems much happier and is trying a lot harder.

Other strategies that were used at home are better use of time-outs and having Brandon and Stephen write about their behaviors. These strategies had great results and life at home has become less stressful and much happier.

The E.P.S.D.T. program can last up to a year. After the first six months of this program my life and my children's lives have become much easier. We are more functional as a family. I am finding myself doing more things with the boys. Brandon is learning to play the piano. I found a piano teacher who works with special needs children. He started lessons in January, 1998. I am taking the lessons with him so that I will be able to work with him at home. This is good because I wanted something that I could do with Brandon alone. I am also spending more time with Stephen, playing games, and working on his karate.

From January of 1997 until January of 1998, I feel my life has really changed. The hospital has signed us up for another six months of this program to work on a few other areas that need to be addressed.

Stephen and Brandon are much happier now and we are functioning much better as a family. I find myself not yelling very often and I am not hitting the boys at all. I have become a firm believer that there is no reason to hit children. The therapist from the hospital has taught me that by learning some simple techniques on dealing with bad behavior, you can make a big difference in your life and your children's lives. I have not been this happy in a long time.

Brandon has come a long way. He has become more independent and he is able to care for himself. Hc has made a lot of accomplishments over the years. He made his First Communion when he was nine years old. In 1997 he participated in the Special Olympics for the first time. On May 7th, Brandon entered the Special Olympics and won a gold medal in the softball throw. He also won a ribbon in the 100-meter dash. Then on May 30th and 31st, he attended the University of Rhode Island State Games. He won a bronze medal in the 4x100-meter relay race. He also won a gold medal in the softball throw and he took a fourth place ribbon in the 100-meter dash.

Around September of 1997 I had Brandon try karate at the same place Stephen takes lessons. The instructor worked with Brandon one-on-one, once a week for about a month to see how he would do. After about a month of private lessons, the instructor felt Brandon was ready to participate with the regular class. He had some problems staying focused but for the most part he did really well. I was so proud at what he was able to do. I stopped the karate lessons for Brandon when I took him off all the medication. When I stopped the medication Brandon's behavior got a little worse and his attention span got shorter. He has since improved a great deal but we are still working on some behavior issues that need improvement. I hope to someday get him back into karate. It is really good for special needs kids. It helps them feel good about themselves.

As far as other people accepting Brandon, that hasn't been a problem either. Everyone loves Brandon. The kids at karate also accepted Brandon and included him in all the activities that took place in class. The staff and students didn't need to give him any special treatment because of his disability. They all praise Brandon and tell him how proud they are of him. His brother, Stephen, has been taking karate for two and one-half years and he spends some time working with Brandon on karate moves, which is good because it is something that they can do at home together.

Brandon still has some weak points that we are trying to work on. He is still afraid of loud noises although he has improved a lot from when he was younger. Not long ago he would scream and cry if he heard a lawn mower or a weed-whacker outside. This would really distract him if he was in school. He was okay if he could see where the noise was coming from. No matter what the noise was when he was younger, if he couldn't see where it was coming from, it would really bother him. He has gotten over that now that he is older. The only thing that still bothers him is balloons, especially when they pop. This really sets him off.

Brandon also is only at the point where he asks questions when speaking to you. He will ask the same question over and over again. He also talks to himself a lot. These are all areas that we were hoping the medication would help to improve. But the medication didn't work, so that is where Roy, from the hospital, is trying to help by using behavior management. This program has certainly helped a lot.

Brandon has strong points also. He is able to read and write. He does this at a slow pace but he can do it. He is also good with math, and is one of the top spellers in his class. He is able to dress on his own and take a shower with little help. These are some of Brandon's strengths that I know will help him later in life.

It has not been an easy road for my two sons and me. Almost on a daily basis I have to make vital decisions. It can get very frustrating and tiring at times. I'm

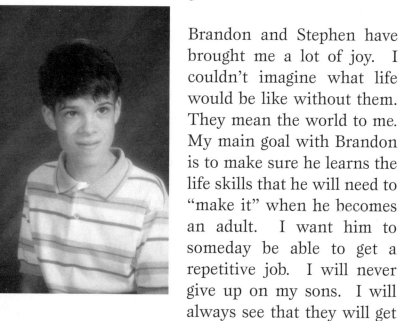

very fortunate that I have parents and my aunt and uncle who give me a lot of help. They support me in the decisions that I make for my sons. They also care for Brandon and Stephen, which helps to give me a break.

Brandon and Stephen have brought me a lot of joy. I couldn't imagine what life would be like without them. They mean the world to me. My main goal with Brandon is to make sure he learns the life skills that he will need to "make it" when he becomes an adult. I want him to someday be able to get a repetitive job. I will never give up on my sons. I will always see that they will get the help they need to succeed in life.

Our local school department has also given me a lot of help and support with both boys. They have a great special education program. Brandon was in a 210-day program for the past four years that has brought him a long way. This program is an inclusion program, which means he spends most of the day in a regular classroom. He has a special education teacher or aide with him in the classroom. The other children and classroom teachers have been very receptive to this type of inclusion program. They have all loved Brandon and he has made a lot of friends. This school year has been a big change for him. Because he is in the sixth grade, he had to change to the middle school. With all of his support, Brandon has handled it well.

There is one other area that is difficult for me. It is not easy for people to date someone who already has children. When you have a

special needs child, dating can be even more difficult. There is a line that is difficult to cross, traveling from just dating to a point of commitment to the whole family. It is painful to have your child not accepted by someone you care about.

Finally the thing I would like to say to other families that have special needs children is, never give up hope. There is always help out there, you just have to keep looking. There is a light at the end of the tunnel. You just have to help your child reach the other end. It's a long, tiring journey, but like I keep telling myself, it will be worth it in the end.

Keeper of My Heart By Kathy Stelik

Kate

date of birth:
October 22, 1979

Phonologic Dyslexia with Central
Auditory Processing Disorder

For many years I have watched as children have grown to be the best that they could possibly be, babies and toddlers, preschoolers and school aged children, adolescents and young adults, all with so many differences, and all with so many amazing gifts and strengths. I have always felt so grateful for having the opportunity to work with people who are so very special.

As an Occupational Therapist I have watched the development of so many children. I have been able to see their dreams, hear their hearts, feel their bodies, sense their frustrations, connect with their spirits and celebrate all of their accomplishments. And every day I learn. Some days the lessons elicit tears of joy while others may teach strength through sadness and disappointment. They have all been lessons that I have had to use over and over again in my personal life while raising my own special children.

I have been blessed with three beautiful, healthy children. Todd, the eldest has

just graduated from college and is working as an Occupational Therapist. Aaron, my middle child, works with special needs children and goes to college part time. He has struggled all through school because he was blessed with the amazing challenge of living with attention deficit disorder. Despite a few trips down the road less traveled, Aaron has evolved unscathed and doing well. Kate, who is the baby of the family, is now nineteen, directed, happy, immersed in her education and with her first love. She is truly the happiest she has been; however, the road to this happiness has been long, treacherous and agonizing. Kate has phonologic dyslexia with central auditory processing disorder. In short this means that she processes all auditory information very slowly, is unable to decode new words, retain vocabulary and read at a level that is equal to her cognitive ability. Many family members, professionals, and educators, who could not seem to get a handle on her problems and why it was hard for her to learn and remember, have marked her childhood. A variety of well-meaning suggestions, which usually began with, "If only she would try harder or didn't get so frustrated, she would…" were a constant theme of any given day. I guess no one ever truly understood how hard she always tried and how, despite failure after failure, she would pick herself up and start again.

Her inability to learn through listening challenged all of the developmental rights of passage for a little girl: singing the alphabet song, learning the Pledge of Allegiance, singing nursery rhymes, taking the Girl Scout oath, committing to memory the Our Father and Hail Mary in preparation for First Communion class, forgetting one-line parts in the school play, raising her hand eagerly in class only to forget the answer in total embarrassment, and always being the little tap dancer in the back row going in the wrong direction.

When she was younger, she would get up in the morning and eagerly get ready for school with great anticipation of what fun the day would bring. I watched her enthusiasm and her ability to play and have fun dwindle as time went on. She had a way of creating safe places for herself. Sitting next to me in our favorite spot with her blanket, staying in her room that was filled with stuffed animals and Lego models that she spent endless hours constructing, and sucking her thumb while watching television, were her areas of comfort. As she got older she replaced her thumb with favorite snacks that seemed also to give her comfort. Kate began the "frequent flier" route to the nurse's station by grade two; this converted to the "frequent absence" route by grade nine. Eagerness slowly turned to avoidance, happiness to frustration, tolerance to anger, and dreams to thoughts of uselessness.

As a child grows, it is not enough for them to get positive input from parents alone. They seek reassurance and approval from friends, teachers, and coaches. It was not enough for Kate to be sent off everyday with a kiss and assurance that everything would be okay, to keep trying hard and it would all fall into place. Oftentimes just the opposite would occur. Sometimes she would try so hard and all of her efforts would go unanswered. Teachers did not recognize the positives but were quick to accentuate the negatives. Attributing lack of success to attitude as opposed to frustration due to lack of understanding. This is when even the strongest love does not seem to make a difference. Kate finally arrived at this place at age sixteen in grade ten. She was unable to read because she could not decode new words and she could not write because she could not spell. She had tried for years to blend in, stay in safe places, hang in the back of the class and speak only when spoken to. Although she's never said anything to me, I'm sure she had spent hours praying that no one would call on her to read out loud or answer a sponta-

neous question and most assuredly she prayed that it would all go away. I can actually count the number of days that she came home with a song in her heart, as opposed to tears in her eyes.

To watch a vibrant, intelligent child lose all hope and dreams and begin to slip away is the worst feeling of all. To know, despite my background in this field, that I was unable to unlock the doors that would direct her to achieve her dreams was tormenting. Sitting together and listening to Kate talk about how difficult life had become, and how school had finally become an unachievable goal, was horrifying. Talking about dropping out of school instead of planning for college, questioning what type of job she could get if she was unable to do simple tasks such as: write down numbers, take messages, and spell effectively, entered the conversation daily. It was the point at which I knew there had to be something else we could do. When I think about how hard she has had to work; doing and redoing, correcting, rehearsing, reading and re-reading, writing and re-writing, cutting up all the paper in the house to make flash cards, thinking she had finally understood only to realize she did not, studying for the big test only to fail, I am in awe. She has always had to spend three times the energy and effort that her classmates did. But she did it. She would get frustrated, become "moody," get angry and retreat to her room but she would eventually emerge with a glimmer of hope and a smile.

Unfortunately, most of Kate's special education had been directed at accommodation, strategies to help her cope, techniques to decrease frustration and ways to build self-esteem. No one understood how important it was for Kate to learn. To learn meant learning how to read and write on a level with her age and grade. This was the key to everything. Learning these basic skills was all she needed. Had someone found the right intervention years ago, her childhood would have been so different. If teachers had only opted for remediation and skill development instead of accommodation and modification she would not be so far behind. Despite years of summer school, special schools,

tutors, and extra hours every night, she persevered. And while she persevered I continued to search for help.

We were very fortunate to have finally found a program that could help her with her unique learning disabilities. The Landmark School is on the North Shore of Boston in the quaint town of

Prides Crossing. This meant she would have to live two hours away. There were many tears shed in the process of deciding to let her go, but we all knew this was her chance to shine and accomplish all she had hoped for. So we packed her up one summer day and she has been there ever since. Since her enrollment, she has blossomed into a more confident, self-assured, happier young woman who has begun to accept her learning disability as a fact of her life. A fact that has made her stronger and more directed, kinder and more understanding and more resilient to the little twists and turns that life can bring.

Kate and I both know that nothing will ever be easy, but things are definitely easier. We both know that some of her dreams may not be attainable, but many more doors have been opened. We understand that for her to go to college means many more

years of hard work, but we also know she now has the skills to do it. Most importantly, we both know that whatever she chooses to do, she will do it well. She will continue to embrace those things that have always brought her comfort: her family, love of the ocean and animals, and her incredible need to laugh and have fun. She is, without a doubt, one of the most remarkable children I have ever known and the keeper of my heart.

What Really Counts By Matt Wright

Matt

date of birth:
October 25, 1982

Learning Disabilities

I am sixteen years old, will be a junior in high school this fall, and I have learning disabilities.

In around third grade we had to learn the multiplication tables. I learned them off and on that year about four or five times. My parents and sisters would use flash cards until I knew them well. But then I would easily forget them. This was frustrating for me and my teachers. Some teachers just could not understand that I really worked hard because I couldn't prove it in class. A lot of the teachers that I think were good, took time out to talk to me, offered me extra help, and gave me the benefit of the doubt. My parents took me for testing at some point and that is when I heard that I had a math learning disability. The good part about finding out that you have a learning disability is that then you can get help. The person testing recommended that I continue to take math classes but be taught to use a calculator. At first some teachers insisted that I shouldn't use a calculator because it wouldn't be fair for the rest of the kids. But once they allowed it my grades improved and I could concentrate on how to find answers in math even though I had trouble with some basic math. The other part of my learning disability is called written language. Even when I was little I had trouble writing as much as the other kids because I was a lot slower at it. I also have been tested for attention deficit disorder. The doctors disagree about this and can't prove it either way. The one thing I know about learning disabilities is that you have to understand that you are as smart as the other kids but you just need help to show it in school.

This is my first year in high school. Having learning disabilities affects my life at school and my homework. For me, learning disabilities means it takes me longer to do assignments because it affects almost everything I do. The good part about high school is that teachers are a lot more understanding because they deal with a lot more kids with disabilities than my other school, just because there are so many kids. In my elementary school I did have some teachers who really understood, but there were just as many who didn't understand and didn't seem to even try to understand how disabilities affected my schoolwork. When teachers don't understand they make you feel stupid and useless. But when teachers try to figure out the best way with you, you feel they care and have confidence that you can do a good job and you work even harder for them.

In high school there is a lot of teacher support. I go to meetings with my teachers and parents, and we work together to make any plans for whatever is needed to help me succeed. My mom is always there for me and sticks up for me until I get what is educationally right for me. Once the plan is set, then I have

to keep my promise to contribute just as much as the teachers. That is my job. I need to make sure I put lots of effort into keeping track of my work. I am also an auditory learner which means I learn best just listening. The problem then is that I have trouble taking notes while listening to teachers talk for a long time and then I don't have good notes to study later.

I have lots of interests. Ever since I was little the three things I loved were music, trains, and being outside. I play the drums in the symphonic band and the

jazz lab band in school. I think it is very fair that my parents let me play the drums starting at six o'clock in the morning, although sometimes I get the urge to play earlier. I joined the Big Brother program and I finally have a little brother after having to put up with three older sisters. He is in the second grade. My favorite hobby is model trains and studying real trains. Some weekends my dad and I go to model railroad shows because now I have him interested in them, too. My second favorite thing in the world is free-style dirt jumping. I have dug up my backyard and have made four jumps but I plan to fill the whole backyard this summer if I can borrow a backhoe. That is, if my mom and dad let me take over the yard. I do a lot of skateboarding, too.

I am a hard worker. I have always enjoyed doing physical work and I am happiest when I am working outside. I have worked driving farm equipment, and I have done some landscaping and construction work. My dad and I have a small snowplowing business that I will be in charge of in a couple of years. I named it, "Matt Wright and Father, Snow Removal." After college I want to get licensed to operate heavy equipment for a construction company.

The neat part about being the youngest in the family is that everybody spoils you and enjoys you to bits. My grandparents think everything I do is wonderful even when I don't do anything. My grandfather calls me his little "dahling" to tease me and we have a special handshake. My Gram Wright is eighty-nine years old but is more tuned into life than some of my friends. When I need new sneakers I can always go to my Gram Perreault but when I need money for McDonald's I go to Gramp. My sisters are always there for me. They've taught me a lot about life—to share my feelings, and how to treat girls right. I know I can always call them if I ever have a problem or just want to talk. Heather and Julie live in Boston, Massachusetts, and Erin lives in Oklahoma. I miss them living here although at times they could get really annoying. We have lots of fun together when they come home. The neat part about having a sister get married is that you get another man around the house to hang out with. My brother-in-law, Juan, loves to bike, listen to music, and play video games with me. Besides family, I think what really counts in life is having a positive attitude, keeping an open mind, and being a good person.

Our Inspiration By Joanne M. Pigeon

Laura

January 12, 1973 - December 11, 1990
Multiple Disabilities

As a child I knew that one day I would have children. The day I married Ray I became a full-time mother to five-year-old Debbie and two-year-old Steven but I still felt the need to bear a child. About a year and a half later, my desire to have a child was fulfilled.

Friday, January 12, 1973 was without a doubt the happiest day of my life. "You have a beautiful, healthy, baby girl," announced my doctor in the delivery room. Laura weighed in at seven pounds fourteen ounces, and she was twenty inches long. She certainly was beautiful!

About a week after Laura was discharged from the hospital, she developed a low-grade temperature. I immediately informed her pediatrician who felt that this was nothing to be concerned about. He told me that she was probably coming down with a cold. However, if it should continue to rise, he wanted to see her.

A few days later, Laura woke up from her nap with a temperature of one hundred and five degrees. She was rushed to the hospital and admitted. Throughout the next four days, she underwent numerous tests. After ruling out meningitis, she was diagnosed as having a virus of unknown origin.

At her follow-up visit about a week later, I mentioned that since being home from the hospital Laura would fuss, but she didn't cry. Her pediatrician told me that I was lucky and that I have "a baby from Heaven." However, now I wish that I had pursued the fact that she did not cry.

At a year old, Laura was very passive. When other children would take a toy away from her, she would not cry or try to grab it back; she would look for something else to play with. I was concerned that she was not progressing at the rate of other babies her age. Instead of crawling she would drag her body along the floor. I was also concerned with the fact that she had not started to babble or respond to certain sounds.

At her one-year checkup, I mentioned my concerns to her pediatrician. I also mentioned that although Laura was older than the babies we had been with recently, she seemed to be developing more slowly. Her pediatrician stated that my other two children were probably doing everything for her. He assured me that this often happens with a younger child. Although I knew that her siblings did anticipate her needs, I still had a feeling that there was a problem. Her doctor also suggested that I should not compare her to other children, as all children develop at their own rate. With regard to her hearing, he experimented with a variety of noises in the office. Most of the time she responded. As a precaution, he referred her to a special children's hospital in Connecticut.

At the hospital it was determined that she had a great deal of fluid buildup in the middle ear. We were referred to an Ear, Nose and Throat surgeon. The surgeon explained that her eustachian tube was underdeveloped, and that she would need tubes in her ears. He also explained that this is very common in children who are under the age of five. The surgery was successful. We were told there was a considerable amount of

scar tissue, and that the amount of hearing loss, if any, would be determined at a later time. After coming home from the hospital, we noticed an improvement in the way she responded when we spoke to her, and an improvement in her response to various sounds. It didn't take her long to discover that crying would get our attention.

Suddenly one day, at fourteen months old, Laura slid out of her high chair, landed on her feet and took a few steps. I believe she even surprised herself. I was ecstatic! However, after that occurrence, I found that I had to encourage her to walk.

As Laura's second birthday approached, although we noticed some progress, she continued to develop at a slower rate. I was becoming concerned with the fact that her gross and fine motor skills were very poor, along with her ability to communicate her needs. As a result, she would sit and cry, sometimes for hours, because she was so frustrated. There were days that I wanted to do the same.

During one of our hospital consultations a few months later, her doctor suggested that we have a workup done to determine if her hearing loss was the only problem. As a result of his evaluation, it was determined that it would benefit Laura to be in a hearing-impaired class.

Laura was two years and eight months old when she entered a hearing-impaired class. Every day was a challenge to get her on the school bus, as she was kicking and crying. However, after being in school for a while, she would calm down. During that year, Laura learned how to communicate with us using gestures and sounds.

The following year tubes were again put in her ears, and again we noticed improvement in her hearing. I anticipated that her balance would also improve, but this didn't happen. Although her hearing improved, her voice continued to sound as if she were hearing-impaired.

A few months later, another complete workup was done at the hospital, to evaluate and compare the level that Laura was at developmentally from the previous year. As a result of this evaluation, I was told that her hearing loss was not significant enough to be the cause for her being developmentally slower. I was then told that my little girl was mentally retarded. Although I knew she was slow, I was taken aback by the news. It felt as though a knife was being hand pierced through my heart. At that point, I didn't know what to think or feel about her future.

Although everyone wanted to be supportive, no one knew what to say or how to interact with Laura. It seemed as though family and friends were expecting much less of Laura now that she had this "condition." As I look back, I think I was more concerned with the label and the limitations that would be placed on her.

That September, Laura was in a special class with other mentally challenged preschool children. Laura loved school and looked forward to getting on the bus each day. She still wasn't talking. As a result, she was getting speech therapy that had been started in her hearing-impaired class. She was still doing well with her gestures and sounds regarding her needs and wants. However, I was looking forward to the day that I could communicate with Laura about her thoughts and feelings.

During Laura's fourth year, I mentioned to her pediatrician that Laura's motor skills were still poor, and she was still not talking. He informed me that her recent tests revealed that this was due to cerebral palsy, and he recommended physical therapy. I was not only surprised, but at that moment I was angry. Why was this happening to my daughter?

The following September, we had physical therapy incorporated into her Individual Education Plan (IEP) at school. Her most difficult task was walking up and down the stairs alternating her feet. Sign language was initiated to help her communicate as well. Some signs were difficult for her to form with her fingers, but we were able to recognize them.

When our older daughter's jazz instructor learned of Laura's cerebral palsy, she suggested that I sign Laura up for the pre-school class, and she would alter the program to include steps for Laura. She assured me that this would be a great form of therapy. Although I agreed, I was concerned about how the other children and their parents would react when Laura could not keep up with them. Laura's movements were slow and awkward, and although she often missed

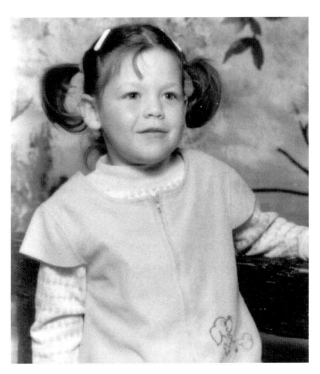

the beat, everyone was very patient and encouraging. Laura loved the classes and looked forward to going each week. I can still recall her practicing to *Greased Lightnin'* by John Travolta. This did wonders for her self-esteem.

I was concerned with the fact that my seven-year-old daughter was becoming increasingly clumsy. I was particularly concerned by the fact that she would fall down the stairs. It's an awful feeling watching your child walk down the stairs and wondering if this would be the time she would fall.

We asked for a consultation by the hospital. A neurologist on the team wanted to meet Laura and do a workup on her. As a result of his workup, it was determined that she had a seizure disorder. He stated that it was petit mal but that some children outgrow this. He was unsure of Laura's prognosis. Learning of her diagnosis was both a shock and a relief. At this point, I was happy that the doctor discovered the reason she was falling. He immediately placed her on medications to be taken each day and told us that Laura would not be restricted from any activities.

Our daughter, Debbie, had been a volunteer for Special Olympics the year before. She convinced us to let Laura get involved. Because Laura was young, and she had only been on her seizure medication a few weeks, I was asked to go along for the weekend to stay with her and be her coach. I boarded the bus, unsure of what to expect from Special Olympics and Laura. I was concerned that this would be too much for her physically and that she would not understand what would be expected of her. She did well at the local Olympics, but now we were at the state level. I was hoping that she would not find this overwhelming.

My husband Ray, along with Debbie and Steven, met us at the university. With all of us on the sideline, we hoped Laura would run to the finish line without stopping. Laura walked away from her first competition with the "Gold Medal!" Although Laura was happy to get the "Gold," we noticed that she was just as

happy to get a ribbon at other events. She was happy to be competing with other children. Special Olympics proved to be an inspiring experience for all of us. These athletes are not judged by their disabilities, but rather by their abilities.

As Laura grew older, we had to make a decision regarding her academics for the following school year. The question we needed to address was, "Would she be going into an educable class or a trainable class?" I knew the final decision would be with Ray and me. I requested to view both classes before making my decision. The educable class was designed to be academically challenging, whereas the trainable class concentrated on daily living skills. After viewing both classes, we decided Laura's needs would best be met with the trainable class.

Laura's medications were working well, and she was becoming more stable on her feet. Her outlook was more positive, and she was using her limited speech and sign language that she had acquired. She was truly a delight to be around.

One summer my eight-year-old daughter came into the house and told us that she wanted the training wheels taken off her two-wheel bike. We bought this bike so that she could get exercise. Frankly, we never intended for the training wheels to come off, but there was no reasoning with Laura on this issue. We knew that if she was determined to do something, she could be stubborn. We took the training wheels off her bike and we stood in the driveway a short distance apart so

that Laura could ride between us. Her first few attempts were as we expected, but Laura was determined to ride her bike. After a couple of hours, we had to admit she was doing better than we had anticipated. By the end of the summer, she was riding as well as any other child. I had never expected Laura to ride a two-wheel bike. The excitement and pride that I felt was overwhelming! Laura's self-esteem skyrocketed.

Laura started in a trainable class that September. It was amazing the things that she learned. For example, her class made cookies as a way of earning money for activities. While baking cookies they were learning basic math skills, as well as daily living skills. She was learning word recognition through baking as well. By volunteering to work with Laura and a classmate, her teacher was able to get the girls into a Brownie Troop. Laura had grown from a little girl into a delightful young lady while in this class.

As a mother of a mentally challenged eleven-year-old girl, I had the responsibility of explaining menstruation to her.

There was no easy way to explain this unpleasant phenomenon that she would experience every month. I decided to skip why this would be happening to her, as she wouldn't understand anyway. I explained that this would happen every month and showed her how she would tend to her needs. I figured that by the time she was thirteen or so she would have this routine down and be ready. Mother Nature was not so kind. Laura started at the age of eleven, just two months after my explanation. I found that I was amazed at her maturity and how well she did considering I had not spent much time preparing her for this.

That June I was called out of work by the school nurse. She thought that Laura had a fainting spell. We watched Laura for the next few days and nothing further transpired. About a week later, I received a call from the day-care center. This time she fell off the swing. I knew this was more serious than fainting. The next day, Laura lost control of her neck muscles. While I was on the phone with her neurologist, Laura somehow got the strength to walk to the front door. She opened the door and fell down the cement stairs onto the sidewalk. Her doctor told me that he would meet us at the emergency room and have her admitted. She was having grand mal seizures at regular intervals at this point. After taking her off all her medications, new medications were started. It was explained to me that Laura might be leaving the hospital with a seizure helmet for her protection. However, during her hospital stay, it appeared that this new set of medications might work for her and a helmet would not be needed. A few months later the medications were adjusted to meet her needs and life was back to normal.

A couple of years later, we bought a house in Westerly, Rhode Island. I knew this move would be difficult for Laura since she had been in the East Hartford school system all her life. Laura had the opportunity to start in a special needs class in either a middle or high school setting. We chose the high school setting because she would have been in the middle school for only one year. We wanted her to establish herself without being moved again the following year.

Laura had a difficult year. School was quite a bit higher functioning than she was used to, but her teacher was wonderful and tried hard to work with us to help Laura adapt. The second year was easier for her. Her class ran a breakfast nook as a means of earning money for activities, along with helping them prepare for the job market. The children each had their own responsibilities appropriately matched to their ability. Laura was a bus-girl. The earnings from the nook helped get the children involved in horseback riding, as well as many other activities.

Laura's favorite was the horses. She immediately fell in love with them. Laura had the opportunity to work as a volunteer for the summer in the stable doing selected tasks which included brushing down one of the horses. Later that year Laura was involved in a competition in which she got a third place

ribbon. Watching her from the bleachers made me nervous, but it was wonderful seeing her up on a horse and knowing how happy she was.

In September 1990, I was given the opportunity to advance in my job by going to school during the day. I needed someone to stay with Laura, who was now seventeen. I was looking for someone before as well as after school for a few hours that Laura would be comfortable with, without feeling as though she had a baby sitter. Melissa was a little younger than Laura. Although they had only been together a few times, Melissa was very caring and mature for her age. It wasn't long before

Laura looked forward to her time with Melissa and Melissa's friends. On occasion, Melissa would do her hair and/or makeup, which Laura enjoyed. She was becoming more cheerful and quite entertaining. At seventeen, Laura had a friend who accepted her as she was.

Holidays were always special times. Traditionally after Thanksgiving dinner, Laura would decorate the tree in her room. Christmas was Laura's favorite holiday. It was a delight to watch her throughout this season. We could see the gleam in her eyes as she decorated the tree in her bedroom and later helped decorate throughout the rest of the house.

As the first week in December approached, Laura had what appeared to be a virus. She showed no signs of excitement, nor did she want to get out of her p.j.'s. I was becoming very concerned as this was very unlike her. All of a sudden a strange look came over her as she asked for help to get to the bathroom. At that point, I noticed she was starting to appear jaundiced. Once into the bathroom, she passed a blood clot and started to hemorrhage. Laura was admitted to the hospital after being stabilized in the emergency room where numerous tests had been performed. She was alert and appeared to be calm asking for her afghan and her baby doll "B," short for Beatrice. Ray and I were told by the hematologist on staff that her platelet count was very low. He said he would order transfusions, but he felt that she was not going to survive this. We were in a state of shock as he repeated the message a few more times, knowing that we did not want to believe what he was telling us.

Laura's next few days were filled with a wonderful network of friends and family but by Sunday morning Laura appeared to be very weak and would not eat anything. My little girl, who was always smiling, no longer had the strength to smile. Although her doctor was sure Laura would not survive this ordeal, some of our family and friends had a very positive outlook and assured us that she would—she was young.

That afternoon when Melissa came to visit, Laura sat up and smiled. She even let Melissa feed her a few cubes of Jell-O. Everyone in the room commented on Laura's sudden surge of energy. However, this did not last long. Although Laura was receiving transfusions we were told her body was rejecting them; she had autoimmune disease. Her seizures were beginning to increase as well.

On Monday although Laura appeared to be getting weaker, she was happy to see her teacher who came with individual get well cards made by Laura's classmates. Later that evening when we asked Laura about visiting friends at their home, we found it puzzling that Laura's response was, "Home?" Suddenly I got the feeling she felt that she wasn't coming home, but she did have a peacefulness about her. Although this made us uncomfortable, we assumed she was tired and we continued to talk about holiday plans for when she came home.

The next morning, we awoke to Laura being cheerful and wanting to watch TV. The last few days had been hectic, and I assumed that this would be her best day. I asked Ray to wake me again in an hour, as they were going to watch cartoons before breakfast. All of a sudden, I was startled to hear Ray shouting, "No, Laura, No!" Laura was having non-stop grand mal seizures. After several hours, her seizures became weaker, so did her breathing. I still recall holding her hand and telling her I love her over and over again.

Laura was pronounced dead on December 11, 1990, at 11:40 a.m. from Thrombotic Thrombocytopenic Purpura (TTP).

To this day, I regret that half-hour of sleep that I got, but I can't do anything to change that. Maybe it was meant to be because she needed that precious time alone with her dad.

The next few days are difficult to recall. I managed to go through the motions at the funeral home and the church. I went back to my full-time job the following week. I thought that by keeping very busy, I would not have time to think about the emptiness and intense grief that was engulfing my body. The first week back, everyone was trying to be kind and understanding. The second week was difficult because of the Christmas parties and the excitement of the holidays that everyone else was feeling. It appeared that everyone was wishing me a "Merry Christmas." I couldn't imagine having a "Merry Christmas" and was sure I never would again!

The following month was Laura's birthday month. She would have been eighteen. The sight of her picture hanging on the wall in her room virtually brought me to my knees. At this time, I was getting by minute by minute, but I knew I couldn't continue on with the immense grief that I was feeling. This was the first time in my life that I had reached a crisis of which I could not get control.

He gave us ideas on how to get through these difficult times. I have also learned that coping with the loss of a child is an adjustment that is continually ongoing through the years. It is not something parents get over; it is a matter of acceptance which will come in time and cannot be rushed. There are ups and downs, as the healing process occurs, but a peacefulness eventually replaces grief.

About a year after Laura passed away, Ray and I were laid off from our jobs due to defense cuts. We both decided to go back to school full-time to fill the void that we were still dealing with and to gain new job skills. We have since both accomplished what we set out to do at school and have obtained new jobs. Melissa is now enrolled in college to obtain a degree in special education.

I contacted a highly recommended grief-counselor. He helped us get our life back together. He explained that birthdays, anniversaries, and holidays will bring about a feeling of emptiness.

As a parent of a special child, I have discovered that these children travel through life much the same as we do. However, they travel at a slower pace.

As a family, we had strived to understand Laura's disabilities and limitations, and recognize her talents and abilities. Laura was and is an inspiration to us. She faced challenges with determination and courage. As I remember my daughter who cherished life, I thank God for the time I had with this *Very Special Child.*

Never Give Up By Tina N. Provencher-Lomas

Amy

date of birth:
December 29, 1978

Cri-Du-Chat Syndrome

Amy Provencher was born on December 29, 1978. She weighed three pounds, twelve ounces, and was thirteen inches long.

Since Amy was born at such a small birth weight, she was immediately transferred to a children's hospital to be cared for in the infant Intensive Care Unit, (ICU). Her heart was not fully developed, which left her in critical condition for the first three weeks of her life. The dedicated nurses and doctors worked with Amy around the clock to help her maintain a healthy weight so that she would be able to leave the hospital.

During her time at this hospital, Amy began to gain weight and her heart was continuously being monitored. After spending three months in the ICU, she was able to go home to begin her life with our family. Amy left the hospital in March of 1978, at the weight of five and one-half pounds.

Once home, Amy began to gain weight rapidly and appeared to be a healthy, normal child. There were frequent visits to her doctor at the hospital. Many tests needed to be performed on Amy's heart to be sure there were no additional defects. At one point there was a possibility of surgery to correct the hole in her heart but as time went on the hole began to decrease and it finally healed.

It was at the age of six months that another problem occurred in Amy's life. Her doctor wanted to do extensive blood-work on Amy. When she cried during the testing, she sounded like a cat. Her doctor feared Amy had a syndrome called "Cri-Du-Chat" which translated in English is "Cry of the Cat." This syndrome is genetic and very rare. The doctor's suspicions were confirmed and

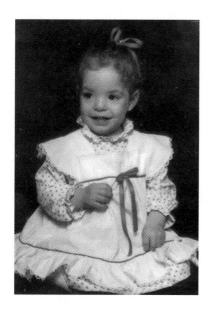

Amy was diagnosed with Cri-Du-Chat Syndrome.

The Cri-Du-Chat Syndrome often slows down all growth. The prediction was that Amy would not walk or talk, and most likely she would not advance mentally past the age of a one-year-old. Amy's future looked dim.

We were devastated by this news, but failed to give up on our hopes for her. We treated her like any other child. At the age of one and one-half she began to walk and was able to speak. Although her speech was not that of a normal one and one-half year old, she was still able to accomplish speaking along with walking.

When Amy was three she began going to special education classes at a school located in our hometown. She rode the bus Monday through Friday, just like any other child. She has attended special education classes for the past fifteen years.

Dedication from our family, the support of the programs at our hospital, her special education classes, and Amy's own strong will, have all helped her to become the happy, adjusted individual

she is today. Amy participates in the Rhode Island Special Olympics. She is a sophomore in the Washington Annex Work-Study Program and actually has a job working two days a week at a hair salon. She truly loves horseback riding and swimming is another of her accomplishments.

At times, Amy appears to be a normal eighteen-year-old. At other times her fine motor skills and speech handicap her, and she becomes frustrated. However, Amy has a wonderful sense of humor, and life on the whole is happy and progressive for her.

Amy is by no means severely handicapped as once diagnosed. She has grown to take her place in society. She has attended school dances, has a good social life, and is looking forward to her graduation in the year 2000.

If you are living your life with a child who has a disability . . .

Patience, caring, understanding, and lots of love for anyone with a disability, be it physical or mental, is the "key" to their happiness and acceptance in this society today. Yes, you will get the occasional stare or comment because your child is "different," but you must try to understand that not everyone has experienced what you are going through. Remember, you were given this special child for a reason, and God must have thought of you as the only person who would be able to take on such a responsibility.🌱

a certain kind of love | Never Give Up

A Special Gift By Christina Allen

Erika

date of birth:
April 11, 1994
Down Syndrome

My daughter Erika is three years old and has Down Syndrome. Tonight, for the first time, she played "Duck Duck Goose." She was able to say each word clearly and played without my husband and I reminding her what to say or do. She even yelled "run" for each person when it was their turn to do so.

Before tonight I had a long five-page piece written that didn't say a whole lot and took me months to write. As I watched my family enjoy each other and I cried with joy for Erika, I realized what I really wanted to share in this book.

Having a special needs child has changed my family and me tremendously. It could have been very easy to give in and ask, "Why us?" every day. Instead we said, "Why not us?" and now take each day at a time and try not to worry about the future. I realized by looking and hoping for time to go by, for changes to happen, and needed skills to be learned, I was wishing away today and missing the little accomplishments along the way.

I have three children and have had, and will have, the same expectations for all of them. I think this is what has helped Erika the most. Things might take more time and work but we are persistent. We have big dreams for Erika.

I want my children to have friends, be invited to birthday parties, for people to be patient with them and for them to be happy. I know my family can give these comforts to my children—I only hope the world can. I think letting them go and losing control as they get older scares me the most. I know how cruel people can be. All I can do is hope in my heart that people will be kind to all of them.

My life has taken many different turns I never thought it would in a million years. I cried a lot when I first had Erika, but with the help of my husband, realized we have to make Erika's life the best we can and move on. I don't cry that often anymore and when I do it's more out of happiness and pride.

I love my family and wouldn't change a thing. I look at life so differently since I've had children. My happiness comes from watching them learn and grow. All the material things don't really matter. Our gift two years ago to my mother, sister, and family was having Erika walk and greet them at the door on Christmas morning. She learned to walk two weeks before the holiday and we kept it secret. It was a gift and memory we will all cherish forever. I would never trade these kinds of feelings or memories for anything.

The things I do wish I could change, I find I often can't and these things hurt the most. I wish I could ask people to take the time to talk to someone who is different, to wait a little longer while a

special needs person bags their groceries, or to embrace a special needs child into the classroom and teach the class what friendship and kindness is truly about. These are things I would like to see happen. I would like for people just to be kind.

Trying to write this has been very difficult. There are a lot of feelings my husband and I share that I came to realize, by trying to put them in writing, are still too personal and private. I know some day my children will read this and I don't want them or others to misinterpret my intentions. Therefore I have left a lot out of this story. Maybe in a few years, once I have grown up with my children, I'll be ready to share more, or each person in my family can share each of their own stories.

I hope by people writing their stories in this book others who read it will hear our messages.

𝄞

When I had Erika, I was given a folder in the hospital from the Down Syndrome Society. I didn't want to look at it until she was about three months old. Inside I found a passage written by another mother of a child with a disability. The passage captured my initial feelings in the hospital when I gave birth. I think it can best explain to someone who does not have a child with a disability what it feels like.

Welcome to Holland

by Emily Perl Kingsley

I am often asked to describe the experience of raising a child with a disability—to try to help people who have not shared that unique experience to understand it, to imagine how it would feel. It's like this…

When you're going to have a baby, it's like planning a fabulous vacation trip—to Italy. You buy a bunch of guidebooks and make your wonderful plans. The Coliseum. The Michelangelo David. The gondolas in Venice. You may learn some handy phrases in Italian. It's all very exciting.

After months of eager anticipation, the day finally arrives. You pack your bags and off you go. Several hours later, the plane lands. The stewardess comes in and says, "Welcome to Holland."

"HOLLAND?!?" you say. "What do you mean Holland?? I signed up for Italy! I'm supposed to be in Italy. All my life I've dreamed of going to Italy."

But there's been a change in the flight plan. They've landed in Holland and there you must stay.

The important thing is that they haven't taken you to a horrible, disgusting, filthy place, full of pestilence, famine and disease. It's just a different place.

So you must go out and buy new guide books. And you must learn a whole new language. And you will meet a whole new group of people you would never have met.

It's just a different place. It's slower-paced than Italy, less flashy than Italy. But after you've been there for awhile and you catch your breath, you look around... and you begin to notice that Holland has windmills... and Holland has tulips. Holland even has Rembrandts.

But everyone you know is busy coming and going from Italy... and they're all bragging about what a wonderful time they had there. And the rest of your life, you will say "Yes, that's where I was supposed to go. That's what I had planned."

And the pain of that will never, ever, ever, ever go away... because the loss of that dream is a very, very significant loss.

But... if you spend your life mourning the fact that you didn't get to Italy, you may never be free to enjoy the very special, the very lovely things... about Holland.

Thoughts On Patti By Carol Leach

Including thoughts by Dad, sisters and brother.

Patti

date of birth:
February 2, 1970
Down Syndrome

When her Dad was in Vietnam and her siblings slept, Patti was born early the morning of February 2nd before the groundhog made his appearance.

I knew I was to have a small baby and that the baby was breech but I didn't know until the birth that my baby had Down Syndrome. The obstetrician said he would have the pediatrician confirm his suspicions later that morning.

I spent a very wakeful several hours before the doctor arrived. He was very kind and supportive. He encouraged me in my decision to take my baby home and advised that she would be no more care than my other babies, although she would be slow in her development. When I told him of my concern about telling my husband and our other five children, he said military men see things either black or white, and sending a pamphlet with pictures explaining Down Syndrome would help him understand

better. His advice was to be straightforward and honest with the children; they would react the way I would react toward their sister. He said that we had a ready-made stimulating environment that is perfect for the growth of a retarded child. Patti was accepted and loved immediately by her siblings and each wanted to help feed and hold her like they would any baby sister.

While the doctor was supportive, one of the nurses upset me by asking if I wanted my baby on display in the nursery window with the other babies, and did I want the announcement in the newspaper. I said of course I did, and without any kindness in her manner she did as I requested. She also refused when I asked to see some literature on

Down Syndrome even though she knew I was a nurse.

In my need I called an army friend who was a parent of a retarded child. She was wonderful and braved a terrible storm to drive an hour to see me in the hospital, bearing gifts and encouragement and hope.

When my husband was in Vietnam we were living near family. One grandparent refused to believe that anything was wrong with Patti. Even so, she and all family members were a tremendous help to me. I did have my difficult moments. One day while my mother was babysitting I took a walk and remember feeling that I would never again be able to enjoy the beauty of the trees and flowers blooming. I thought I was burdened with something that would make me forever sad.

The pediatrician recommended that I visit a special-education class at a local school. I was uncomfortable around a Down Syndrome child, realizing that my baby would grow up to look like this.

The role of parenting a retarded child was difficult for me to accept. Still, I knew I would take this responsibility because I knew that it was mine to take and I would do the best I could. Perhaps not "the best," but *my* best.

Through the years I never forgot that someone might not feel comfortable around a retarded child just as I hadn't. I tried to help ease that feeling by initiating or assisting with conversation so that it would flow in the direction most comfortable for everyone. Also, by trying to show how Patti was like other children rather than focusing on how she was different.

Since we were a military family we moved quite often and Patti was exposed to different programs. She was enrolled in an infant stimulation program at Georgetown University at the age of thirteen months. Besides teaching the children, parents were also taught the skills. The parents met as a group to provide support for each other before the idea of support groups was even devised.

Patti's next formal training was at the age of three, in Kansas, at a child development center. She entered public school at age six when the public law 94-142 was passed, which allows disabled children the right to public education from age three to twenty-one. We moved several times and she had good teachers and good experiences in most of her schooling. She remained in a self-contained classroom environment, not mainstreamed, except for reading in her earlier years with first and second graders. She was exposed to art, music, and physical education outside the class-room. This suited her needs and she was happy; thus we were content.

Special Olympics was a highlight for Patti. In her youthful years, Patti won medals in running, throwing the softball, and the long jump. In later years she also won for bowling. The family, including brothers and sisters, all went to cheer her on, just as she and the whole family went to our other children's sports events. Patti also attended adaptive aquatics classes and learned to swim. One spring she was on a soccer team. Patti and a Down Syndrome boy were the only retarded members of the team.

We did things as a whole family, Patti always being a part of all our functions. Friends and neighbors treated Patti like the rest of our children, but as the baby of the family. This was our family and to Patti's brothers and sisters this was a normal family, even though they knew Patti was special.

Wherever we lived, everyone knew Patti. One advantage of being different is you stand out above the rest. Fortunately for us, this has always been a positive thing with Patti.

It only happened once, but on a Sunday morning when Patti was four years old she stayed at home with her dad while the family went to church, which was across the street. During Mass, Patti came walking down the middle aisle of our church, still in her pajamas. I wished to ignore her because of my embarrassment, but she innocently said "Hi, Mom," and I got up and quietly took her home.

Being a Catholic family we wanted Patti to be able to receive the sacrament of Holy Communion. A nun volunteered to come to our home once a week to teach Patti what she needed to understand, as best she could, in order to receive Communion. Patti's First Communion day was her own along with one other Down Syndrome boy and the priest made it very special. After Mass many of the parishioners came to have cake and congratulate the two new communicants.

One feat Patti accomplished, to our amazement, occurred when I was in Germany for the birth of a grandchild. Patti was sixteen years old. The overseas phone number was on the refrigerator for my husband's handy reference. Quite late one evening, German time, the phone rang and it was Patti asking for Mom. We had a several minute conversation and she was content. My husband then talked with me and said he didn't know she was phoning. She had dialed about fifteen numbers by touch-tone all by herself!

The most surprising thing Patti ever did was at her graduation from high school. Prior to the all-school graduation, which Patti participated in, a small ceremony and party was held in the special-education classroom for her and another graduating class member. The principal, school committee president, several teachers, students, and parents were present. After the presentation and plaques were given out, Patti asked everyone to sit down. Addressing everyone from the front of the class, she gave a spontaneous farewell speech, thanking particular teachers that she asked to come forward and expressing her feelings of gratitude to all. It was sincere and heartwarming. Neither her teachers nor we, her parents, knew beforehand that she was going to do this.

Patti has settled into being an adult, functioning at a mild to moderate retarded range, and living at home with Mom and Dad. She works in a sheltered workshop three days a week. She enjoys recreational activities with fellow workers two or three times a month, and joins some of them weekly for a walk in the park. She's responsible for the care of her person, her clothing, and her room. She has various house chores, among which are setting and clearing the table, partially loading the dishwasher, and helping Dad in the yard on occasion.

She loves music, especially country western and Garth Brooks. TV favorites are country music videos, ballgames and award shows. Patti likes time alone in her room listening to music on tapes while playing "air guitar" or beating the rhythm with drumsticks. She sits at her desk with pencil and paper, or typewriter, listing the top country tunes of the week and the names of the singers. Besides music she likes bowling and playing catch or whiffle ball. Once a week Patti has a one-hour reading lesson with a tutor and the help of a computer. Her reading ability is at a third grade level. Also weekly, she volunteers at church helping the ushers by passing the collection basket. Patti remembers everyone's birthday and reminds us to call her sisters and brother on their birthdays, as they all live far away.

As I mentioned earlier, we have found wherever we have lived that you can't be anywhere with Patti and not realize that she attracts attention. We are constantly aware of this feeling of being noticed in a special way. This has almost always been a positive response from strangers, acquaintances and professionals, and we feel, too, that Patti has been a positive influence in their lives.

Hopefully, I have succeeded in conveying my message that the beauty of the trees and blooming flowers have continued through the years to bring me more joy than I could ever have imagined.

The following passages are written by Patti's family.

Jackye Leach, Sister

Being raised in a home with a handicapped sister was a rewarding and strengthening experience. I learned to not focus solely on the handicap but to see the person rather than the condition. The experience made me very tolerant with remarkable understanding and maturity in dealing with handicapped individuals. It was not the tragedy that people imagine since my parents talked openly about the condition, making it quite natural. I have strong bonds of affection for Patti and feel I benefited from growing up with her. She proved to me that her problems were different rather than greater.

Cheryl Bergman, Sister

Having a younger sister with special needs due to mental retardation (Down Syndrome), has added so much to our family. It has taught us compassion for others, unselfishness, tolerance, and patience. Patti has given more to the family than she could ever get back herself. Being who she is will influence generations as her nieces and nephews also learn those important lessons of relating to those persons who look and act differently than they do.

Our family is large, and all the siblings are intelligent, successful, attractive, and independent. We have been "truly blessed" so to speak. But Patti, without possessing hardly any of these qualities is unaware of the horrible things that occur in our world today. She is almost sheltered from the worries and fears that we all go through on a daily basis, and above all she is assured of her place in heaven when her time comes. Sometimes it makes you think, *who is the truly blessed one*???

Phyllis G. Leach, Sister

Having a sister, Patti, with Down Syndrome...

—has made me more aware of others who struggle with disabilities or hardship in their lives.

—has made me more caring, more patient, and more appreciative of simple gifts that are often taken for granted.

—has never made me ashamed. If someone is mean to Patti or ignores her, it just tells me that this person lacks the right values.

—keeps you young, because Patti still believes in Santa Claus, loves to ride the roller coaster, and gets excited about going out for an ice cream cone!

—keeps you grounded and genuine. You can't be phony or pretentious with Patti; it's lost on her. She's not impressed that you make $200,000 a year or know the President. Patti loves you for the right reasons—you're nice to her, you take time for her, and you show her you care about her.

—has brought our family closer together and closer to God.

Johann Salas, Sister

Growing up with a handicapped sibling creates many mixed feelings and emotions. In one way you want to protect them from any cruel people or encounters, yet on the other hand you want them to "be just like everyone else" and teach them to stand their own ground. I was never embarrassed to be with my sister—in fact she taught me a lot about what is really important in life—to be truthful, accepting, and non-judgmental of people.

Jay Leach, Brother

"Blessed are the meek, for they will inherit the earth." Matthew 5:5

"Meek" in the dictionary is defined as "showing patience and humility; gentleness." I think this definition closely matches the personality of Down Syndrome individuals.

My sister Patti taught me many invaluable lessons to help me in my personal life. One lesson she helped me understand is that there will always be greater and lesser people than yourself, but that everyone is very valuable, has a purpose, and can make a special contribution to society.

Patti helped me understand the concept of unconditional love. No matter what I did behaviorally, she would always love and have time for me. When I was younger, Patti was someone I could always go to to cheer me up when I was feeling down. She never had a grumpy disposition. Instead she always had a smile on her face. She was willing to spend time with me, to help me forget for a moment life's stresses and worries, in her own special way. I remember going away with a joyful feeling and a lesson on not to take myself too seriously. She taught me that there are more important things in life than gaining power, prestige, and wealth. Besides our relationship with God—people, and our relationships with them, are what is most important.

If I had a chance to rewrite the above Bible verse to include those wonderful children who affect our lives so much, it would be the following—

"Blessed are the "special" children, for they will inherit the earth… and your heart." Jay 1:1

John Leach, Patti's Dad

I was in Vietnam when I first learned of Patti's condition. My first feelings upon becoming aware that I was the father of a Down Syndrome daughter were concern and doubt. They were not of the nature of questioning "Why me?" or thinking that I was being punished by God for any wrongdoing, nor were they feelings of guilt. I can honestly say that I'm not a person who dwells on negative thoughts or situations, and I try to handle life's occasional trials as they come. My concerns and doubts centered on my wife and our other children. I didn't know how they would initially handle the situation, nor did I know how we all would deal with the situation over the long run. I had serious doubts as to how we could care for Patti and how much attention she would require.

Over the years, all my concerns and doubts have long been put to rest. I feel all of Patti's siblings, Carol, and I, have greatly benefited by having Patti in our lives. She truly has been a blessing. We all are more tolerant, we show more respect, and share more love and understanding for those who are less fortunate than ourselves. I can't imagine life, certainly in this family, without her. Unknowingly, I believe she has impacted our children's career choices. Almost all are in health services professions.

Now that all our other children are grown and have moved on, Patti is still "our child, living at home and keeping us young." 🌳

A Letter to My Son By Christine Kenyon

Chuck

date of birth:
September 15, 1968

Cerebral Palsy

The months of preparation and varied, important last minute decisions were almost completed. What wonderful memories your wedding rehearsal and the dinner, which followed, would make—a prelude to the joining of two people, two families and two cultures. Raquel had lived the first half of her life in Mexico City; you had lived in Rhode Island except for the ritual of our yearly vacation. Tomorrow would be your wedding day, a joyful time for all. You and Raquel had begun the final stages of preparation and were ready to begin your new life together.

Your wedding day had arrived, but you had difficulty focusing on the excitement of the morning. The day before, you realized that serious pain was developing in your foot—a tiny fold in your sock, between your foot and brace, had caused a very painful callus. You and Dad squeezed in an emergency appointment at the podiatrist's office before we could leave for your ten o'clock wedding. But why should this surprise us? And how could you dance at your wedding?

Dad and I were married on July 2, 1966. In May of the next year Heidi was born. How precious it was to have our first child. Our families shared in our joy. Dad and I really loved being a family and we were anxious for Heidi to have a little sister or brother. In the winter of '68 we were pleased that we were expecting another child. Heidi would have someone to grow up beside her. We looked forward to another little family member. But this time things would be quite different.

Under the deep sleep of anesthesia, I heard a voice somewhere in the distance saying, "Mrs. Kenyon, Mrs. Kenyon." …I thought someone was calling your Grammy Kenyon. Then, when I heard my first name being called, I somehow responded and heard him say, "It's a boy!" I felt a leap of joy in my heart that I can still vividly remember, then I immediately went back into a deep sleep. Later, when I heard Daddy's voice, I told him, "It's a boy." He whispered, "Shh, you're yelling. They'll hear you down the whole corridor!" And I think they did!

We had three stays in the hospital that summer and fall, so that medication could be given to slow down your early attempts at arriving into this world. As anxious as you were to join us, it was obvious that much more time was necessary for your healthy arrival. But you were as determined then, as you are now, and on September 15, 1968, you were born by caesarean section, eleven weeks early. Perhaps you wanted to avoid December's cold and snow.

You were born eleven weeks prematurely, weighing three pounds nine ounces, a very good weight for your weeks of prematurity. The doctor said it was a good thing I had big babies. Soon, as with most newborns, your weight would decrease to two pounds fifteen ounces.

When feeding you, the nurse could hold you in the palm of one hand with her fingers supporting your head. The doctor said we would take one day at a time.

We had looked forward so much to your birth, but now it was scary to think you might not survive. My hospital room was across from the nursery and that first evening I saw your pediatrician running down the corridor to the nursery. I called out to no one in particular, "That's my baby! I know it is!" I just knew he was running in to help save you. My roommate peered out the door to observe what was going on in the nursery and confirmed my fears. I wondered and worried what effect my problematic pregnancy and your difficult early birth would mean for your little soul.

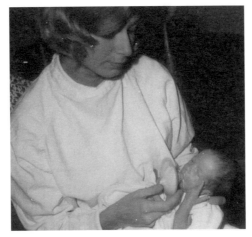

Later the doctor came in to explain what had happened. You had experienced difficulty breathing and had turned blue. A nurse had given you a shot before he arrived and you were now breathing normally. We talked for a while; I told him that I had been trying to stay awake, believing that if you needed me, I would somehow "be there" for you. Some of my fears had been calmed and he convinced me to take a sleeping pill and get some rest.

Before I fell asleep, I remember praying—really talking with God. "God, if you choose to allow this baby to live, I'll do everything I can to see that he knows you. I realize I can't control what he will do or believe in his life, but I will do my best. Please take care of him." Then I fell asleep, somehow comforted by putting your care into His loving hands.

We named you Charles Robert: Charles after your dad, and Robert after your Grampy Perreault. But after lots of suggestions from the nurses, we called you Chuck—a nickname that would remain forever.

The nurses found you unusually determined, and told me that preemies (at least back then) would usually have many gains and losses as they developed. With one or two exceptions you continually gained and were able to come home just in time for Thanksgiving—a true day of thanks. How excited, yet actually frightened, we were to welcome you home. Your sister, Heidi, at eighteen months, thought you were a little doll for her to play with. Actually you were smaller than many of her dolls.

Dad was excited but so very nervous holding you. I thought I wasn't nervous at all, just excited, until I was awakened by your 2:00 a.m. cry. The nurses weren't with us anymore. Now I was the nervous one! What did I know about you? I hadn't held you enough—or fed you enough—or been alone with you at all. I was uncertain that I could be as good a mother to you as the nurses had been in my place. There had always been a backup for you, skilled nurses at your side. But the longer you stayed, the more you became a part of their family, too. Now Dad and I were the only ones left to

care for you. And what did we know about taking care of a baby who had struggled to get this far. Were we capable of providing the care you needed? Anxiety ruled!

I can tell you this now, because you do know how much you are loved, but at that time I had trouble bonding with you. Realistically or not, I was afraid to get close to you because I feared that at any moment you might die. I felt tremendous guilt for feeling that way, but as a young mother of two children under fifteen months, and with the pressure of your constant illnesses, I wasn't even sure how to cope, except minute to minute, myself.

But your survival, and even our survival as a family, depended on both of us becoming a team and gathering strength together every single day. As each day passed I began to realize how cute you were as well as how much each day was a struggle for you. Focusing on this, it became easier to meet your needs despite the problems. Your sweet little eyes struck a chord in me. Somehow, I knew you were reaching out and trusted me to meet your needs. I began to feel more like your mom, and finally a strong bond had developed. I was loving you unconditionally. No matter what else would occur from then on, we could handle it together.

With support and encouragement from the family, especially your grandparents, we continued on. Despite your numerous colds and illnesses, at six months of age you finally reached thirteen pounds. We were elated but for only a short while. You entered the hospital because of a respiratory infection and you lost one of those precious pounds. However, in some ways that seemed like a turning point because weight was never a major concern after that hospitalization.

Thank heavens we had a caring family who lived nearby. Your three grandparents, Aunt Lyn, and Aunt Debbie helped by caring for Heidi during shopping, helping with housework, and in general cheering up Dad and I. Heidi was almost two and needed lots of attention as well.

Heidi just loved you and didn't allow your limitations to interfere with playing. At first you were "her" baby then later you became her playmate.

Around the time of Heidi's second birthday, you really enjoyed playing with each other. There was a lot of laughter from both of you. You were beginning to sleep longer through the night, and so were we. But the least sound from you would awaken me. I never quite relaxed until I could check your breathing and know whether or not you were okay. We began to recognize certain signs; bright red ears meant a cold, ear infection, or respiratory infection within a day or two—always. Even one cough usually meant illness would follow.

Your dad loved you dearly, yet wasn't comfortable holding you for long, concerned with your fragile appearance and frequent crying and illnesses. He was (and still is) a person who loved being outdoors, whether working on the farm or in the woods, and he wanted very much to share that part of his life with you. Dad was kept busy working at his job and taking care of our small farm. It was hard for us to fulfill your needs since you still had that "startle reflex" which would always cause you to cry, seemingly without reason.

Despite a lot of sickness that first year, you were developing into an observant, comical, beautiful child. You did have difficulty holding your head up for long periods of time and although you had observant eyes, one did cross. I thought you looked adorable. You grew more special every day. But I don't know if anyone could understand how much you had grown in my heart. How difficult to believe that after your birth there was ever any trouble bonding. We really had begun to communicate.

I began to recognize your needs before you "asked." In retrospect, I realized that focusing so much on you, Heidi and Dad weren't getting all the attention they deserved and needed; they were a part of our family, too. As a wife and mother, life required a true balancing act. Whoever needed the most attention at a particular moment seemed to receive it—

unless those needs overlapped. Then the balancing really began.

When you were nine or ten months old the doctor mentioned that if you didn't show greater growth or more age appropriate responses by your next visit, we might have to see another doctor or group in Providence. I was startled by this, but then thought of how far you had already come and I wouldn't let this discourage me. It was obvious that you were always "thinking." And, after all, you were eleven weeks premature; that was holding back your development, or so I wanted to believe. You had even begun to speak—saying Mama, Dada, juice, and a tooth had even come in, which seemed normal to me. You weren't sitting unassisted, or standing yet, but that didn't worry me. We focused on what you could do. When my mom and dad were visiting one day and you asked for juice, I was surprised at my Dad's response. He said, "How on earth did you know Chuckie wanted a drink?" I said, "Didn't you hear him ask for juice?" Dad replied, "I heard him say 'something' but it didn't sound anything like juice to me." This caused me to ponder a bit, but I decided that a mother was often the first to understand her child's words and didn't spend too much more time thinking about it.

When your first year checkup arrived, I knew that the doctor would be pleased with your progress. I was anticipating his pleasure at the growth you'd shown. But, instead of excitement he looked quite serious. As I recall, he explained that preemies are generally developmentally delayed as many weeks, or months, as they are premature. Using that guide you should have been exhibiting the markers of a nine-month-old yet you still had an infant's "startle reflex." He recommended that we go to a children's clinic. He further said to be prepared; they may find any number of things about you—you might never feed or dress yourself, walk, talk, or be toilet trained. Of course, at that point, I didn't focus on the word "might." I just felt as if my eyes had been opened for the first time, forcing me to look into a frightening future for you. Now I saw some realistic possibilities that I really didn't want to face!

What about how you laughed when Heidi or Dad did something funny? What about those words I clearly heard? What about that "thinking" I could see going on inside you? But… what about your droopy head, those beautiful eyes that so frequently crossed, your inability to sit up on your own? The way you pulled yourself around by your arms in your "army crawl," dragging your legs behind you, must have meant something really was wrong. What about all of that? Why didn't we see this before?

I had great faith in your pediatrician. He was a wonderful man and doctor. Uncertain of what your exact potential and diagnosis would be, he was preparing us for all that might truly occur. I managed to get as far as Aunt Judy's home, which was quite near the doctor's office. As I tried to tell her, I just sobbed. I can't remember our conversation. I can't remember the drive home or even what I told Daddy. But, when I came home and told him, he cried. I felt as if a great curtain had been pulled down over your future. I was aware of the sorrows ahead, but at that moment, unaware of the joys that would continue.

An appointment was made at the child development clinic for your evaluation. As time passed, and we anxiously awaited the appointment, we began to look closely at you, thinking of all those scary possibilities. We began a series of visits to Providence; waiting in so many clinics, seeing so many doctors. But finally there was a name for your condition, cerebral palsy-spastic quadriplegia. As concerned as we felt for you, we at last had a name for your condition and could somehow move ahead from there. More testing, doctors' visits and physical therapy treatments began in earnest. Sometimes we made three visits a week to Providence. You and I would both be exhausted—you physically and I emotionally. We'd often drive into our yard, with you already asleep, and I would take a

nap right in the car before gathering you up and going into the house.

When you were two and one-half you had your first surgery on your legs. When we went in to see you, you whispered that you needed a drink. Although it was on your chart that you were unable to use a straw, it was the only way anyone had attempted to give you something to drink. We learned right then that during hospitalizations we needed to be with you as much of the time as we possibly could. It was different then—parents could only see their child at prescribed times. Six weeks after your surgery, you had to go back and stay in the hospital for extensive physical therapy. Fortunately, you were ready to come home after about one month, not the three months originally thought. Parents were only allowed very limited visits. This was emotionally painful for us and equally so for you. How wonderful that things changed and now parents can stay twenty-four hours a day if they wish, in most hospitals.

When you arrived home, you were particularly quiet for quite a few days, which we did not expect. But Heidi and your cousin Rae Jeanne could always make you laugh and you were soon moving around, keeping up with whatever they were playing. It was great seeing you become your funny old self!

And how wonderful that we changed doctors as the years went on. In spite of your surgery at two and one-half, another when you were in first grade, and lots of physical therapy, your muscles continued to tighten. After years of walking with your body so bent over that you were constantly looking at the ground, (unless you stopped and made a concerted effort to force an upward glance), a "knight in shining armor" arrived. We had been told at six-month intervals, visit after visit, that you would likely need surgery the next time. Peter, your caring physical therapist, had been gently suggesting for a while that a new doctor at the clinic, who was very highly thought of by the staff, might look at you in a new way. Dr. H. didn't hold the five to ten minute visits to which we

had become accustomed. For the first time, a doctor spoke with you at length, not us.

He asked what you enjoyed doing and what plans you, as an eighth grader, had for the future. He examined you and spoke with you for almost an hour. Just days after that eventful visit, you were scheduled for long overdue surgery, which gave us all hope, and more than a little fear of the unknown. At long last, by the end of eighth grade you were standing straight and were eight inches taller!

We all learned a lot over the intervening years:

—though a child may only know a few words, his mind is recording much of, if not everything, that is happening around him (Traveling to Jamestown at age six, you recalled driving down that very same road, even though you were much less than two years of age at the time. You even convinced us by remembering the farm had a lot of sheep and that you and Dad had gone for hay in the old, green Chevy pick-up.)

—if vacuum cleaners could pick up lots of things from the floor, then for a child who spent most of his time playing there, it might just pick up the little child watching

—while physical therapy is so necessary, to do something daily that causes her child pain goes against everything a mother is

—for a three-year-old, who wasn't particularly fond of his new glasses anyway, glasses make great roads, especially with the lenses side down scraping the roadway in the gravel

—standing and climbing on the furniture had always seemed wrong—but when you jumped your very first jump ever, from the couch to the chair during a reading association meeting, everyone applauded

—chocolate can be a great motivator (Remember the time when you were six and you crawled under two fences, walked through the barnyard, opened Uncle Arch's gate and knocked for ages at the door, asked for a chocolate bar, thanked him, and headed home, clutching the candy, all in freezing weather?) Where was that mother of yours???

—if you find a note on your child's bed saying, "I've jumped out the window!" but there are no opened windows in the room and crutches are left on the floor, look under the bed before looking outside under the windows

—also, if a note saying your child has run away appears from under the bedroom door, express great concern quite loudly—don't dial 911—look under the bed again

—standing up and laughing hard don't necessarily go well together—at least if you want to remain standing

—don't wear your brand new, light colored jacket when you drive your three-wheeler around the barnyard

—when elementary school gets to be "just too much," it's convenient to have a Grampy who will pick you up from school, ask if you're really sick, and if not, take you to the cycle shop for the rest of the day

—when you have two full leg braces, don't flip over backwards doing a wheelie in your wheelchair—especially when your mother is in the room— you add five years to your life with the daring act and laughter but your mom has five deducted from hers

Everyone loved your sense of humor and the way few things seemed to bother you. Not everyone knew that your great smile and frequent joking and teasing hid some of your deeper sad feelings— feelings about where you fit in—fears of what your future would hold. Going to counseling as a family and individually gave you the ability to see your strengths, not just your weaknesses—which we all have.

You did well, Chuck! Dad, Heidi and Neil, Gram and Gramp, and I are proud of you, along with the rest of your family and your many friends and acquaintances. You had lots of bumps and bruises along the way but you shine today, in part, because of them. You wondered where your life would take you; you already know some of the answers. We know the path hasn't been smooth but it was worth traveling together. Now Dad and I will enjoy watching as you and Raquel continue along, making your own path.

After you joined Campus Crusade and came to know the Lord in a personal way, you gradually matured in a deeper sense and even returned to the university. You developed a large circle of friends, one of whom became the most important friend in your life, Raquel. Yes, Raquel—which brings us back to where I began.

Your wedding day, May 1998, was eons away from September 15, 1968… an immeasurable number of years, joys and sorrows—all truly a lifetime apart. Somehow you made it to your wedding on time—with a sore foot, but on time! This would appear a major inconvenience to some, but you took it in stride as you had done in so many different instances in your life. You walked down the aisle, out of the church and on to the wonderful reception your new in-laws had prepared; it was truly a memorable time for all.

And what a dance it was! 🌳

My Journey By Charles Robert Kenyon

(Son of Christine Kenyon, *A Letter to My Son*)

Chuck

date of birth:
September 15, 1968
Cerebral Palsy

My name is Charles Robert Kenyon, "Chuck." I was born on September 15, 1968 to Charles Dickens Kenyon and Christine Perreault Kenyon. I have one sister, Heidi, who was fifteen months old when I was born. I was born by caesarean section, eleven weeks premature, a not quite so healthy baby boy. My mother had been hospitalized for hemorrhaging off and on during the previous five weeks and during the twenty-four hours or so prior to my birth. She had received transfusions of roughly three pints of blood that thankfully kept both of us alive. I weighed in at a paltry three pounds nine ounces, and at one point dropped to two pounds fifteen ounces, before I gained any weight. My mother, Christine, as she was awakening from her recovery room stupor, was told that her baby was a boy. I'm told at this point my mom broadcasted the fact quite loudly over and over, "IT'S A BOY, IT'S A BOY," as she was wheeled to her room. Shortly after birth I stopped breathing momentarily but thanks to some miraculous work on the part of God, and some very gifted nurses and physicians, I survived and slowly but surely began to thrive. Some time after birth I was diagnosed with cerebral palsy.

My Childhood

One of my earliest memories was of being left at the hospital at the age of two and one-half. At that time the doctors thought that the best way for children to receive frequent and proper care and therapy they needed on a daily basis, was for the parents to leave the children at the hospital for a month or sometimes even longer. They felt the child's physical condition would be improved by the daily regimen of therapy. The child's parents were allowed to visit only two or three times a week. My physical condition may or may not have improved through this, I don't really know. I do know that emotionally this experience had a profound effect on me. I would say that I felt abandoned when I was left at the hospital.

I remember when my parents would come to visit and I would be really excited to see them, but very soon after that they would leave again and not come back for a few days. I learned quickly this would become the pattern. I would be very lonely and frightened at the hospital, and then my mom and dad would come to stay and then they would leave again. This would occur all in the course of about an hour. So it wasn't long before, when they would come, that I remembered what would happen and I would quickly become sad, even while they were still there, because of the dreaded anticipation of their leaving

again. So soon I was just sad, and scared, and confused. After all, did anyone think to ask how I felt about all this?

My feelings may sound extreme to you, and they even do to me, too, especially when I contemplate this event with my twenty-nine-year-old mind. Then I take a step back and say, "Wait a minute, when this happened I was the ripe old age of two and one-half!" So at that age, for me, it was pretty traumatic. Of course this must have been really hard for my sister and parents, too.

I would undergo two surgeries and spend about six months in the hospital either recovering from surgery, receiving therapy, or being treated for several bouts of asthma, all before the time I turned seven. I still struggle with asthma but thankfully it is largely kept under control with medications. The rest of my childhood was fairly normal and by about age four I began to walk with the aid of crutches.

Grammar School

I grew up in a small town of approximately five thousand people. I started school at the age of four and attended nursery school for two years. One of the best decisions my parents, Charles D. and Christine, (the aforementioned, aspiring hospital recovery room singer), made early on was to enroll me in the local elementary school with my sister, Heidi. At that time, many children with disabilities were sent to special schools. For the most part I remember being treated pretty much like everybody else by the other kids. I do remember on one occasion one friend kicked my crutch out from underneath me and he laughed and thought it was funny. Being a young thinker, "think" is what I did. I got up, brushed myself off, laughed with everybody else, and then whacked him in the knee with my crutch. Needless to say, he never tripped me again, and we really did end up good friends after that. I attended elementary school with a lot of absences from repeated bouts with asthma until I was twelve years old.

I wasn't the type of person to talk very much about what was going on inside myself. That is, I didn't share very much with others with regard to what I thought about myself, my friends, and the world around me. Most importantly I seldom shared, verbally anyway, the disappointment that I felt at being more physically limited than my classmates.

I remember quite vividly most of my grammar school life. I remember especially at around age seven or eight that I was able to run with the aid of crutches that I still use to this day. Being able to run made me feel pretty free.

At this time I also remember that a lot of the time I felt like I was "in a fog," so to speak. I don't think that I was very aware of my community, at school or otherwise. I think this was due to being sick so often or because of my medications. I always seemed to be the one who was said to be "not paying attention." When instructions were given I needed to have somcone explain them again to me, after everyone else seemed to know what was going on. One example is when I was in the third or fourth grade. I can remember our class being called to the cafeteria at our school, and the custodian got up and thanked everyone for sending him cards and letters when he was out sick for the last couple of months. I remember not even knowing that he had been sick and this was a man I cared a lot about. Around this same time, in the winter, I often missed many days of school due to repeated bouts with asthma and a couple with pneumonia. Oftentimes, when I was sick, I stayed at my grandparents' who lived one mile from my home. That is where I first learned to play cards. I would always let my grandmother sit with her back to the picture window so I could use the reflection in the window to see her cards.

I also remember that I was not included very often in class activities. For instance, when I had gym class, I would attend the class with everyone else but instead of participating in the activities with the rest of the class I would often sit by myself. I can recall many times when the teacher or one of my classmates would ask me how I was doing. I would often try to smile or fake a laugh so that others would think I was enjoying myself too. I did this in the same way that you laugh at a joke when you have no idea what the punchline meant but you laugh anyway, just so you can appear "with it." Looking back, I wish I had let someone know how it felt. I wish I had talked about it. For the most part though, I would often sit by myself and sometimes bounce a ball on the floor or just twiddle my thumbs until gym class ended. I think that another area of great struggle for me was riding the bus back and forth to school. When I first began to ride the bus I would sit in the very front seat. It was easiest to sit there because it would be somewhat of a struggle to get on the bus using my crutches. As I got a little older I would often meet up with a friend at school and go to get on the bus with him or her. Except for a few rare occasions, when I was allowed to sit in the back of the bus with a friend, I was usually told to sit in the first row of seats. I really disliked this because most of the time the older children would tend to sit in the back or middle rows of the bus and I was unable to sit with them. You see, when we were in school, the only times you could really talk to someone were when you were on the playground at recess, eating lunch, or riding the bus. Riding the bus was one activity where I felt I wasn't physically limited, however the bus insurance company said that because it would be a hazard for me in the case of an accident, I would be required to sit in the front row seat of the bus. Throughout most of my grammar school years, that was the way it was. I wasn't able to sit with and talk to friends my own age and I felt very limited by this. I hope this rule has changed for kids on the bus today.

Some Favorite Pastimes

As I had mentioned, for almost all of my life my maternal grandparents, Robert and Ethel Perreault, have lived only a mile from my home. My grandparents always loved their grandchildren, as was quite apparent when especially in the summer months, several of us grandkids would be there at any one time on what seemed almost a daily basis. Up until I was thirteen years old, when my cousin Matthew was born, I was the only boy out of nine grandchildren.

Needless to say, at times I felt just a tad outnumbered. On almost a daily basis I spent time with my grandfather. You see, my grandfather and uncle had a motorcycle dealership conveniently located across the street from my elementary school. So I would frequently get picked up from school and would stay with my grandfather at work, often until the end of the day.

From quite an early age my grandfather taught me to drive, and eventually mow, with his riding lawn tractor. This may sound like it may have been boring, but especially when I was very young, it provided a fun outlet for me and gave me a real feeling of confidence at a period in my life when I really needed it. At one point he had a lawn tractor that had an extra wide seat, and I remember riding with him while he cut the grass on many occasions. My grandfather found mowing his lawn to be quite a relaxing activity, especially when faced with the pressures of running a business. He often said this provided him an opportunity to think without any distractions. My grandmother and I, for many years, would play cards in the afternoons. We would also drink lots and lots of tea, as was normal in their home and mine, because my grandmother and my mother were originally from England.

I think the reason that my grandparents have been so special to me is because much of the time I felt as though anything was possible when I was around them. Secondly, I think being able to run the lawn tractor was good for me because at a very young age it gave me a real feeling of accomplishment. At about age ten I traded the lawnmower for a three-wheeled ATV which would provide me with much enjoyment too, not to mention a few bumps and bruises over the next three or four years.

As a Teenager

Right about the time that I turned thirteen a new doctor came to Rhode Island Hospital. I went for my first meeting with him, accompanied by my mother. He asked me what my hopes and aspirations for myself were. He later determined that if I was to accomplish any of my dreams, and to accomplish them while being able to walk, I was going to require some surgery. This surgery was called a hamstring release. Having cerebral palsy, one of the difficulties I have is that my hamstrings are tight and require me to perform stretching exercises in order for me to stand straight.

At that point in my life, walking had gradually become extremely difficult for me. Day by day I could feel myself becoming less and less able to walk without extreme difficulty. Little did I know what a huge difference this surgery would make in my life. The hospitalization period was about three weeks longer than originally anticipated but when all was said and done the results of the surgery were quite remarkable. Prior to the surgery I stood approximately five feet one and one-half inches tall. At the end of the surgery I was approximately eight inches taller, about five foot nine and one-half, and for the first time I was seen as a big guy. My own father who I always had to physically look up to was now eye to eye with me. This was a great feeling!

The recovery from this surgery was painfully slow. I missed all of the eighth grade, except for tutoring at home, save for the first and last month of school. So it was very difficult for me to form friendships at that time.

At the start of puberty, around thirteen, like most boys my age, I was very self-conscious about my appearance. I turned all of my frustration inward and never shared it with anyone. I was just too ashamed to talk to anyone about how I was feeling. I thought it was just a fact that because I had cerebral palsy, no girl would ever find me attractive, physically or otherwise. I felt that everyone who knew me knew this was true but they were just too polite to tell me so. As far back as I can remember I never shared these feelings with anyone and they became an extremely heavy emotional load that I would carry for much of my young adult life.

In seventh grade I met a girl that I wanted to ask out. However, I convinced myself that there was no way she would ever date me simply because of my disability. Then I asked her out and she said no. I was crushed. For me, all this confirmed what I had thought all along. And I turned all the hurt inward and never discussed it. The best way to describe this is, that for most of my life, I felt horrible shame for having a disability and felt certain that I was ugly and unattractive solely because of my having cerebral palsy. I agonized over how to get up enough courage to express to a girl that I was romantically interested in her. On many occasions, when the ball was in my court, I would simply not speak up. I was basically trapped in a self-fulfilling prophecy, where I was sure no one would date me because of my disability, so I purposely drove any possible dates

away. I didn't ask anyone else out for a date or tell any woman how I felt about her until fourteen years later. Over the years I longed for a relationship with someone but wrongly convinced myself early on that having cerebral palsy had somehow branded me, if you will, as undesirable to members of the opposite sex.

The High School Years

Like many teenagers, I thought that my high school years were the toughest that I had ever encountered. This was a time in my life, where socially at least, I knew that I just didn't fit in.

When I was fourteen I entered my local regional high school. Upon entry I felt that I was ill prepared. I had spent the previous year being tutored at home and found it a hard transition to go to school full time. One of the first things that I discovered was that many of the friends I had made in grammar school had all made new friends and I felt as though I didn't know anyone.

Another very difficult period of life started during this time for me. Most of my high school career I longed for friends. I just wanted friends who would call me on the weekend, or ask me to go to a party, or out for pizza. With the exception of two, maybe three occasions, no one ever called.

I did find a group of local guys that I could have lunch with nearly every day. They would talk about the girlfriends they had, the parties they went to and the beer they drank. As far as I knew they didn't do drugs or get into fights. They were just good ol' American boys, a group that I wanted to be identified with, to belong to, if you will. A few of the guys would talk about getting together and would often say that they would like me to tag along too. So I'd wait for the call. But no one ever called. How did I ever make it? Probably because of persistence, I just never gave up. Looking back now it seems like I thought about giving up every day, but somehow I never did!

After High School

One of the toughest milestones in my life was getting through my eighteenth year. Like many eighteen-year-olds I thought that I was supposed to have all the answers and yet I really had no idea what I would be doing the very next day, let alone the rest of my life.

For years I was able to be devastated inside while smiling and keeping up appearances on the outside but now it was even more of a struggle. This time period was a milestone in my life because it was during this time that I felt my lowest, even contemplating suicide on almost a daily basis. Not being sure what I wanted to do in life, I attended the University of Rhode Island but dropped out after one semester, vowing never to return. When I did this I really felt like I blew my one and only chance for college and a future.

Wanting to give me some help, my uncle in the Midwest talked me into trying to sell equipment trailers to contractors.

This went really well for three or four years and I had a successful part-time business for myself. But due to a downturn in the local economy eventually I found my business had ceased. I felt that because I didn't have physical abilities I wouldn't be hired by any other business. Then, just when I needed it, a local businessman hired me as an office clerk. You would think by the time I had run my own business and then had a job that I would see for myself that I did have great value and potential as a person, but I still didn't believe it.

I wandered around somewhat aimlessly, or maybe it just felt like I was aimlessly wandering. You see, I now think all along I've been just like everybody else—trying to find my way in life. At the time though, I thought that all the struggles I was encountering were merely by-products of my having a disability. I realize now that while some of the insecurities were unique to my having a disability, many more of them were just the same thoughts and feelings as any scared, young adult has going through major changes in his life.

A New Beginning

Previously I had mentioned that my eighteenth year was a very difficult time, and it was, but as I said it was also a milestone year. It was a milestone because it was the year that I became a born-again Christian. My mom had become a born-again Christian a couple of years before and had convinced me to attend church with her on occasion. One morning when I had attended church with her the pastor was preaching about the need to ask Jesus into your heart in order to have eternal life. He went on to say that this would be a life-changing experience for anyone who did this. I remember thinking that this seemed right for me, that I was ready for a change, so on that very morning I prayed a simple prayer and asked Jesus into my life. Slowly but surely He has changed my life for the better. Some of these changes were painfully slow in coming but over the last ten years I have grown much. It was through my involvement at church that I became involved in 1992 with a campus ministry organization, Campus Crusade for Christ, at the University of Rhode Island.

It was at these meetings that I met many men and women who are still great friends to this day. Real friends. One of these friends was John. He had a huge impact on me, I believe, because he was my age and still not quite done with college. This got me thinking that maybe I should consider going back to school. It wasn't too late. With John's encouragement I began to entertain the idea of returning to college. I also met and befriended quite a few women and even started to date a few on occasion. One woman I met was Raquel who would become a close friend to me as well as be my date for many weddings, dinners, and other special events.

During the past four years I have also spent some much needed time in counseling and have been able to work through many of the hurts that I had gone through in the past. I realize that many of these experiences that I have been through, although quite gut-wrenching for me at the time, have made me a stronger person for just having gone through them. One of the biggest pieces of advice I could give to anyone with a disability, or to anyone who knows someone with a disability, is to encourage them to speak about it, express how they feel, and tell how the disability impacts their life.

In the summer of 1992, I completed a course at the university, which was the same course that I originally took and failed in the fall after high school. This time I received a "B." I've had to work really hard. I have taken many courses, often only one or two a semester, and often while working as well. It has not been easy going back to school, but by doing so I am slowly learning and finally believing that I am an intelligent man. I am planning to graduate in 2000 with a degree in psychology and a minor in philosophy.

Raquel—the woman that I mentioned becoming best friends with—well, I told her that I loved her dearly on Valentine's Day, 1995 and that although I had never done this before I wanted to date her so that we would know if we could ever marry. Most of the anxiety that I had carried around with me for all those years disappeared.

It turned out that on that Valentine's Day, at that moment, Raquel did not quite have the same revelation, if you will, that I had…

Or did she? We celebrated our second wedding anniversary on May 17th, 1999.

One of the major challenges facing my parents was that while there was much advice and seemingly endless amounts of literature informing parents how to raise children who were not disabled, there wasn't much available about children with disabilities. There just wasn't enough material about cerebral palsy for my family to read, that could show them how to face the seemingly insurmountable challenges of raising me. Hopefully today, with ever increasing amounts of information available to new parents on the Internet, they will never face a shortage of information that will help their child. It is my hope that with the release of this book, young parents and their extended family will feel encouragement and hope.

Our "Uptown Girl" By Michael R. Grills

Annie

date of birth:
January 11, 1990

Multiple Disabilities

So it was, on January 11th, 1990, Annie Darling Grills was born. Daughter to Michael and Laurie, sister to Benjamin, Annie was named after her recently deceased great-grandmother, Anne Belle Coon Grills, who had been an icon within the extended family for many years. After putting Laurie through twenty hours of fun-filled laborious contemplation (obviously Dad's point of view), Annie decided to enter the world. Sporting a full head of black hair and bright rosy cheeks, she, along with all her other new friends, laid in the nursery for all to see. Within two days Annie checked out of the nursery and came home with us to take up residency in Benjamin's old bassinet. Once home we were thrilled in the realization of having a boy and a girl. Let the games begin!

What Happened

Laurie, who was breast-feeding, took on the role of the tireless mom who looked after all the children's needs. I was back at work glowing about the new addition to our family. I had always wanted to have a large family and my dreams were beginning to come true. Laurie also wanted to have a large family and was really enjoying the role of a new mother.

Just as we had begun to settle into our new routine something went terribly wrong. It was on the sixth night, as Laurie recalls, that for some unknown reason she awoke sensing a need to feed Annie out of her normally scheduled time. Upon entering Annie's room she noticed that her skin-tone had turned to a yellowish blue and she felt very warm. After taking her temperature, which was 105 degrees, she quickly phoned our pediatrician. At this point I was awoken with Laurie explaining the situation to me. We were to rush Annie to the hospital where our pediatrician would meet us.

Our doctor met us at the emergency room and took Annie while Laurie and I were led off to a small adjacent room. As we sat in the room it became apparent that something was seriously wrong with Annie. Soon the doctor re-emerged telling us that Annie was going to be transported to our city hospital. Annie's condition was serious and we should quickly make arrangements to meet her there. In a fury we raced home, made some calls for Benjamin's care, and were at the city hospital in what seemed like minutes. The ambulance transporting Annie was just arriving. Enclosed in an incubator, she was taken from the ambulance and rushed to the pediatric intensive care unit. Laurie and I were led to a room across the hall where we were told to sit and wait. There we sat worrying, wondering, frightened of what was happening.

I remember staring out the window of the room after midnight, thinking of how cold and dark the night had become. Anxiety began to seep through my body as I noticed the word "meningitis" scratched on a dusty chalkboard in the middle of the room. I wondered what Laurie was thinking as we both waited silently. After what seemed like hours the door opened and in walked a doctor. She looked tired and weathered from what was probably a long day. She introduced herself while pulling up a chair next to us. Once seated she looked at both of us and said that Annie had contracted a form of meningitis and may not make it through the night. At that moment we were overwhelmed as our anxiety had turned to an uncontrollable pain from within. Why? What had we done? These were our thoughts as our emotions spilled out on a platter for all to see. Once gathered, she led us off to see our daughter. Time stood still.

Walking into the pediatric intensive care unit with Laurie was terrifying. Annie was in a small room adjacent to the main room clinging to life. Her beautiful hair had been shaven. She had tubes and needles seemingly coming out of everywhere while the veins in her entire body were enhanced by the poison flowing through them. Her head and shoulders were constantly jerking as if she was being electrocuted. As Laurie and I watched in horror, it became just a question of whether she would survive. I remember thinking I could be stronger, faster, smarter, work longer, make more money, and climb higher mountains, but none of that mattered anymore. For the first time in my life I felt completely helpless, unable to help my only daughter as her life hung in the balance. Now Annie's life was in their hands, the doctors and the Lord, and not necessarily in that order.

We hoped and we prayed as the doctors would come and go, seemingly waiting for the inevitable. They were pumping a concoction of drugs through a vein in her ankle. The drug mix would become stronger as the weaker ones failed to stabilize Annie's blood pressure and heart rate. It was decided that Annie should be baptized. Laurie and I watched through the blurred vision of tear-filled eyes as the baptism was performed. Then we waited. A day passed. We waited some more. During the second day I began shuttling back and forth to the room while communicating to family and friends as to Annie's condition.

It was at this time that I began to notice the other children located in the main part of the unit. Some looked terribly sick while others were plagued with gross abnormalities. This was no place for the faint of heart. What a truly humbling experience. Meanwhile, Laurie did not leave Annie's side. Then, ever so slowly, Annie's vital signs began to stabilize. By the afternoon of the second day it became clear that Annie would refuse to succumb to the disease. While she would survive this vicious bacterium, and we were relieved, we knew Annie would never be the same.

On the third day Annie was placed in the main part of the PICU, and as she slowly began the recovery process, our questions mounted. What would she be like? Would she walk, talk, and see like any other child? Only one person could answer these questions: Annie.

Annie spent the next six weeks recuperating at the hospital. It was during this stay that we learned, for the first time, just what happened to her. Doctors informed us that Annie had contracted Group B Streptococcus from the vaginal wall during her birth. They went on to explain that thirty-five percent of all women carry this bacteria but ninety-nine percent of the time it has no effect on the child once born. Then came the most difficult news. This all could have been avoided if Laurie had been fed a simple antibiotic during her labor. (Laurie and I have since become members of the Group B Strep Association which is striving for mandatory screening of all expectant mothers for the bacteria.)

As can be imagined this was a difficult time for us. Laurie stayed at the hospital the majority of the time while I shuttled from work, home, and then back to the hospital most of the days. We were slowly coming to grips with what our "new" life would be like with Annie. There was little good news coming from the various doctors. The main concerns centered around the amount of brain damage that had occurred and the possible loss of her eyesight. Also, her right ankle had a large burn from where the drugs were fed into her body intravenously. No one knew for sure the extent of her brain injury because of her age. Before long it was time to bring Annie back home.

Within the next few years we pretty much had a handle on Annie's condition. The state of Rhode Island's early intervention program provided physical therapy at our home on a routine basis. The therapist would come and loosen up Annie's muscles and joints so she would have a better chance at improving her motor skills. A subsequent MRI revealed that Annie, in fact, had damage to parts of her brain, including the cortex. The prognosis from the doctors for her acquiring eyesight became pessimistic.

She also would revisit the hospital on three occasions to undergo extensive reconstructive surgery on her badly burned ankle. Her ankle was so bad that one surgery required the removal of a muscle in Annie's upper back so it could be "transplanted' on one side of the ankle. Obviously, along with everything else, this has hindered Annie's ability to walk. Today Annie is able to take steps with the help of plastic leg braces in conjunction with a walking apparatus.

The Highlights

For Laurie and I, as we look back at her first seven and one-half years, we find there have been many memorable moments. Some are full of joy, others painfully sad, yet as we learn how Annie thirsts for life there becomes a realization that some things were just meant to be. Annie now has two brothers and one sister. Along with Benjamin, now Adam and Chandler help Annie better understand the world around her. It's the highlights of this world that I would like to touch upon now.

Early on it became painfully apparent that Annie didn't like riding in her car seat. While I assumed it was precipitated by the motion of the car, along with her inability to see, it seemed there was nothing Laurie or I could do to keep her from crying during trips. Then one afternoon, as Laurie recalls, she was traveling with Annie and decided to play a Billy Joel cassette tape during which the song "Uptown Girl" came on. Suddenly, for the first time, Annie stopped crying while riding in the car. After a little experimentation (Annie would begin to cry again at his other songs) Laurie realized that it was this particular song that apparently was "hip" to her. Well, needless to say, "Uptown Girl" not only became the number one song in our home but we also found that the phrase "don't leave home without it" took on a new meaning! Whenever we went anywhere, from that point on, you could be sure there would be a copy of "Uptown Girl" close by.

During this time our own "Uptown Girl" began to attend a school in Westerly, RI. Her class was designed for special needs children. They attempted to train Annie to play ball, feed herself, and use the bathroom, along with many other things. It was at this point that the facilitators of the class realized that the song "Uptown Girl" also motivated Annie to accomplish tasks. The song had become so important to her that they decided to contact Billy Joel's manage-ment people to see if he could possibly meet her. Although the contact was made, the teachers were informed that Billy was just embarking on his "River Of Dreams Tour" and he would be unable to adjust his schedule. I then wrote back to Billy Joel's management people and along with describing Annie's condition asked if we could meet him at one of his concert stops. Well, about a month went by when, upon arriving home from work one day, Laurie told me she had received a phone call from Billy Joel's manager. He explained that the tour was going to stop in Worcester, Massachusetts, and that if Annie could be there Billy would love to meet her. Well, sure enough, all the arrangements were made for Annie's special night. Following a fascinating limo ride we were led backstage. Once there, with cookies in hand, Billy Joel and his band members met, spoke to, and had pictures taken with the "Uptown Girl."

Subsequent to Annie's program she was located at another elementary school to begin kindergarten. It was determined that this school was the best equipped, within the district, to handle her needs. Annie became part of a program developed by an area school, which attempts to mainstream disabled students. Once there, Annie began to improve upon her living skills (maneuvering her wheelchair, taking steps, feeding, communicating and toilet training) while making quite a name for herself among the other students. In addition, The Providence Journal newspaper, had contacted the school explaining that they were interested in writing an article describing this town's inclusion program. At this point, Laurie and I were contacted by the school. They asked if we would allow Annie to be featured in the article. With our blessing, Annie was featured in what was a heartwarming article describing basically how the school included Annie in the various daily activities. It went on to describe how Annie enlightened her classmates and teachers alike.

Annie loves the water. She spends one morning every week at the local YMCA as part of her program at school. Even with all her limitations, Laurie, who accompanies her, is amazed at how she will slide off the side of the pool and into the water on her own. Even though Annie is supported by inner tubes, it is fascinating to see how she thoroughly enjoys the experience.

If you have never been able to witness the Special Olympics I can tell you from my first experience that you really are missing something. Recently, Annie participated in her first Olympics, held in the Tootell Gymnasium located at the University of Rhode Island athletic complex. She competed in simulated bowling, baseball, and basketball, along with a few other special events. The thrill that all the children expressed in competing through the day proved to me that these Olympics are truly "special."

The last highlight I would like to share took place on Christmas Eve night, in 1995. We traditionally have some of the family over for food, spirits, and exchanging of gifts. During the evening we decided to strap Annie's braces on to see if she could walk across our main living room. Since none of the family had seen her walk, coupled with the knowledge that they could cheer her on during the attempt, Laurie and I figured it was a perfect time for her to try the long walk. With the help of her walker, Annie proceeded to walk step by agonizing step, across the living room. It was the best Christmas present we could have had. There wasn't a dry eye in the house.

Annie Our Daughter

As Annie approaches her tenth birthday Laurie and I can pause and reflect on how far she has come. Having a disabled child changed our world. We have watched as Annie has struggled to learn about the world around her. She has made us all laugh and cry. She has taught us patience and understanding. But most of all she has displayed that willingness to never give up, no matter what.

Whatever life we are given, we are to live it to the fullest, however that may be. While Annie continues to require full-time care, she is the type of person who loves to hug you, loves to kiss you, and loves to show that we're all special in some way.

The Most Powerful Teacher in the World

By Elizabeth Pinto

Michael

date of birth:
January 3, 1968

Multiple Disabilities

I'm thirty-four years old and the oldest of three children. I have a younger sister, Deb, and a younger brother, Michael. He is twenty-nine and the focus of this chapter. Michael is the most powerful teacher in the world. He has shaped my destiny and his influence has greatly contributed to who I am today. The way I perceive the world is largely because of the experiences I share with my brother. My most precious beliefs and values all correlate to what Michael has taught me, not just in childhood but as we continue to live and grow today. Michael was my dearest teacher, who lead me to my current world view. As is often the case with leaders, they lead by example. His life has done just that. I can assure you as I sit here today and type this chapter, Michael has touched more lives and developed more human spirit in others than I could ever hope to.

Michael's ability to teach can't be measured in percentages or even dollars. He taught me that life is valuable, and time is precious and we shouldn't waste it. He showed me that life is full of opportunities to learn, and there is something to learn in every struggle. Michael taught me that intuition is reality-based, and nonverbal communication signals are more powerful and direct than words. He taught me that

facial expressions and the turning of a lip, or the tilt of the head, or the pace of breathing—all connote meaning to the keen observer, the observer who wants to see and communicate. He taught me all of this without saying a word. Michael does not talk.

Perhaps I jump to my concluding thoughts first because the message is so clear to me every day. But I will begin at the beginning, as I remember it with the memories that shaped my childhood, recognizing that memories differ, even within the closest knit families, like mine. When discussing my rendition with others it is clear that differences exist in perception.

It was the late 1960's, and my mother was pregnant with Michael. Everyone in the family became sick. To my parents horror we were all diagnosed with German Measles. I believed that I was the person who brought the measles into our home. I thought my brother Michael's birth defects were because I was sick, and until recently I operated under this assumption. One year ago I found out that my assumption was incorrect; I did not expose my family.

I was five when Michael was born. He was affected by the German Measles in utero. Doctors warned our parents that there was a possibility of birth defects. Some even suggested that Mom should abort. Our parents decided to proceed with the pregnancy. When Michael was born, doctors tried to convince them that

he would need to live in an institution. They decided to bring Michael home.

When Michael came home from the hospital, our parents did not hear the typical comments about new babies. People seemed uncertain about what to say. It wasn't too long after he came home that I noticed he had two different colored eyes. One eye was a light blue and the other a cloudy gray. There was a pervasive mood of sadness and anxiety not knowing what the future would bring. Family members cried or remained silent. I had turned five just a few days before Michael was born, and had no idea of the devastation people felt by not having a perfect baby. I was just curious about Michael's eyes.

I remained curious throughout our childhood. I tried to assimilate the information I had been told in our home with the outside world. The word cataract was not in many five-year-olds' vocabularies. The concept of pupils being dark spots in everyone's eyes and cataracts as spots covering pupils, eluded me. A kindergarten classmate of mine went running home one day when I diagnosed her pupils as cataracts. I was told the story years later and felt awful that I had scared her.

Michael was referred to as a "Rubella Baby." I'm sure today he would be called a child who is "rubella-affected." He was born during the second wave of Rubella. The first wave was in the early to mid 1960's. The children born earlier had been diagnosed with brain damage and were deaf and/or blind. There were some children born with heart defects, too. Michael was diagnosed with similar challenges; deaf, blind, and mentally retarded with a heart murmur.

I could not understand why he was called handicapped. Our parents always said that everybody has strengths and weaknesses, Michael's are just more apparent. I relied on this explanation for my entire early life. Actually, I rely on this explanation every day of my life. When people questioned Michael's retardation, I questioned their lack of understanding. When people questioned his sight, I questioned their lack of

foresight and vision. When people questioned his ability to hear, I questioned their ability to listen. When people questioned the quality of Michael's life, I questioned their ability to understand the human spirit. If you didn't like Michael or felt uncomfortable around him, you couldn't be my friend

and I didn't have time for you. He was the dividing line between me and the world.

Growing up, Michael was the center of my universe, the filter for all interactions. He was the screen for all understanding. If people didn't understand him, I had no desire to share time, space or experiences with them.

Michael is a powerful person with a beautiful soul. He heard more of my thoughts about the world when we were growing up than anyone. I ached to learn about his experience of the world, his experiences of our family. He taught me so much. By the time I was six, Michael had taught me that gender and color are not reasons for exclusion, and should have no place in the world. This lesson was further developed as we grew up. The message he gave me at the time was—accept differences—differences should be valued. How boring the world would be if we were all the same: same color, same gender, same strengths, and same weaknesses.

I know what you're thinking. How could this blind, deaf, and retarded kid do all she says he did? I need and want you to know he taught me even more. He taught me to live, listen, and see with my heart. What I'm trying to say is that sight and hearing can be limiting, but our hearts and souls are endless and connected. It may seem surreal, but the message was clear to me before I could write in cursive.

My brother Michael was born blind. When he was two years old, surgery was recommended to correct his cataracts. Few doctors would work with people with multihandicaps. In fact, there was only one physician in Rhode Island that worked with kids like my brother. The only place to have the cataract surgery was in Boston at Massachusetts's Eye and Ear. There were a total of three eye surgeries and they worked on one eye at a time. I don't remember anyone predicting that he would have sight. I remember thinking that the cataract would be gone or smaller, making his sight improve. He was two or three years old at the time. His blindness was the easiest handicapping condition for me to understand.

Visiting him in Boston was scary. We parked across the street from the hospital and had to cross a pedestrian bridge over Storrow Drive. The corridors of the hospital appeared huge. His room was down at the end of the hall. It was a long, dark, and smelly walk. I believed that awful hospital smell meant bad things. I hated it there. I hated that my brother was there. He was in a big crib. His arms and hands were restrained so he wouldn't get at his stitches. I hated seeing him like that and I'm sure our parents did, too. I couldn't understand what I had seen. I cried and asked questions. I remember the part about not ripping out the stitches. I hated the thought of my brother having stitches in his eye. We brought Michael home. The Doctors recommended wrapping magazines around his arms, and securing them with our Dad's neckties to prevent him from touching his eyes. Time had to pass to know if the surgeries were successful, and his sight would improve.

Michael's heart murmur did not require surgery. I was thankful for that. Doctors believed it may close as he matured. It was not life threatening and could go untreated.

Michael did not meet developmental milestones like other children his age. Those charts in doctors' offices that parents look forward to bragging about brought no such right to our parents. His ability to walk, talk, and eat were all delayed. For many months he laid on his back making patterns in the sunlight with his little hands. He wasn't pulling to stand or even rolling over as the charts predicted.

Social workers, occupational therapists, physical therapists, and special education teachers all came to our house to talk to our parents. I hovered around these professionals with their screens and flashlights, and listened. I was always listening. Sometimes I would offer my observations. I wanted to be heard.

I remember discussions about movement, vision, eating and feeling. I also remember discussions about glasses, hearing aids, and sensory integration. Would he tolerate wearing the glasses or hearing aids? The professionals thought if his hearing or vision improved enough and he found them helpful, he would wear them. I especially remember the hope that our parents voiced, "Will he be able to scratch a mosquito bite? Swat at a fly that lands on his arm?" A simple hope, but the possibility of it happening was unclear at the time. The things most people take for granted, my brother would need to be taught.

For quite a while, years in fact, Michael ate only soft food. Giant jars of baby food were his staple. There was nothing organically wrong with him, but he wouldn't eat hard foods. The professionals convinced our parents that he could eat hard food and if he was hungry enough, he would. Our parents consented to a trial with two meals a day. The details of the story differ depending on whose recollection you hear. Michael came home from school one Friday night and ate his large jar of baby food. The following morning hard food was placed in front of him. He refused to eat or be fed. Our parents, although distraught, agreed to let him go hungry. Lunchtime rolled around, and again hard food was put in front of him. He ate it. Our father was overjoyed and ran to tell a neighbor. The saga of soft food was over. Onward to munching on Spaghettios, fruit cocktail, and Rice Krispies. Another lesson was learned. Sometimes fear controls the options and choices we give others. Giving choices is critical to proceeding to the next level of development, self determination, and self sufficiency.

Michael started attending Meeting Street School when he was three years old and left in his twenty-first year. The small special education bus would come around 7:00 a.m. He waited in a small chair in the kitchen and when the bus pulled in the driveway, Mom, Dad, or Deb and I would go out and load him on. We knew all the kids, monitors, and driver. They were nice people, and loved my brother dearly. Sometimes when I went to my brother's school I would ride the bus and learn some sign language.

His day started early and finished late. He wouldn't return home until almost dinnertime, hours after Deb and I would be home from school. We would look in his book for notes about his day. What did he do at school today? Did he feed himself? Did he go swimming? He couldn't tell us. He never complained.

Michael attended what we all thought at the time was the best school in America for children with multihandicaps. The school did address his needs, and it is a given that he wouldn't have the skills he has today if it was not for their persistence and Michael's tenacity. He has mastered many activities of daily living skills and can feed, dress, and clean himself. He can go to the bathroom independently. All of these things were incredibly important to his self- sufficiency.

The piece that was missing for him was friends. Leaving home before seven o'clock in the morning, and returning after four o'clock in the afternoon didn't leave him any time to make friends. In the early days, families of Michael's classmates would get together for cookouts at school. Our family knew other families and it was a great support. But looking back, he was a victim of Meeting Street School. He never had the opportunity to be with children who were his own age who were not disabled. Sending him away for school meant he could not have access to neighborhood kids. Michael only had Deb and me; we were his nondisabled peers. If there is a message here, and I believe there is— every child should have the opportunity to make friends and build relationships naturally. Michael did not have this opportunity.

Michael is a visitor in his hometown. This is a tragedy. People should have had the opportunity to know him growing up so they would know him as an adult. All this should have happened naturally. People in the neighborhood lost on this account. The challenge the adult agency that supports Michael faces is reconnecting him to his community, his hometown.

He went everywhere with us. There was no stopping the family. Our parents had a station wagon and before Michael could sit, a playpen was put in the back of the car, and off we would go. I'm sure the sight of him flapping his hands in the sunlight to make patterns in front of his eyes was quite something to see. It never phased us. If we took a trip, Michael took a trip. If we went to the beach, Michael went to the beach. If we went shopping at Filene's Basement, Michael came. In fact, the joke our parents told was that we would get the best seats wherever we went because people would give us space. Even at the beach on weekends, space galore.

When we needed a babysitter, I would do all of Michael's care or teach the babysitter what they needed to know. We went through a lot of babysitters. I began to realize that not everybody was cut out to babysit us. When I was a teenager, I babysat when our parents went out. While other kids my age were going to the movies, I was home with Michael. I swear I saw every episode of "The Love Boat." The truth is I

preferred Michael's company to that of many others.

I could not understand why people gave us space or stared at us. It was just the way it was. I would get frustrated by their apparent fear and obvious ignorance. I could not understand why they wouldn't come up and ask whatever they were thinking.

I believe I became an astute observer of people by the time Michael was three or four years old. One day our mother, Michael, and I were at the mall. He could not walk yet and was being pushed in his stroller. I was tuned into the stares of many people that day. I was angry. I wondered why people that curious would not seek answers by asking questions. I asked Mom, and she replied that she thought they could be scared. Scared of Michael? I could not fathom it.

As I have shared, growing up with Michael was a point of reference for me. I would choose friends who liked my brother and could deal with him. I was aware that my life was different than

many kids my age. At school, on the playground, when I heard kids call each other "retard" my blood would boil. I would rush in and say, "Don't call him/her retarded. They aren't retarded. My brother is retarded." My belief that many people do not understand or value differences was further developed. Differences were used as dividing lines to separate people. I could not understand why separating people from other people was so important. I could not see the value in it. In fact, I could not understand why it happened at all.

Michael meant more to me than anyone or anything growing up. I cherished our time. I would sing and play with him. Each year on his birthday I would make up a song about the upcoming year and he would laugh and smile. He has some old favorites to this day. When I whisper the verses in his ear I have no doubt that he knows who we are and who we were. I believe we both recognize the specialness that was "us" growing up.

In the mid 1970's, I had the opportunity to attend several conferences about siblings. I found them helpful, though it was very hard to discuss my desire to give my eyes to my brother so he could see, or share the wish to get inside my brother's head to know what he was thinking. I remember being overcome with emotion and shedding tears as I told our story. Many siblings' experiences were similar.

I was fourteen when I wrote a passionate letter to Michael's school principal. The letter was published in the school newspaper. It was about my questioning, "Why Can't People Just Understand?" I just could not accept the concept that people who were different were on the "outside," and there were whole groups of people on the "inside" that would not accept people with differences. I questioned why we all could not just be part of the community. I was so proud of the letter; I still am.

The year I went away to college, Michael went to live in a group home. He has lived in

several homes in several communities. Currently, he lives in a group home that is about one mile from my house, which makes it easy for him to come home most weekends. He has chores that he performs with our dad and grandfather and he enjoys that routine.

I see Michael about once a week. We go to the beach together on weekends in the summer. I attend all the meetings that are held to review his progress and appropriate supports. The adult agency knows that at least three family members will attend every meeting.

For the last few years Michael has not been himself. He has faced challenges around depression and anxiety. We have faced these challenges with him, yet no one has answers. Meetings have been frequent. When I was a child, I wished I could get into my brother's head to know what he was thinking. Now, I wish for a quick fix, and a way to know what is going on in his world. I wish for a remedy to return Michael to the happy and smiling person I grew up with. Continuing to search for answers is a slow and arduous process. It is difficult to remain patient when he struggles so openly to help us understand his dilemma.

As our parents mature, I realize my role will change. As they approach retirement and begin traveling more, I will need to assume more day to day responsibilities. I will continue to be involved and advocate for and with Michael. I urge other families to be vigilant advocates to help insure their loved ones are safe and have positive supports. I have lived with my brother for just about thirty years. Twenty years have passed since I first wrote my plea to include all people in the community. I have had various jobs working with children who have had cognitive, physical, sensory, and emotional challenges. I have worked in three New England states in a variety of school systems and am currently the Assistant Director of Special Education in a small town in southern Rhode Island. Each day I work to change practices that exclude people with disabilities, and increase opportunities that are inclusive. I think of my latest career challenges as a mission rather than a job. Each day I work to make changes and increase choices for children with disabilities.

Michael has been my most powerful teacher. I would never be the person I am today if it was not for him. He has made me aware of my mission in life; to promote an all-inclusive community that excludes no one. I continue my advocacy of inclusive practices. To accept less than a community that includes everyone is to do a disservice to my brother and all he has taught me.

Love, Patience, & Joy By Jean Joy Crowley

Joy

date of birth:
January 28, 1976

Cornelia DeLange Syndrome

It was January 27, 1976; the score was 53 to 53, less than a minute to go, and we needed this win to advance to the play-offs. Within that minute I felt a warm dampness begin to trickle down my legs and I knew my water had broken. I wrapped my warm-up jacket around my waist and continued to coach the high school varsity girls' basketball team through what would be their final game of the season. While the girls' team and I were ending one chapter in our lives, another one began on that bench. Her name would be Joy!

Throughout my pregnancy I was told this baby appeared to be very small. I was five days overdue now so how could that be? This was my first, so I told myself that it was probably because I was very tiny and therefore I would have tiny children. I entered the hospital that evening and went through the process all women do of preparation, monitoring, asking questions, breathing deep, and praying that everything was going to go like it's supposed to. The moment arrived, the cry was strong, "It's a girl" was announced; "She's very small, let's

incubate stat," came from the doctor's voice. The dream of a perfect baby was shattered. Now a new dream had to begin.

Joy was four pounds six ounces and only fourteen inches long. I kept saying to myself, "That's only two inches longer than a ruler." Her x-rays showed some spots on the lungs and a murmur could be heard in her heart, but everything else seemed okay internally. We would find out at a later date that she had a hole between the main pulmonary artery and the aorta. This was called patent ductus. Feedings were a nightmare. Everything kept trickling out of her nose. I continually asked the nurses for help and they also had difficulty. Thank goodness it wasn't just my inexperience. Come on, how hard is it to give a baby a bottle? The doctor was called and she came right away. Being a close friend of my family she took a great deal of time to help and comfort me. She spent time in the nursery and then came to my room. Knowing her well, I knew by the look on her face there was more for me to deal with. She informed me that Joy had no hard or soft palate in her mouth and that's why formula was running out of her nose. This was called cleft palate. I had heard of this but did not know anyone who had a child born with this problem. We now had to figure out how to get nourishment into Joy without using an I.V. The doctor gave me nipples that are used to feed baby lambs and we attached them to medicine bottles. They were very long and therefore would bypass the open roof of Joy's mouth. They also had a large opening, which was important, because Joy, without a

roof in her mouth, had no ability to suck. This worked, except the hole being so very large allowed the formula to pour out of the opening causing Joy to choke often. I had to get the knack of tipping and pulling back so this would not happen. Every time she choked, my heart would race and my hands would sweat. I finally became adept at the procedure.

The doctor decided it would be best if we transferred Joy to a hospital that dealt with children born with disabilities. She would be close to those who could care for her better and we would begin what was to be a long medical and emotional journey. The first order of business was to touch base with a plastic surgeon to get an indication as to how we should proceed in repairing the cleft palate. It was decided that the hard palate would be repaired first but not until she was a year old. That meant a full year of lambs' nipples and choking episodes.

Joy had to remain in the hospital until she reached the weight of five pounds, five ounces. As I would soon find out, almost everything about Joy took longer than usual. The hour drive to the hospital each day was excruciating because I was allergic to the stitches in my episiotomy. I had to be very conscientious about positioning. Ouch! The only good thing about Joy being away from me was that I now had a chance to rest and heal. I knew the days ahead were going to be rough and I would need all the physical and emotional strength I could muster.

That first year proved to be very interesting. It seemed like most of the time was spent feeding Joy and trying to sleep while she was sleeping. It took so long to get through one bottle that by the time one feeding was done the next wasn't far behind. I wasn't one to stay still for very long so being locked into staying home all the time was difficult for me. No one felt comfortable babysitting for Joy so my only outlet was grocery shopping, while Dad stayed with Joy. I hate grocery shopping!

I had taken a year's maternity leave from teaching and originally had planned to return to work in January of '77. In September I noticed a little bulge on Joy's lower abdomen. It turned out to be the first of two inguinal hernias that would need to be surgically repaired. Also in September I realized that I was pregnant and discovered my due date was in March. Any hope of returning to work certainly needed to be put on hold.

Also during that first year several of Joy's orthopedic abnormalities were discovered. Some of her fingers were extra long and the others were missing whole segments so they were very tiny. Her toes had the same problem and both of her feet were club. Her lower leg bones were not aligned properly so she was casted from her knees to her toes. It was also discovered that she had no hip sockets to hold her upper leg bones, so walking would never happen unless this was corrected. She was put in what was called a pillow splint with her legs in a frog position. They would remain that way for as long as it took the tibias to groove sockets into the pelvic bones. A year would be the minimum.

With the onset of spring and good weather came a reprieve for Joy and me. At least we could go outdoors. While she slept in her carriage I would work in the garden. What a break. It was great. I remember one spring day especially well; it didn't turn out so great. It was raining and what I was about to find out would put yet another dark cloud over Joy's life. I was vacuuming the rugs and it was almost time for Joy to wake from her nap. I decided to vacuum her room figuring it would awaken her. It didn't! I kept running the machine back and forth in front of her crib expecting her to roll over and smile at me. Was she in such a deep sleep or was something wrong? My gut feeling wasn't good. We mothers do have that innate ability to surmise things that others can't when it concerns our children. I began clapping my hands and making loud noises. Nothing worked. I reached into the crib and gently poked her until she woke up. I let her lay for a few minutes to give her time to perk up. I moved to the other side of the room and when I could see that she was not looking at me I clapped my hands as loud as I could.

No response! My knees weakened and I collapsed to the floor and cried. I couldn't believe this was happening.

I went to a specialist and had Joy tested in a sound lab. It's amazing how accurate the results can be on someone so young. It was determined that she was moderately deaf but that hearing aides would greatly benefit her. The molds were made and the aides attached. Now to try to get her to wear them. It was a struggle at first but when she realized what the aides were doing for her I then had trouble getting her to take them off to go to bed at night. The first of many battles was won.

In December of 1976 Joy's hernia became strangulated and had to be operated on immediately. The first hernia had been taken care of in September. We were now gearing up for the initial palate reconstructive surgery in January. I was very apprehensive. Joy had tripled her weight in the first year but still only weighed a meager twelve pounds. I was now seven months pregnant and getting fat. I had gained too much weight this time. I figured that if I gained a lot of weight I would have a big baby and everything would be okay. I was scared to death that a repeat of Joy's difficulties might happen.

On January 20, 1977 Joy was admitted to the hospital and was to be operated on the next day. The doctor had explained how he would graft skin from the inside of her cheeks to create a hard palate. If you run your tongue along the roof of your mouth you can feel all the bumps and ridges. That's what they constructed for Joy. It's unbelievable how at one time there was just an empty space and now she would have a roof in her mouth almost the same as the rest of us.

I insisted on staying at the hospital throughout this whole episode. The best they could do for me was a reclining chaise since all of the cots were taken. I spent most of that night staring at my little twelve-pound bundle. My eyes filled with tears wishing it were me and not her. It's hard to watch someone you love dearly go through so many things, one right after the other. I was scared that they would give her too much anesthesia and she would never wake up. I guess it's natural to have negative thoughts when you're under pressure and stressed. I thought the night would never end but I was thankful for that because it meant more time with Joy.

The morning arrived and with it came a bustling of activity in preparation for surgery. The doctor came to see Joy and made an attempt to comfort me. I walked, holding the side bar of the crib, as far as the elevator with a lump so hard in my throat I could hardly swallow. As the door closed all I felt was fear and the coldness of tears running down my cheeks. The surgery was going to take anywhere between three and five hours. It would seem like years. There is nothing worse than waiting and not being able to do a thing except be with your thoughts. Much of the time I let my thoughts get carried away to places I shouldn't have gone to. I had to keep reassuring myself that all was going fine, it soon would be over, and little Joy would be here for me to nurse back once again to healthiness.

As they rolled Joy's crib into the room I could see how swollen her face was. She was barely awake but managed a tiny smile when her eyes met mine. Her arms were in full splints so that she couldn't bend them at the elbows. This was to guarantee she wouldn't put her hands in or near her mouth. Infection was the critical issue at this point. Her mouth was filled with stitches that had to be kept clean. Only clear liquids would pass through her lips for at least one full month. Was feeding Joy going to be another nightmare? Would she be crying all the time because of hunger? How would I put the bottle in her mouth without touching the stitches? These fears subsided as I became comfortable feeding Joy at the hospital. The nurses were helpful and encouraging so, except for feeling and looking like a seven-month pregnant stuffed pig with swollen ankles, things were looking up.

On the eighth day in the hospital the doctor became concerned, not with Joy's progress, but with mine. I had been sleeping upright for a week and my hands, feet, and ankles were exploding.

He was fearful that I was developing toxemia. I refused to leave Joy and go home so his only alternative was to discharge her to my care. He felt assured that I was ready to take over and he knew that I needed to get home where I would be able to take better care of my own pregnant needs.

It was January 28, 1977, Joy's first birthday. Everyone was awaiting her arrival home from the hospital. There were flowers, presents, food and a very special group of friends and family to greet us. We had made it through a very trying first year but here we were and it was great to be back in the comforts of our home. I looked at little Joy with hearing aides in each ear, casts from knees to toes, legs pinned up like a frog, splints on both arms and God knows how many stitches in her mouth and I was thankful for having such a special little angel.

The next eight weeks were filled with busy days and nights. Feedings were stressful and long, and the pregnancy was beginning to take its toll. Joy's dad and his mother were my salvation. Together we rotated feedings, trips to the hospital for checkups, and the decorating of another nursery for our soon to be second child. By the middle of March Joy was eating baby cereal and fruits and was slowly gaining weight. She learned to crawl even with her legs up like a frog. At fourteen months most children are already walking but for Joy it still wasn't clear whether walking would ever be a reality. The second plastic surgery, to close the soft palate, was scheduled for May. This would give me a little time with my new baby before having to take special care of Joy after surgery.

Amy was born on March 31, 1977. This made her fourteen months younger than Joy. She was twenty-one inches long and weighed eight pounds, two ounces. She was a beautiful blue-eyed, blond-haired, plump, healthy baby. Thank you God! Amy was an easy baby to care for although what wouldn't be easy after that first year with Joy? She ate like a champ and slept like a bear. The perfect baby! This dream wasn't shattered.

May was creeping up on us and I had to prepare for another plastic surgery. This one was going to be much easier than the first. It only entailed pulling the skin of the soft palate closed and stitching it together. The difficult part was the clear liquid regimen but at least I was now experienced at that. Joy was slowly growing and gaining weight, she was pulling herself up, and she and Amy had each other to play with. By the middle of that summer of '77 I felt that my situation at home had become all-consuming. I needed some diversity in my twenty-four hour day, just to maintain my sanity. I craved adult

a certain kind of love | Love, Patience, & Joy

companionship and the continuation of my career. I could obtain both, along with my sanity, by returning to work, so in September I was back teaching full time.

During that year x-rays showed that the sockets in Joy's hips had developed enough to take the pillow splint off. She was free at last. It was amazing how well she had learned to maneuver with such a cumbersome object between her legs. Now she had to learn, all over again, how to move around without it. The hope was for her to build up enough strength to walk. It was a long waiting game. Joy turned two in January of '78 and still had not taken her first step. Another whole year passed, it was her third birthday, and she still hadn't taken that step. She was moving more securely and confidently but her sense of balance was shaky. I could tell that those steps were going to happen and I certainly wasn't going to lose faith now. It was just taking longer than anticipated. Joy's inability to walk wasn't really a problem except for

the fact that she and Amy had to be carried everywhere. My upper arms were beginning to look like those of a weight lifter.

Love and patience always ends up being rewarding and in this case the rewards were magnificent. On a hot summer day in July of 1979, we were sitting in the living room watching Joy and Amy play. Amy was running about as usual and Joy was pulling herself up along the side of the couch. In one beautiful instant she let go and walked alone down the hallway with a grin so huge it seemed ear to ear. To her own amazement she was finally walking! Joy was now three years and six months old and a new world was

| a certain kind of love | Love, Patience, & Joy

opening up for her. I began telephoning everyone who had been so supportive and loving throughout the previous years so they could share in this wondrous excitement. The cars began rolling in and a party was about to ensue. We opened champagne and toasted our Joy and were thankful that another battle in her life had been won.

The laws protecting children with disabilities provides for them to go to school from age three to twenty-one. It was now time for Joy to begin in a preschool for special needs students. She loved being with little kids and learned by their model. The time had come to do some educational testing to see what Joy's cognitive abilities were. I always knew that she was developmentally delayed but when testing proved it true, it was a tough pill to swallow. We all want our children to be intelligent, critical thinkers, and have a thirst for knowledge so they will grow to become prosperous and independent adults. This would not be the case for Joy. The psychologist who tested her explained the results and concluded that she was globally mentally disabled. From that day on I couldn't tolerate the word global.

After two years of preschool it was time for more decision making. Should Joy be placed in a self-contained class or was there something better for her? The school system chose the self-contained class. We disagreed. Being a teacher and knowing my rights as a parent of a special child, I asked for a hearing. We hired a lawyer and went to battle for Joy. We felt that because she was moderately deaf the Rhode Island School for the

Deaf would be better able to meet her needs. It would be there that she could learn to communicate through sign language. At age five she was still basically non-verbal. The hearing lasted until four o'clock in the morning. It was a hot August night and the combination of stress and heat caused perspiration to pour down everyone's foreheads. It all became worth it when the hearing officer ruled in our favor. Another battle was won.

Before Joy began the trek to the School for the Deaf in the fall, the doctors decided to do a heart catheterization to check on the hole. The murmur could still be heard and they felt a closer look was needed. That summer of 1981, Joy once again was admitted to the hospital. The procedure didn't take as long as expected and a nurse, who I became friendly with through previous ventures at this facility, came running into Joy's room smiling from ear to ear. "It closed by itself, after four years it usually doesn't, but hers did. Can you believe it?" She was babbling so fast with excitement that I asked her to slow down. She explained that the doctor wanted word sent down to us about this fantastic news. Heart surgery would not be needed. Another battle was won.

The next eight years were good ones but the days were incredibly long for Joy. The bus picked her up at 6:15 in the morning for the hour-long ride to Providence, RI. She was returned home at 4:30 each evening. The progress made was worth the efforts for now she was fluent in sign language and was able to communicate her needs. During these years she grew at a snail's pace and only weighed about forty pounds at age twelve. She was dwarf size but cute as a button.

Joy always had difficulty keeping food down and never had a regular bowel movement. It was time to bring her to more specialists to have another thorough going over. We chose to bring her to a facility in Connecticut that specialized in children with disabilities. No one had ever given us a label or a reason for Joys' difficulties and we never asked. After many days of poking, prodding, and testing, the results were in. Joy was diagnosed with a rare syndrome called Cornelia DeLange (CDLS). These children are very small in stature, have many orthopedic abnormalities, have bowel and reflux problems and usually are mentally delayed. The expected life span is young adulthood. Throughout the next few years, different doctors disagreed with the diagnosis. One felt she had Charge Syndrome, one CDLS, and another felt she had her own syndrome and he called it Joy's Syndrome. Joy was Joy and no matter what label was given to her, it wasn't going to change how she was cared for or loved; it made no difference.

Joy inherited my mother's maiden name, "Joy," and it has always broken my heart that my mother passed away before she could know my special angel. And what a joy she is! She always wants everyone to be happy. If I raise my voice to scold Amy, Joy gets upset and says, "happy mom?" She wants to make sure that my unhappiness with Amy is only temporary. Joy tries to make her world

and the world around her as perfect as she can. Of course this "perfect world" is just in her mind. For example: if one pillow on the couch is down, she puts all of them down. If a door is slightly ajar she must shut it. If the toilet seat is left up she puts it down. And don't think you can walk around the house without your shoes on because Joy, (the "shoe police") will tell you, "shoes on right now!" She has us in stitches when she goes through this routine and it's at these times that we realize what a special "Joy" she is.

After attending the School for the Deaf for eight years it was time to bring her back to our hometown high school. They had given her what she needed, the ability to communicate. The only disability of the majority of the children at that school was their deafness, so they would enter their high school academically sound. Joy was not of that caliber. It was time to come home. She entered a special needs class in the high school and seemed to be content.

The next battle was one I had been fighting since toilet training and it turned out to be life threatening. The bed-wetting battle! It was November of 1992. Joy was sixteen years old, weighed ninety-four pounds, and was four feet tall. I had tried everything to correct this situation but to no avail. Joy was not able to do the buzzer routine because she couldn't hear it. No drinks after a certain time failed. Getting her up at midnight didn't work, so morning baths, and washing bed covers and sheets became a daily routine before going off to work.

I had read an article about a new medicine that had some success in curing the bed-wetting fiasco. Its dose was given in the form of a nose spray. Joy and I went to the doctor and discussed if we should try it. He first did some urine tests to make sure there was not a medical reason for her wetting. It was determined that Joy just had a very tiny bladder. He wrote out the prescription, we had it filled and began that evening. The warning on the package said, "have physician check electrolyte count after ten days," so that was in the plan. Glory be and hallelujah, a dry bed the next morning. It works! The following two mornings brought about the same results. I was ecstatic, but this battle wasn't really won!

On that third evening I had to attend a meeting, so I went into Joy's room to say good-bye to her and Amy. Joy said "Mommy, stay home." I told her I wouldn't be long and would come in to kiss her goodnight when I returned. Amy thought Joy's eyes looked funny and we should bring her to the hospital. I said, "Oh sure, we will just walk into the emergency room and tell them Joy's eyes look funny." We had been through such difficult episodes with Joy that the fact that her eyes looked funny wasn't a red flag to me. But, Amy was right! I went to my meeting and when I returned home Joy was sleeping. Before watching the news I went in to check on her and was happy that I didn't have to wake her to go to the bathroom because the new medicine had taken care of that problem. When I walked in she was having a grand mal seizure! There was vomit everywhere and then she stopped breathing. I yelled to my husband to call 911 and I proceeded to give her CPR, which I was trained in. When we arrived at the hospital Joy's doctor was already there. He had an electrolyte count done, which showed that Joy's was 114. The normal count should be approximately 145. She lapsed into a coma. It was just unbelievable how within minutes I went from being elated to devastated.

The next two days and nights were filled with fears of losing my special little angel. Joy's temperature shot to 105 and she had to be placed on a cold-bed. The seizures continued but the temperature finally came down. Her blood pressure was low and the doctor asked that dreadful question: Do you want life support? I had to leave the room before I completely broke down. I just needed time to think. But did I have time, and if so, how much? I needed air, please give me some air. I did a few laps around the hospital grounds. It was dark and cold, not just from the night, but from inside my heart.

I lay by her side for two nights, my hand holding hers, praying that she would squeeze it. Anything God, please let her do anything to give me a sign that she will be okay. During the second afternoon, all of Joy's family held hands around her bed and prayed that somehow she would survive this horrific ordeal. That evening I fell asleep for the first time since entering the hospital. I was physically and emotionally spent. At 3:20 a.m., fifty-three hours after finding her in that awful state, I opened my eyes and Joy was up on her knees staring down at me. I jumped up, screamed, and hurdled over the bed rail to hug her. At that very moment I didn't ever, ever, want to let her go. God had given me my special angel back again. Thank you for the miracle, God. Another battle won.

From the moment we left the hospital it seemed like we were on a medical downhill slide. Something was different, Joy was different. Before she was tossed into that horrible coma she had a routine that was unbreakable. She was a creature of habit so intense that it was beyond normal. Each day for breakfast she would have Rice Krispies and a banana with cream. Since she awoke from her coma that breakfast has not passed her lips. I've tried and tried but it's a "no go." Certain things that she had obsessed about have been replaced with new ones. It's like she has forgotten things that were a huge part of her life.

Her eating habits were also altered. Before the coma she weighed ninety-four pounds, which was too heavy, being only four feet tall. She was not eating very much and when she did it often came back up. Her bowel movements were sporadic but they were at least occurring. She slowly began losing weight, pound by pound until she was thirty pounds lighter. It was time to go to Boston again. The scheduled appointment was moved up when Joy had yet another seizure. I don't know what triggered it, but it put us in the emergency room once again. The doctor didn't like the feel of Joy's belly so an x-ray was taken. It showed what appeared to be a large mass filling her whole abdomen. I had also noticed that her breath was intolerable. At the time I didn't make any connection. We immediately went to Boston where the doctors had much experience with CDLS children. They knew right off the bat what the problem was, but testing would be done to confirm their suspicions.

The first order of business was to clean Joy's bowel. The large mass that filled her abdomen was excrement. That attributed to the horrendous breath. Imagine it, she was filled with waste. The bowel movements she had been having were not emptying her, so after months of time there was no more room. This seemed unbelievable to me, but is not uncommon in CDLS children. The second order of business was to determine the acid production in Joy's stomach. CDLS children tend to have severe reflux problems, too, which means that the food taken in often comes back through the pyloric valve at the opening of the stomach. Thin wires were fished through Joy's nose until they rested inside her belly. A monitor was attached to her side to record how much acid was being produced and after two days the results were in. Joy's acid count was off the graph and the lining of her esophagus was severely burned. No wonder she didn't want to eat. It must have been terribly painful. The only time she ate well was when hunger was more painful than swallowing. Now we knew the problem and it was time to begin the cure. Joy took two types of medicine each day, one to curtail the acid production and one to coat the stomach and esophagus, so they would heal. She also began a regimen of laxatives to keep her bowels regular. Within two months she was eating regularly and having bowel movements every couple of days. It was best that I keep her weight to about sixty pounds so I became more cognizant of her eating habits. She looked wonderful and felt great. Another battle was won!

In 1997, when Joy was twenty-one, there were two battles that we hadn't yet won. The first was how to deal with menstruation. Throughout Joy's life everything developed at a much-delayed rate. Walking took forever, communication was a struggle, growing was slow, learning was far behind, but not her period, oh no, that came early! The one thing I hoped would be delayed the most, arrived before schedule. She doesn't have a routine time for this event. The problem with this whole situation is that she refuses to wear protection. What a nightmare! I put a pad on her and as soon as I leave the room it's off and in the trash. I've tried sewing two pair of undies together and slipping a thin liner in-between but she got a grip on that real quick and in the trash it went. The flow is light and only lasts for a couple of days. Sometimes months are in between so it's not something we have to deal with on a regular basis but it is a definite problem. I've looked for specialists in this area but to no avail. There are two valid concerns that I have, one being that menstruation is an unpleasant ordeal for Joy and myself, and two, I am fearful that there is always that slight chance that someone may take advantage of her. No matter how many times she may have been taught about good touches, bad touches, she would never be able to ward off an aggressor. I had hoped to find a doctor that would agree to a partial hysterectomy. Without a medical reason for this procedure it becomes a moral issue. Wouldn't you know, the one area of her physical being that doesn't have an identified problem. Oh well, this battle definitely hasn't been won.

The second battle is her obsessive compulsiveness that is causing self-injurious behaviors (SIBS). As Joy gets older her obsessions seem to be getting worse. Those things that we used to laugh at, like shoes on, toilet seats down, doors open or shut all the way, are now putting her out of control. If these minor issues are not perfectly the way she wants them she scratches her face until it bleeds. They certainly are not minor to her! She is to the point where she will only wear turtlenecks and sweatshirts, even in the summer, and only white low-cut sneakers will she allow on her feet. When it's time for dinner I make sure to call her to the kitchen way ahead of time because if she's watching a video she must rewind it back to the beginning, put it in its jacket, and place it in the appropriate place on the shelf. If some-one has borrowed one of Joy's seventy-some videos and has randomly put it on the shelf without her seeing it, she will notice and put it back in its proper place instantly. It's not funny anymore.

As Joy matures she has many of the same needs as other adolescents. The most important thing missing in her life is companionship. Everyone needs it, and most of us have the ability to make that happen. In Joy's case others have to make it happen for her. She is depend-ent on those around her to plan her life and I think that is causing a very high level of frustration for her. I try to meet her needs in this area as much as possible by letting her call friends on the phone, visit their homes, and have them come to ours. But the amount of times this occurs certainly isn't as often as most teenagers and young adults would have it. When plans can't be followed through, she scratches herself. I have been working with a behavior specialist on modifications to stop this behavior but none of them have really worked. Her obsessive compulsiveness is a reality and no modification will make it go away. I have been told that there are new medications that are having great effects on obsessive compulsive behaviors and am in the process of researching them. I am really skeptical of medications after what happened previously but if they will help Joy and give her some relief it certainly is worth trying. There is nothing worse than watching your child injure herself, yet it is beyond your control. I wish I could get inside of her head and fix whatever needs to be fixed so she won't hurt, but I can't, so now we are both frustrated and sad because this battle has not been won.

Planning for a special child's future is imperative. Transition planning is crucial so that at the age of twenty-one a plan is already in place. Joy has been working three days a week as a preschool classroom aide, in the school where I am the facilitator. The other two days she attends the high school. It's come full circle because that very preschool she started in at age three, with the very same teacher, is where she now works.

Living arrangements must also be accounted for. Joy lives at home now but I sometimes wonder if she would be happier living with other adults with disabilities. I am struggling with that concept but maybe that's being selfish. I'm so afraid that there is no one who can care for her like I do, and there probably isn't. I guess that doesn't mean it can't work or make Joy happier. I must remember that it's Joy's needs that must be met, not mine.

If Joy was to move to different living arrangements and was happy with them, it would ease my deepest fear—the fear that her dad and I will die before her. I'm afraid that if this happened Joy would never understand. Forever is not a concept that she can grasp. When I think of her asking and waiting for us every day and never having it come to fruition it wrenches at my insides.

We must not pretend that having a special child doesn't alter our lives; it does. Those alterations are sometimes very difficult but they also can be very rewarding. Most of it depends on having a positive outlook no matter how rough the road gets.

When that road does get rough, never lose sight of all the wonderful times and memories your children bring to you. Because Joy has an incredible love for music, our home is always filled with her favorites. Sometimes it's classical, other times it's the sound track from one of her favorite movies, and often it's opera. Her ultimate favorites are Christmas Carols. You can ride or walk by our house in July and hear "White Christmas" blaring from the windows. I always wonder what some of the joggers and walkers must think as they pass by. Her love of music extends to playing the keyboard, and she isn't too bad either. She has a very good ear for music and it brings her and us a great deal of pleasure.

Our family has grown over the years to include her collection of dolls. We talk to them as if they were living members of our household. That is very important to Joy and her friends, Sara, Jamie, Michael, Judy, Sally, and of course, let's not forget Cricket. Her other friends are in the form of elastics. She has a collection to beat all. They consist of all sorts of colors and sizes. It is mind boggling to see how she manipulates them between her thumbs and index fingers. She rolls and twists them, without even looking, in such a way that when people watch they are in amazement. At night the whole bag of them is emptied under her pillow. There they stay until the next morning when they get put back in the bag and accompany her along with one of her special doll friends throughout the day.

Besides books, babies, and animals, Christmas has extra special meaning for Joy. We have always made so much of this beautiful time of year and Joy can sense the happiness in the air. Remember, Joy craves for everyone's happiness. She will believe in Santa Claus forever, so our home always will be a Christmas for kids, filled with our special child, our special family, and our special love.

Raising children certainly is a challenge. Raising special children is the ultimate challenge. There are times when I have to smile and keep my feelings to myself, like when people say to me, "God only gives 'special children' to those who are strong and can handle it. You are a chosen one and it's His way of testing you." I despise those statements! There are times when I feel I don't have any strength at all! There are times when I ride to work with tears in my eyes because of a difficult morning. There are times when I wonder how I am ever going to get through this. And there are times when I feel so very inadequate in providing for and taking care of Joy's needs. There are plenty of instances when I wish someone else was chosen, and if this is a test, how am I doing, and when is it over? Fortunately, these fleeting moments of self-doubt and anger are short lived and I

groups, and caring physicians have and will continue to help us through our struggles. They will aid us in our attempts to win all of Joy's battles. No matter what obstacles arise we will face them head on, because we have family, courage, patience, love, and Joy.

have learned to face my challenges with courage and hope. I am very honored to be part of the life of such a beautiful human being.

In today's world, those families whose patience, courage, and love are being tested every day, now have so much more help than in years past. These families must reach out and allow others to give them support and guidance. Throughout Joy's life so far, and however much more of life she has, the one thing I know is that family, friends, special support

When I wrote Joy's story in April of 1997, I began my journey with the pending onset of Joy's birth, while coaching the high school girls' basketball team. On that team was a top-notch player named Brenda. Who would have dreamt, back in January of '76, she would play a crucial part in Joy's future happiness?

It is now twenty-three years later and Brenda is the director of a group home in our town. She, and many others who knew our family, had often tactfully suggested that maybe we should consider allowing Joy to move into a group home. They were certain that Joy's life would be more fulfilled. I cried at the thought, as you know from reading my story. I couldn't let go. I didn't want to let go. No one could take care of Joy as well as mom!

Joy moved into "Brenda's House" (as Joy calls it) on January 30, 1999. There are seven other disabled adults and an incredibly competent twenty-four-hour staff. She has the friends she so desperately needed, activities every day, and a loving atmosphere to keep her heart happy. The staff has dubbed her, "The Little Princess." Joy's attitude has greatly improved, she is talking more than ever, and guess what—she still loves all of her family.

Thank You Brenda!

I feel that Joy has been set free, and now she can share with others, *A Certain Kind of Love.*

Epilogue By E. Deborah Wright

Journal Entry 4:47 a.m., Thursday

I awoke as I often do, thinking about the very special people writing for our book. They have shared such precious family stories and have put their heart and soul into each. As I write by my window I hear so many songs of birds, none the same. They remind me of the children in our book, in our lives—all different songs yet all beautiful to hear.

In the 1950's, when I was young, there weren't any children like those in this book. Well, that is how life was, as I saw it. These children were not in my neighborhood or school. They were not in stores. They were not at playgrounds. They were not in movie theaters. They were not even in my church. Of course they existed—but not in everyday life.

Think about it!

As a teenager I learned there were special places where these children were sent to live. The belief was that this was best for the children and their families. I grew up when most moms generally didn't work outside of the home. They had the time to spend with their child yet they were often encouraged or coerced by well-meaning medical professionals, family, and society, to give their babies away. Yes, they were told to give away the babies who were deemed less than perfect, physically and/or mentally. Now most moms and dads work outside the home yet they keep these babies in their care. Many single parents tackle this monumental task alone.

Think about it!

When these children were institutionalized we all lost. My generation grew up believing it was alright to send imperfect babies away. I remember a couple who adopted a baby that was later "sent back" when it became apparent that something was wrong. Sent back to where? They traded the baby in for a new, perfect baby. I wondered and worried about what happened to that first little baby. Maybe that is what led me on the path to adoption. We adopted our fourth child. When you adopt a baby it is always possible that as the child grows you may discover a disability that was not known at the time of the adoption. My husband and I knew the risks but we also knew that no matter what challenges the future would bring, we would face them together with our son.

I have had discussions with friends and colleagues about the impact that children with special needs have on our schools. My school system began an inclusion program a few years ago and I felt the impact might be too great. How would I be able to teach the rest of the children? How would I divide my time? What I hadn't seen yet was how children with special needs help the class and how their classmates learn compassion, tolerance, and love for others.

Children today have begun to grow up with neighbors and friends who have special needs and they usually just take it in stride. Often they don't see their peers as different. Classmates care, befriend, and assist each other. If children are encouraged to socialize with children who are in some way different, then they will grow to understand each other and become friends. But it is up to teachers and parents to create this kind and caring atmosphere. We can't just tell this to our children. The examples we set—how we live and how we treat others—will decide our children's future.

   Think about it!

Some community members have felt it costs too much money to educate children with special needs. Try to imagine the cost if we had continued to use tax dollars for institutionalizing children from infancy on, twenty-four hours per day. Then set the money issue aside and think of this cost: Many of the children institutionalized at birth were presumed to be unable to learn or function and were never given the chance to live up to their potential. They were locked away as babies because they were different. Remember… "It was for the best."

   Think about it!

I think that some individuals feel that people who have a child with a disability have somehow caused it, perhaps by some unhealthy lifestyle. It certainly is a feeling that at some point crosses our minds, if we are parenting such a child. We think, "What could we have done to prevent this?" So these individuals go along their merry way, feeling sorry for those who are less fortunate but also feeling it's not really their problem. And although it is not often verbalized, they may think to themselves, "Thank God I'll never have to deal with that!" If you have had these thoughts, consider this: You can live the healthiest of lives and your child can still be born with a disability. You may have the healthiest child today, who gets an illness tomorrow… or has a sports injury… or is in an accident that causes your child to live every day hereafter with a disability.

Some day the story of your child, grandchild, or someone else you love might fit into the parameters of this book and you will have the opportunity to share a *certain kind of love*.

> *Think about that!*

❦

As teachers, Jean and I encourage and prod our schoolchildren to accept differences and care about others. Hopefully our stories have made you contemplate the message of each family, especially the love they have for their child. I hope you will share the book with co-workers, family, and friends—and talk about it. We all need to hear their voices and listen with our hearts. Perhaps you will find a way to show your support for someone with special needs in your community. Everyone can make a difference. YOU can make a difference.🌱

National Resources for Special Disabilities

The following pages are reprinted with permission from *Exceptional Parent Magazine*. <www.eparent.com> e-mail: EPLIBRARY@AOL.com

We hope that you will find this list of National Resources for Special Disabilities helpful.

To order a complete copy of *Exceptional Parent* magazine's 1999 Resource Guide please call 1-800-535-1910 or send a check for $15.50 (includes shipping and handling; New Jersey residents add tax) to:

Exceptional Parent
P.O. Box 1807
Englewood Cliffs, NJ 07632-1207

This directory includes national groups and organizations that can serve as resources for parents and professionals seeking information and support regarding specific disabilities and conditions. Please note that information on some specific disabilities may also be available from Federal and Federally-Funded Information Resources, Parent to Parent Programs, or certain National Information and Advocacy Resources (see Table of Contents for page numbers). In addition, Matching Resources, at the end of this directory, may also be useful.

CROSS-REFERENCING

Categories have been cross-referenced where appropriate.

Many conditions are known by more than one name. Readers are directed to "See" other relevant category names where resources are also listed. Under CHROMOSOME 4P-, for example, readers are referred to WOLF-HIRSCHHORN SYNDROME.

Some specific disabilities are not covered by a specific national organization. These conditions may be cross-referenced to a broader category that includes organizations that can provide helpful resources. For example, the metabolic condition ARGINASE DEFICIENCY is cross-referenced to UREA CYCLE DISORDERS. In some cases, the reader may be directed to a similar (but not identical) condition, when groups for that condition have indicated the ability and willingness to provide appropriate information and support. For example, 45,X SYNDROME is cross-referenced to TURNER'S SYNDROME and HYPOPIGMENTATION.

In cases where resources are available for both a general category of disability (for example, VISUAL IMPAIRMENT), as well as specific conditions within that general category (for example, ALBINISM; GLAUCOMA; MACULAR DISEASES; RETINITIS PIGMENTOSA; RETINOBLASTOMA; SEPTO-OPTIC DYSPLASIA; and USHER SYNDROME), cross-referencing goes in two directions. Under VISUAL IMPAIRMENTS, for example, readers are informed of the types of visual impairments for which specific resources exist; and under each specific type of visual impairment, readers are referred back to the more general category. The only exception to this type of cross-referencing is the general category MENTAL RETARDATION, which is not used as a cross-referencing term.

In cases where one specific condition usually includes other conditions, but those other conditions do not necessarily include the first condition, cross-referencing goes in one direction only. For example, under LAURENCE-MOON-BARDET-BIEDL SYNDROME (LMBBS), readers are directed to "See also" KIDNEY DISORDERS and RETINITIS PIGMENTOSA, though neither of these conditions refer back to LMBBS. This is because LMBBS typically includes kidney complications and retinitis pigmentosa, but a primary diagnosis of either one of these conditions does not typically include LMBBS.

Cross-referencing assistance came from the organizations listed in this directory, from the National Organization for Rare Disorders (NORD) and their *Resource Guide* (third edition, 1997, available for $43.50 through the EXCEPTIONAL PARENT Library [800] 535-1910; catalogue number NO200D), and from the *Physician's Guide to Rare Diseases* (second edition, 1995, edited by Jess G. Thoene, M.D., which is also available from the EXCEPTIONAL PARENT Library).

USING THIS DIRECTORY

A description of services provided by individual groups follows each listing in this directory. Numbers correspond to items listed in the **Key to Services**, which appears on every other page. When available, World Wide Web sites and e-mail addresses have been included. Web sites are listed beginning with their addresses, so remember to include the standard **http://** before each. E-mail addresses are indicated by the symbol, ✉. (Unless otherwise indicated, all telephone numbers are for voice only.)

11-ß-HYDROXYLASE DEFICIENCY
See: Adrenal Hyperplasia, Congenital

17-20-DESMOLASE DEFICIENCY
See: Adrenal Hyperplasia, Congenital

17-ALPHA-HYDROXYLASE DEFICIENCY
See: Adrenal Hyperplasia, Congenital

17-HYDROXYLASE DEFICIENCY
See: Adrenal Hyperplasia, Congenital

21-HYDROXYLASE DEFICIENCY
See: Adrenal Hyperplasia, Congenital

3-ß-HYDROXYSTEROID DEHYDROGENASE DEFICIENCY
See: Adrenal Hyperplasia, Congenital

45, X SYNDROME
See: Turner's Syndrome; Hypopigmenation

A-BETA-LIPOPROTEINEMIA
See: Tay-Sachs Disease

ABDOMINAL MIGRAINE
See: Cyclic Vomiting Syndrome

ACHONDROPLASIA
See: Growth Disorders

ACID MALTASE DEFICIENCY
See also: Glycogen Storage Diseases; Muscular Dystrophy

(AMDA) Acid Maltase Deficiency Association
PO Box 700248
San Antonio, TX 78270-0248
(210) 494-6144
(210) 490-7161 (fax)
www.members.aol.com/amda-page/index.htm
✉tianrama@aol.com

ACIDEMIA, ISOVALERIC (IVA)
See: Acidemia, Organic

ACIDEMIA, METHYLMALONIC
See: Acidemia, Organic

ACIDEMIA, ORGANIC
See also: Fatty Oxidation Disorder; Maple Syrup Urine Disease; Metabolic Disorders
Organic Acidemia Association
14600 41st Avenue N.
Plymouth, MN 55446
(612) 694-1797
(612) 594-0017 (fax)
www.oaanews.org
✉oaanews@aol.com
1,3

ACIDEMIA, PROPIONIC
See: Acidemia, Organic

ACOUSTIC NEUROMA
See also: Balance Disorders & Dizziness; Brain Tumors; Hearing Impairments; Neurofibromatosis; Neurofibromatosis, Type 2; Vestibular Disorders

Acoustic Neuroma Association
PO Box 12402
Atlanta, GA 30355
(404) 237-8023
(404) 237-2704 (fax)
www.anausa.org
✉anausa@aol.com
1,2,6,9

Acoustic Neuroma Association of Canada
PO Box 369
Edmonton, AB CAN T5J 2J6
(800) 561-2622 (V/TTY, Canada)
(403) 428-3384 (V/TTY)
✉anac@compusmart.ab.ca
1,2,3,4,5,6,7; French materials

ACQUIRED IMMUNE DEFICIENCY SYNDROME
See: AIDS

ACROCEPHALOSYNDACTYLY, TYPE I
See: Apert Syndrome

ACROCEPHALOSYNDACTYLY, TYPE II
See: Crouzon Disease

ACROFACIAL DYSOSTOSIS, NAGER TYPE
See: Nager & Miller Syndromes

ACROMEGALY
See: Multiple Endocrine Neoplasia I; Pituitary Tumors

ACTH DEFICIENCY
See: Adrenal Disorders

ACYL-COA DEHYDROGENASE DEFICIENCY, MEDIUM-CHAIN
See: Fatty Oxidation Disorder

ADDISON DISEASE
See: Adrenal Disorders; Adrenal Hyperplasia, Congenital

ADIPOGENITAL-RETINITIS PIGMENTOSA-POLYDACTYLY SYNDROME
See: Laurence-Moon-Bardet-Biedl Syndrome

ADRENAL DISORDERS
National Adrenal Diseases Foundation
505 Northern Blvd.
Great Neck, NY 11021
(516) 487-4992
medhlp.netusa.net/www/nadf.htm
✉nadf@aol.com
1,2,3,4,5

ADRENOCORTICOTROPIC HORMONE DEFICIENCY
See: Adrenal Disorders; Pituitary Disorders

ADRENOLEUKODYSTROPHY
See: Leukodystrophy; Tay-Sachs Disease

ADRENOLEUKODYSTROPHY, NEONATAL
See: Leukodystrophy; Tay-Sachs Disease

AGENESIS OF COMMISSURA MAGNA CEREBRI
See: Agenesis of the Corpus Callosum

AGENESIS OF THE CORPUS CALLOSUM
See also: Aicardi Syndrome
ACC Network
5749 Merrill Hall, Rm. 18
University of Maine
Orono, ME 04469-5749
(207) 581-3119
(207) 581-3120 (fax)
✉um-acc@maine.maine.edu
3

AGYRIA
See: Lissencephaly

AICARDI SYNDROME
See also: Agenesis of the Corpus Callosum; Epilepsy; Visual Impairments
Aicardi Syndrome Awareness and Support Group
29 Delavan Ave.
Toronto, ON CAN M5P 1T2
(416) 481-4095
2,3,4,7,9

Aicardi Syndrome Newsletter
PO Box 398
Fletcher, OH 45326
(937) 368-2137 (voice/fax)
www.Aicardi.com
✉AICNews@aol.com
1,2,3,4,6,7,8,9

AIDS
CDC National AIDS Hotline
American Society Health Assn.
PO Box 13827
Research Triangle Park, NC 27709
(800) 342-2437
(800) 344-7432 (Spanish)
(800) 243-7889 (TTY)
(919) 361-4855 (fax)
www.ashastd.org
2,4; Spanish materials

National Pediatric & Family HIV Resource Center
30 Bergen St. -ADMC- 4
Newark, NJ 07107
(800) 362-0071
(973) 972-0410
(973) 972-0399 (fax)
www.wdcnet.com/pedsaids
✉nphrc@daiid.umdnj.edu
1,2,4,7; Spanish/Creole materials

ALAGILLE SYNDROME
See also: Heart Disorders; Liver Disorders

Alagille Syndrome Alliance
10630 SW Garden Park Pl.
Tigard, OR 97223
(503) 639-6217
www.athnet.net/~luxhoj/
alagillesyndrome.html
✉cchannn@worlnet.att.net
1,2,3,4,9

ALANINURIA
See: Lactic Acidosis; Acidemia, Organic

ALBINISM & HYPOPIGMENTATION
See also: Visual Impairments
NOAH (National Organization for Albinism and Hypopigmentation)
1530 Locust St., # 29
Philadelphia, PA 19102
(800) 473-2310
(609) 858-4337
www.albinism.org/
✉noah@albinism.org
1,2,5,6,7,9; Spanish materials

ALBRIGHT SYNDROME
See: McCune-Albright Syndrome

ALGONEURODSTROPHY REFLEX
See: Sympathetic Dystrophy Syndrome

ALLERGY
See: Asthma & Allergy; Food Allergy; Latex Allergy

ALLERGY, FOOD
See: Food Allergy

ALLERGY, LATEX
See: Latex Allergy

ALOPECIA AREATANATIONAL
Alopecia Areata Foundation
710 C St., Ste. 11
San Rafael, CA 94901
(415) 456-4644
(415) 456-4274 (fax)
✉74301.1642@compuserve.com
1,2,3,4,5,6,7,8,9;
Spanish materials

ALOPECIA UNIVERSALA-ONYCHODYSTROPHY-TOTAL VITILIGO
See: Ectodermal Dysplasias; Vitiligo

ALOPECIA-ANOSMIA-DEAFNESS-HYPOGONADISM
See: Ectodermal Dysplasias

ALOPECIA-ONYCHODYSPLASIA-HYPOHIDROSIS
See: Ectodermal Dysplasias

ALPHA-1-ANTITRYPSIN (AAT) DEFICIENCY
See also: Liver Disorders; Lung Disorders

Alpha-1 National Association
4220 Old Shakeopee Red, Ste. 101
Minneapolis, MN 55437
(612) 703-9979
(612) 885-0133
www.alpha1.org
✉brandley@alpha1.org
1,2,3,4,5,6,7,9

ALPHA-GALACTOSIDASE DEFICIENCY
See: Fabry Disease

ALPORT SYNDROME
See: Hearing Impairments; Kidney Diseases, Hereditary; Vision Impairments

ALSTROM SYNDROME
See also: Diabetes Mellitus; Hearing Impairments; Kidney Disorders; Retinitis Pigmentosa; Visual Impairments
Alstrom Syndrome Newsletter
1006 Howard Rd.
Warminster, PA 18974
(215) 674-1936
www.jax.org/alstrom
✉sasg@voicenet.com
1,3,9

ALTERNATING HEMIPLEGIA
See: Hemiplegia, Alternating

AMELOCEREBROHYPO-HIDROTIC DYSPLASIA
See: Ectodermal Dysplasias

AMELOONYCHOHYPO-HIDROTIC SYNDROME
See: Ectodermal Dysplasias

AMNIOTIC BANDS
See: Craniofacial Disorders

AMPUTATION
See also: Limb Disorders
American Amputee Foundation
PO Box 250218
Little Rock, AR 72225
(501) 666-2523
(501) 666-8367 (fax)
1,2,4,5,9

Amputee Coalition of America
900 E. Hill Ave., Ste. 285
Knoxville, TN 37915-2568
(888) AMP-KNOW (267-5669)
(423) 524-8772
(423) 525-7917
www.amputee-coalition.org.
✉ACAOne@aol.com
1,2,3,4,5,6,7,8,9,
Spanish materials

National Amputation Foundation
38-40 Church St.
Malvern, NY 11565
(516) 887-3600
(516) 887-3667 (fax)
1,2,3,4,7,9

AMSTERDAM DWARF SYNDROME OF DE LANGE
See: Cornelia de Lange Syndrome

AMYLO-1, 6-GLUCOSIDASE DEFICIENCY
See: Glycogen Storage Diseases; Muscular Dystrophy

AMYLOPECTINOSIS
See: Glycogen Storage Diseases

AMYOPLASIA, CONGENITA
See: Arthrogryposis Multiplex Congenita

ANAL ATRESIA
See: Anorectal Malformations

ANAL STENOSIS
See: Anorectal Malformations

ANATHALMIA
International Children's Anathalmia Network
Genetics: Albert Einstein Medical Ctr.
5501 Old York Rd.
Philidelphia, PA 19141
(215) 456-8722
(215) 456-2356 (fax)
www.ioi.com/ican

ANDERSEN DISEASE
See: Glycogen Storage Diseases; Anderson-Fabry Disease; Fabry Disease

ANDERSON-WARBURG SYNDROME
See: Norrie Disease

ANEMIA, APLASTIC
See: Anemia, Fanconi; Bone Marrow Transplant
Aplastic Anemia Association of Canada
22 Aikenhead Rd.
Etobicoke, ON CAN M9R 2Z3
(416) 235-0468
(519) 235-1756 (fax)
www.aplastic.ualberta.ca
1,2,4,7,8,9

Aplastic Anemia Foundation of America
PO Box 613
Annapolis, MD 21404
(800) 747-2820
www.aplastic.org
✉aafacenter@aol.com
1,2,3,4,5,6,8,9; Spanish/French/Japanese materials

ANEMIA, AREGENERATIVE
See: Anemia, Aplastic

ANEMIA, COOLEY
See: Cooley Anemia

ANEMIA, ERYTHROBLASTIC
See: Cooley Anemia

ANEMIA, FANCONI
See also: Anemia, Aplastic; Heart Disorders; Kidney Disorders; Leukemia
Fanconi Anemia Research Fund/Support Group
1902 Jefferson, #2
Eugene, OR 97405
(800) 828-4891
(541) 687-4658
(541) 687-0548 (fax)
✉fafund@rio.com
1,2,3,6,8,9; Spanish/Portugese/French materials

ANEMIA, HEMOLYTIC
See: Cooley Anemia

ANEMIA, HYPOPLASTIC
See: Anemia, Aplastic

ANEMIA, MEDITERRANEAN
See: Cooley Anemia

ANEMIA, REFRACTORY
See: Anemia, Aplastic

ANEMIA, TARGET CELL
See: Cooley Anemia

ANEMIA, TOXIC PARALYTIC
See: Anemia, Aplastic

ANGELMAN SYNDROME
See also: Epilepsy
Angelman Syndrome Foundation
414 Plaza Dr., Ste. 209
Westmont, IL 60559-5507
www-chem.ucsd.edu/asf
1,2,4,5,6,9

Canadian Angelman Syndrome Society
PO Box 37
Priddis, AB CAN T0L 1W0
(403) 931-2415 (voice/fax)
✉caff@cadvision.com
1,2,3,5,6,9; French materials

ANGIO-OSTEOHYPERTROPHY SYNDROME
See: Klippel-Trenaunay Syndrome

ANGIOKERATOMA CORPORIS DIFFUSUM
See: Fabry Disease

ANGIOMA
See: Hemangioma; Vascular Malformations

ANGIOMATOSIS RETINA
See: Von Hippel-Lindau Syndrome

ANIRIDIA
See: Visual Impairments

ANKYLOSING SPONDYLITIS, JUVENILE
See: Arthritis

ANOPHTHALMIA
See also: Visual Impairments
International Children's Anophthalmia Network
5501 Old York Rd.
Philadelphia, PA 19141
(800) 580-4226
(215) 456-2350 (fax)
1,2,3,4,6,9

ANORECTAL MALFORMATIONS
See also: Intestinal Pseudo-Obstruction Syndrome
Pull-Thru Network
4 Woody Ln.
Westport, CT 06880
(203) 221-7350
(203) 221-9212 (fax)
www.members.aol.com/pullthrunw/Pullthru.html
✉pullthrunw@aol.com
1,2,3,4

APECED SYNDROME
See: Ectodermal Dysplasia; Hypoparathyroidism

APERT SYNDROME
See also: Craniofacial Disorders
Apert Support and Information Network
PO Box 1184
Fair Oaks, CA 95628
(650) 961-1092 (voice/fax)
✉apertnet@ix.netcom.com
1,2,3

Apert Syndrome Pen Pal Network
PO Box 115
Providence, RI 02901
(401) 421-9076
3,4

Apert Syndrome Support Group
8708 Kathy St.
St. Louis, MO 63126
(314) 965-3356
3,4,5

APHASIA, ACQUIRED
See also: Brain Injury; Stroke
National Aphasia Association
156 Fifth Ave., Ste. 707
New York, NY 10010
(800) 922-4622
(212) 989-7777 (fax)
www.aphasia.org
✉klein@aphasia.org
1,2,3,4,5

APLASTIC ANEMIA
See: Anemia, Aplastic

APNEA, INFANTILE
See: Apnea, Sleep

APNEA, SLEEP
American Sleep Apnea Association
1424 K Street NW, Ste. 302
Washington, DC 20005
(202) 293-3656
sleepapnea.org
✉asaa@nicom.com
1,2,4,5,7,8

APRAXIA
See also: Language Disorders; Learning Disabilities
National Organization for Apraxia and Dyspraxia
7675 Charter Oaks Dr.
Pensacola, FL 32514
(904) 478-4895 (voice/fax)
(904) 494-1444 (TTY)
✉dyspraxia@aol.com
1,2,3,4,7,9

AQUEDUCTAL STENOSIS
See: Hydrocephalus

ARACHNODACTYLY
See: Marfan Syndrome

AREGENERATIVE ANEMIA
See: Anemia, Aplastic

ARGINASE DEFICIENCY
See: Urea Cycle Disorders

ARGININOSUCCINASE DEFICIENCY
See: Urea Cycle Disorders

ARGININOSUCCINIC ACID SYNTHETASE DEFICIENCY
See: Urea Cycle Disorders

ARGININOSUCCINIC ACIDURIA
See: Urea Cycle Disorders

ARNOLD-CHIARI MALFORMATION
See also: Spina Bifida; Syringomyelia
Arnold-Chiari Family Network
c/o Maureen & Kevin Walsh
67 Spring St.
Weymouth, MA 02188
(617) 337-2368
2,3

ARTERIOHEPATIC DYSPLASIA
See: Alagille Syndrome

ARTERIOVENOUS MALFORMATIONS (AVMS)
See also: Epilepsy; Stroke; Vascular Malformations
AVM Support Group of Nevada
PO Box 1261
Fernley, NV 89408
(702) 575-5421
2,3,4

ARTHO-OPHTHALMOPATHY
See: Stickler Syndrome

ARTHRITIS
American Juvenile Arthritis Organization
1330 W. Peachtree St.
Atlanta, GA 30309
(800) 283-7800
(404) 872-7100
(404) 872-9559 (fax)
✉jiaustin@arthritis.org
1,2,4,7,8; Spanish materials

Arthritis Society
393 University Ave., Ste. 1700
Toronto, ON CAN M5G 1E6
(800) 321-1433 (ON only)
(416) 979-7228
(416) 979-8366
www.info@arthritis.ca
✉jkonecny@arthritis.ca
1,2,6,8; French materials

ARTHROCHALASIS MULTIPLEX CONGENITA
See: Ehlers-Danlos Syndrome

ARTHROGRYPOSIS MULTIPLEX CONGENITA
See also: Growth Disorders; Muscular Dystrophy
AVENUES: A National Support Group for Arthrogryposis Multiplex Congenita
PO Box 5192
Sonora, CA 95370
(209) 928-3688
www.sonnet.com/avenues
✉avenues@sonnet.com
1,2,3,4

CAST: Canadian Arthrogryposis Support Team
365 Fiddler's Green Rd. S.
Ancaster, ON CAN, L9G 1X2
(905) 648-2007
✉cast@freenet.hamilton.on.ca
1,2,3,4,5

ASCENDING PARALYSIS
See: Guillain-Barré Syndrome

ASPERGER SYNDROME
See: Autism

ASTHMA
See: Asthma & Allergy

ASTHMA & ALLERGY
See also: Food Allergy; Latex Allergy; Lung Diseases
Allergy/Asthma Information Association
30 Eglinton Ave. W., Ste. 750
Mississauga, ON CAN L5R 3E7
(905) 712-2242
(905) 712-2245 (fax)
1,2,4,5,6,7,9; French materials

KEY TO SERVICES
1 Periodical/newsletter
2 Informational materials
3 Networking/matching
4 Referrals to local resources
5 Local chapters
6 National conferences
7 National advocacy efforts
8 Fund research
9 Maintain research registry

Allergy and Asthma Network Mothers of Asthmatics, Inc.
2751 Prosperity Ave., Ste. 150
Fairfax, VA 22031-4397
(800) 878-4403
(703) 641-9595
(703) 573-7794 (fax)
www.aanma.org
✉aanma@aol.com
1,2,3,4,6

Asthma and Allergy Foundation of America
1125 15th St. NW, Ste. 502
Washington, DC 20005
(800) 727-8462
(202) 466-7643
(202) 466-8940 (fax)
www.aafa.org
✉info@aafa.org
1,2,3,4,5,7,8; Spanish materials

Asthma Society of Canada
130 Bridgeland Ave., Ste. 425
Toronto, ON CAN M6A 1Z4
(416) 787-4050
(416) 787-5807 (fax)
1,2,3,4,8

ATAXIA
See also: Ataxia Telangiectasia;
Charcot-Marie-Tooth Disease;
Friedreich Ataxia; Von Hippel-
Lindau Syndrome

National Ataxia Foundation
2600 Fernbrook Ln., Ste. 119
Plymouth, MN 55447-4752
(612) 553-0020
(612) 553-0167
www.ataxia.org
✉naf@mr.net
1,2,3,4,5,6,8

ATAXIA, FAMILIAL
See: Ataxia; Friedreich Ataxia

ATAXIA, FRIEDREICH
See: Ataxia; Friedreich Ataxia

ATAXIA, SPINOCEREBELLAR
See: Ataxia; Friedreich Ataxia

ATAXIA TELANGIECTASIA
See also: Ataxia; Autoimmune
Disorders; Cancer; Immune
Disorders; Leukemia

Ataxia Telangiectasia Children's Project
1W Camino Gardens Blvd., Ste. 212
Boca Raton, FL 33432-5966
(800) 543-5728
(561) 395-2621
(561) 395-2640 (fax)
www.med.jhu.edu/ataxia/
✉betsy@atcp.org
✉rosa@atcp.org;
✉bradmargus@atcp.org
2,3,4,5,6,8,9

ATAXIA WITH LACTIC ACIDOSIS II
See: Ataxia; Leigh Disease

ATRESIA
See: Microtia

ATRIAL SEPTAL DEFECTS
See: Heart Disorders

ATROPHIA BULBORUM HEREDITARIA
See: Norrie Disease

ATTENTION DEFICIT DISORDER
The ADHD Challenge
PO Box 488
West Peabody, MA 01985-7277
(800) 233-2322
(978) 535-3276 (info)
✉koplow@grs.net
1,2,4; prescription drug
discount program

AD-IN: Attention Deficit Information Network
475 Hillside Ave.
Needham, MA 02194
(617) 455-9895
(781) 444-5466 (fax)
www.infonetwork.com
✉adin@gis.net
2,3,4,5,6,9

CHADD—Canada, Inc. Children and Adults with Attention Deficit Disorder
1376 Bank St., Ste. 214
Ottawa, ON CAN K1H 1B3
(613) 631-1209
(613) 257-1563 (fax)
www.tripod.com/~chaddcanadain-dexhtml
✉dty_mada@concentric.net
1,2,3,4,5,6,7,9

CHADD: Children and Adults with Attention Deficit Disorders
499 NW 70th Ave., Ste. 101
Plantation, FL 33317
(800) 233-4050
(305) 587-3700
(305) 587-4599 (fax)
www.Chadd.org
✉national@Chadd.org
1,2,3,5,6,9; Spanish materials

National ADD Association
PO Box 972
Mentor, OH 44061
(800) 487-2282
(440) 350-9595
(440) 350-0223 (fax)
www.add.org
✉NATLADDA@aol.com
1,2,4,6

AURICULO-OCULO-VERTEBRAL SYNDROME
See: Goldenhar Syndrome

AUTISM
See also: Autism and Sensory
Impairments; Language Disorders
Autism Research Institute
4182 Adams Ave.
San Diego, CA 92116
(619) 281-7165
(619) 563-6840 (fax)
www.autism.com/autism
1,2,4,9

Autism Society of America
7910 Woodmont Ave., Ste. 650
Bethesda, MD 20814
(800) 328-8476
(301) 657-0881
(301) 657-0869 (fax)
www.autism-society.org/
1,2,4,5,6,7,8; Spanish/French/
Vietnamese/Chinese materials

Autism Society of Canada
129 Yorkville Ave., #202
Toronto, ON CAN M5R 1C4
(416) 922-0302 (voice/fax)
(416) 922-1032 (fax)
1,2,4,7; French materials

Center for Study of Autism
PO Box 4538
Salem, OR 97005
(503) 363-9110 (voice/fax)
www.autism.org/
✉autism@euphora.com
2,6

More Advanced Autistic People
PO Box 524
Crown Point, IN 46307
(219) 662-1311
(219) 662-0638 (fax)
✉chart@netnitco.net
1,2,4,6

National Autism Hotline/Autism Services Center
605 Ninth St.
Prichard Bldg.
PO Box 507
Huntington, WV 25710-0507
(304) 525-8014
(304) 525-8026 (fax)
1,2,3,4,5,7; Spanish/Italian/
French materials

AUTISM AND SENSORY IMPAIRMENTS
See also: Hearing Impairments;
Language Disorders; Visual Impairments
The Autism Network for Hearing & Visually Impaired Persons
c/o Dolores and Alan Bartel
7510 Oceanfront Ave.
Virginia Beach, VA 23451
(804) 428-9036
(804) 428-0019 (fax)
3,4,7,9

AUTOIMMUNE DISORDERS
See also: Immune Disorders; Vitiligo
American Autoimmune Related Diseases Association
Michigan National Bank Bldg.
15475 Gratiot Ave.
Detroit, MI 48205
(313) 371-8600
(800) 598-4668
www.aarda.org
✉aarda@aol.com
1,2,4,8

AUTOIMMUNE MYOCARDITIS
See: Autoimmune Disorders

AVM
See: Arteriovenous Malformations (AVMs)

B12 METABOLISM; INBORN ERROR OF
See: Cobalamin (B12) Deficny

BAISCH SYNDROME
See: Ectodermal Dysplasias

BALANCE DISORDERS & DIZZINESS
See also: Vestibular Disorders
EAR Foundation
1817 Patterson St.
Nashville, TN 37203-2110
(800) 545-4327 (voice/TTY)
(615) 329-7807
(615) 329-7935 (fax)
www.theearfound.org
✉ityiear@aol.com
1,2,3,4,5

BANNAYAN, RUVALCABA, RILEY-SMITH SYNDROME
See: Sotos Syndrome

BARDET-BIEDL SYNDROME
See: Laurence-Moon-Bardet-Biedl Syndrome

BATTEN DISEASE
See also: Tay-Sachs Disease
Batten's Disease Support and Research Association
2600 Parsons Ave.
Columbus, OH 43207
(800) 448-4570
(614) 927-7551
www.infolane.com/bdsra
✉bdsra1@bdsra.com
1,2,3,4,5,6,8,9;Spanish/Portugese/
German/French materials

Batten Disease Support and Research Association, Canadian Chapter
c/o Bev Maxim
17 Bell St.
Regina, SK CAN S4S 4B7
(306) 789-9047
www.bdsra.org
✉bdsra1@bdsra.org
1,2,3,4,5,6,7,8,9

Children's Brain Diseases Foundation
350 Parnassus Ave., Ste. 900
San Francisco, CA 94117
(415) 566-5402
(415) 565-6259
(415) 863-3452 (fax)
2,8

National Batten Disease Registry
1050 Forest Hill Rd.
Staten Island, NY 10314-6399
(800) 952-9628
(718) 494-5201
(718) 982-6346 (fax)
✉jdockteeb@nyucomr.em1.com
2,3,4,5,6,8,9; genetic counseling,
diagnostic testing

BATTEN-MAYOU SYNDROME
See: Batten Disease

BATTEN-SPIELMEYER-VOGT DISEASE
See: Batten Disease

BATTEN-VOGT SYNDROME
See: Batten Disease

BBB SYNDROME
See: Opitz Syndrome

BBBG SYNDROME
See: Opitz Syndrome

BECKER MUSCULAR DYSTROPHY
See: Muscular Dystrophy

BECKWITH-WIEDEMANN SYNDROME
Beckwith-Wiedemann Support Network
3206 Braeburn Cir.
Ann Arbor, MI 48108
(800) 837-2976 (Parents only)
(734) 973-0263
(734) 973-9721 (fax)
✉A800BWSN@aol.com
1,2,3,4,6

BEDWETTING
See: Incontinence

BEHCET'S DISEASE
See: Autoimmune Disorders

BELL'S PALSY
Bell's Palsy Research Foundation
9121 E. Tanque Verde, Ste. 105-286
Tuscon, AZ 85749
(520) 749-4614
(520) 749-0489
✉BellsPalsy@aol.com
2,3,4,8,9

BENIGN CONGENITAL HYPOTONIA
See: Spinal Muscular Atrophy

BEREAVEMENT SUPPORT
Center for Loss in Multiple Birth
PO Box 1064
Palmer, AK 99645-1064
(907) 746-6123
✉climb@pabox.alaska.net
1,2,3,4,7

Compassionate Friends
PO Box 3696
Oak Brook, IL 60522-3696
(630) 990-0010
(630) 990-0246 (fax)
www.compassionatefriends.org
✉tcf_national@prodigy.com
1,2,3,4,5,6; Spanish materials

Pen-Parents
PO Box 8738
Reno, NV 89507-8738
(702) 826-7332
(702) 826-0632 (fax)
www.pages.prodigy.com/nv/fgck08
a/penparents.html
✉PenParents@prodigy.com
1,2,3,4

Pregnancy and Infant Loss Center
1421 East Wayzata Blvd., #30
Wayzata, MN 55391
(612) 473-9372
(612) 473-8978 (fax)
1,2,4; Spanish materials

BETA THALASSEMIA MAJOR
See: Cooley Anemia

BEUREN SYNDROME
See: Williams Syndrome

BIOTINIDASE DEFICIENCY
See: Metabolic Disorders

BIRTHMARK
See: Nevi, Giant Congenital;
Vascular Malformations

BLEEDING DISORDERS
See: Hemophilia

BLEPHAROPHIMOSIS, PTOSIS, EPICANTHUS INVERSUS SYNDROME (BPES)
See also: Craniofacial Disorders
Blepharophimosis, Ptosis, Epicanthus Inversus Support Group
c/o Lynne Schauble
SE 820 Meadow Vale Dr.
Pullman, WA 99163
(509) 332-6628
✉schauble@wsu.edu
1,2,3,7,9

BLEPHAROSPASM
See: Dystonia

BLINDNESS
See: Visual Impairments

BLOCH-SIEMENS-SULZBERGER SYNDROME
See: Incontinentia Pigmenti

BLOCH-SULZBERGER SYNDROME
See: Incontinentia Pigmenti

BLOOD VESSEL MALFORMATIONS
See: Vascular Malformations

BLOOM SYNDROME
See also: Cancer; Immune Disorders;
Growth Disorders; Short Stature
Bloom Syndrome Registry
Laboratory of Human Genetics
NY Blood Ctr.
310 E. - 67th St.
New York, NY 10021
(212) 570-3075
(212) 570-3376
(212) 570-3195 (fax)
✉mproytch@server.nybc.org
8

BONE MARROW TRANSPLANT
See also: Cancer
BMT Newsletter
1985 Spruce Ave.
Highland Park, IL 60035
(847) 831-1913
(847) 831-1943 (fax)
www.bmtnews.org
✉bmtsnews@transit.nyser.net
1,2,3,9; legal referral for
insurance problems

**BONE TUMOR-EPIDERMOID
CYST-POLYPOSIS**
See: Peutz-Jeghers Syndrome; Polyposis

BONNEVIE-ULRICH SYNDROME
See: Turner Syndrome

BOOK SYNDROME
See: Ectodermal Dysplasias

**BOURNEVILLE PRINGLE
SYNDROME**
See: Tuberous Sclerosis

BOWEL DYSFUNCTION
See also: Gastrointestinal Disorders
**International Foundation for
Functional Gastrointestinal
Disorders (IFFGD)**
PO Box 17864
Milwaukee, WI 53217
(888) 964-2001
(414) 964-1799
(414) 964-7176 (fax)
www.iffgd.org
✉IFFGD@iffgd.org
1,2,4,6,9

BRACHIAL PLEXUS INJURY
See: Erb Palsy

**BRACHMANN-DE LANGE
SYNDROME**
See: Cornelia de Lange Syndrome

BRAIN ATTACK
See: Stroke

BRAIN INJURY
See also: Aphasia, Acquired
Brain Injury Association
105 N. Alfred St.
Alexandria, VA 22314
(800) 444-6443 (family helpline)
(703) 236-6000
(703) 236-6001 (fax)
www.biausa.org
1,2,3,4,5,6,7; Spanish materials

BRAIN STEM MALFORMATIONS
See: Arnold-Chiari Malformation;
Joubert Syndrome; Syringomyelia

BRAIN TUMORS
See also: Acoustic Neuroma; Brain
Injury; Cancer; Epilepsy; Pituitary
Disorders; Von Hippel-Lindau Syndrome
American Brain Tumor Association
2720 River Rd., Ste. 146
Des Plaines, IL 60018
(800) 886-2282
(847) 827-9910
(847) 827-9918 (fax)
www.abta.org
✉info@abta.org
1,2,3,4,6,7,8; Spanish materials
**Brain Tumor Foundation
of Canada**
650 Waterloo St., Ste. 100
London, ON CAN N6B 2R4
(519) 642-7755
(519) 642-7192 (fax)
oncolink.upenn.edu/disease/brain/bt
fc/btfcped.html
✉eallman1@juno.com
1,2,3,4,6,8,9; French materials
**Brain Tumor Foundation
for Children**
2231 Perimeter Park Dr., Ste. 9
Atlanta, GA 30341
(770) 458-5554
(770) 458-5467 (fax)
✉eallman1@juno.com
1,2,3,4,7,8
Brain Tumor Society
84 Seattle St.
Boston, MA 02134-1245
(800) 770-8287
(617) 783-0340
(617) 783-9712 (fax)
www.tbts.org
✉info@tbts.org
1,2,3,6,7,8
Children's Brain Tumor Foundation
274 Madison Ave., Ste. 1301
New York, NY 10016
(212) 448-9494
(212) 448-1022 (fax)
peds-neuro-web.med.nyu.edu/cbtf
/cbtf_hp.htm
1,2,3,4,6,8
National Brain Tumor Foundation
Cathy Clarence
785 Market St., Ste. 1600
San Francisco, CA 94103
(800) 934-2873 (info line)
(415) 284-0208
(415) 284-0209 (fax)
www.braintumor.org
✉nbtf@braintumor.org
1,2,3,4,6,8

BRANCHED CHAIN KETONURIA
See: Maple Syrup Urine Disease

BRANCHER DEFICIENCY
See: Glycogen Storage Diseases

**BRANCHIO-OTO-
RENAL SYNDROME**
See: Craniofacial Disorders; Hearing
Impairments; Kidney Disorders

BRITTLE BONE DISEASE
See: Osteogenesis Imperfecta

**BROAD THUMB-
HALLUX SYNDROME**
See: Rubinstein-Taybi Syndrome

BURKE SYNDROME
See: Shwachman Syndrome

BURNS
Phoenix Society for Burn Survivors
33 Main St., Ste. 403
Nashua, NH 03060
(800) 888-2876
(603) 889-3000
(603) 889-4688 (fax)
www.burns-phoenix-society.org.
1,2,3,4,5,6,7,9

CALLOSAL AGENESIS
See: Agenesis of the Corpus
Callosum; Aicardi Syndrome

CAMARENA SYNDROME
See: Ectodermal Dysplasias

CAMPTOMELIC SYNDROME
See: Growth Disorders; Short Stature

CANAVAN DISEASE
See: Leukodystrophy; Tay-Sachs Disease

CANCER
See also: Bone Marrow Transplant;
Brain Tumors; Leukemia; Polyposis
American Cancer Society
1599 Clifton Rd. NE
Atlanta, GA 30329-4251
(800) 227-2345
(404) 320-3333
(404) 982-3676
www.cancer.org
2,4,5,7,8; Spanish materials
Canadian Cancer Society
10 Alcorn Ave., Ste. 200
Toronto, ON CAN M4V 3B1
(416) 961-7223
(416) 961-4189 (fax)
www.cancer.ca
✉lfernand@cancer.ca
1,2,3,4,5,7,8; French materials
**Candlelighters Childhood
Cancer Foundation**
55 Eglinton Ave. E., Ste. 401
Toronto, ON CAN M4P 1G8
(800) 363-1062 (Canada only)
(416) 489-6440
(416) 489-9812 (fax)
www.candlelighters.ca
✉staff@candlelighters.ca
1,2,3,4,5,6,7;
French/Polish/German materials

CANCER; BRAIN
See: Brain Tumors

CANCER; GASTROINTESTINAL
See: Peutz-Jeghers Syndrome; Polyposis

**CARBAMYL PHOSPHATE
SYNTHETASE (CPS) DEFICIENCY**
See: Urea Cycle Disorders

CARDIAC DISORDERS
See: Heart Disorders

**CARDIO-FACIO-
CUTANEOUS SYNDROME**
See also: Heart Disorders; Ichthyosis
CFC Support Network
183 Brown Rd.
Vestel, NY 13850
(607) 772-9666
(607) 748-0409 (fax)
✉cliffordIV@juno.com
1,3,9

CAREY SYNDROME
See: Ectodermal Dysplasias

**CARNITINE DEFICIENCY
SYNDROMES**
See also: Acidemia, Organic; Fatty
Oxidation Disorder; Muscular Dystrophy
**Assistance for Babies and
Children with Carnitine
Deficiency—ABCD Inc.**
1010 Jorie Blvd., Ste. 234
Oak Brook, IL 60521
(800) 554-2223
(630) 571-9608
(630) 472-1744 (fax)
1,2,3,4,7,8,9

**CARNITINE PALMITYL
TRANSFERASE DEFICIENCY**
See: Acidemia, Organic; Fatty Oxidation
Disorder; Carnitine Deficiency
Syndromes; Muscular Dystrophy

CARPENTER SYNDROME
See also: Craniofacial Disorders
Carpenter Syndrome Network
c/o Cathy Sponsler
26661 Bear Valley Rd.
Tehachapi, CA 93561
✉carpenter.syndrome@php.com
1,3,4,6

CARTILAGE-HAIR HYPOPLASIA
See: Dwarfism; Growth Disorders;
Short Stature

**CARTILAGNOUS
ENCHONDROSES, MULTIPLE**
See: Ollier Disease

CAT'S CRY SYNDROME
See: Cri Du Chat Syndrome

CAUSALGIA SYNDROME
See: Reflex Sympathetic
Dystrophy Syndrome

CELIAC DISEASE
See also: Celiac Sprue; Gluten Intolerance
Canadian Celiac Association
190 Britannia Rd. E., Unit 11
Mississauga, ON CAN L4Z 1W6
(905) 507-6208
(905) 507-4673 (fax)
1,2,4,5,6,7,8,9; French materials
Celiac Disease Foundation
13251 Ventura Blvd., #1Studio City
Los Angeles, CA 91604-1838
(818) 990-2354
(818) 990-2379 (fax)
www.celiac.org/cdf
✉cdf@primenet.com
1,2,3,4,8

CELIAC SPRUE
See also: Celiac Disease;
Gluten Intolerence
American Celiac Society
58 Musano Ct.
West Orange, NJ 07052
(973) 325-8837
(973) 669-8808 (fax)
1,2,4,5,6; speakers bureau
**American Celiac Society Dietary
Support Coalition**
58 Musana Ct.
West Orange, NJ 07052
(201) 325-8837
(973) 669-8808 (fax)
✉bentleac@umdnj.edu
1,2,3,4,5,7,8
Celiac Sprue Association
PO Box 31700
Omaha, NE 68131-0700
(402) 558-0600
(402) 558-1347 (fax)
✉celiacusa@aol.com
1,2,3,4,5,6,8

**CENTRAL HYPOVENTILATION
SYNDROME, CONGENITAL**
See also: Apnea, Sleep; Intestinal
Pseudo-Obstruction Syndrome;
Ventilator Use
**Congenital Central
Hypoventilation Syndrome
Parent Network**
71 Maple St.
Oneonta, NY 13820
✉vanderlaanm@hartwick.edu
1,2,3,6,7,9

CEREBELLAR HYPOPLASIA
See: Joubert Syndrome

**CEREBELLAR VERMIS
APLASIA/HYPOPLASIA**
See: Joubert Syndrome

**CEREBELLO-OCULOCUTANEOUS
TELANGIECTASIA**
See: Ataxia Telangiectasia

**CEREBELLORETINAL
HEMANGIOBLASTOMATOSIS**
See: Von Hippel-Lindau Syndrome

CEREBRAL GIGANTISM
See: Sotos Syndrome

CEREBRAL PALSY
**Ontario Federation for
Cerebral Palsy**
1630 Lawrence Ave. W., Ste. 104
Toronto, ON CAN M6L 1C5
(416) 244-8003
(416) 244-6543 (fax)
www.ofcp.on.ca
✉ofcp@ofcp.on.ca
1,2,3,4,5,6,9; French materials
United Cerebral Palsy Associations
1660 L St. NW, Ste. 700
Washington, DC 20036-5602
(800) 872-5827
(202) 776-0406
(202) 973-7197 (TTY)
(202) 776-0414 (fax)
www.ucpa.org
✉ucpainc@aol.com
1,2,3,4,5,6,7,8; Spanish
materials, provides direct services
through 158 affiliate programs

**CEREBROOCULORENAL
DYSTROPHY**
See: Lowe Syndrome

CEREBROSIDE LIPIDOSIS
See: Gaucher Disease

CEREBROTENDINOUS
See: Xanthomatosis Leukodystrophy;
Tay-Sachs Disease

CHAGAS' DISEASE
See: Autoimmune Disorders

CHALASODERMIA
See: Connective Tissue Disorders

KEY TO SERVICES
1 Periodical/newsletter
2 Informational materials
3 Networking/matching
4 Referrals to local resources
5 Local chapters
6 National conferences
7 National advocacy efforts
8 Fund research
9 Maintain research registry

CHANARIN-DORFMAN SYNDROME
See: Ichthyosis

CHANDS ASSOCIATION
See: Ectodermal Dysplasias

CHARCOT-MARIE-TOOTH DISEASE
See also: Ataxia; Muscular
Dystrophy; Myelin Disorders
Charcot-Marie-Tooth Association
601 Upland Ave.
Upland, PA 19015
(800) 606-2682
(610) 499-7486
(610) 499-7487 (fax)
www.charcot-marie-tooth.org
✉cmtassoc@aol.com
1,2,4,6,8,9; Spanish materials
Charcot-Marie-Tooth International
1 Springbank Dr.
St Catharines, ON CAN L2S 2K1
(905) 687-3630
(905) 687-8753 (fax)
www.cmtint.com
✉cmtint@vaxxine.com
1,2,3,4,8,9; scholarship program

CHARGE ASSOCIATION
See also: DiGeorge Syndrome; Heart
Disorders; Hearing Impairments
Velo-Cardio-Facial Syndrome;
VATERL Association; Visual Impairments
CHARGE Syndrome Foundation
2004 Parkade Blvd.
Columbia, MO 65202-3121
(800) 442-7604
(573) 499-4694 (voice/fax)
www.chargesyndrome.org
✉marion@chargesyndrome.org
1,2,3,4,6,8

CHEMKE SYNDROME
See: Hydrocephalus; Lissencephaly

CHIARI MALFORMATION
See: Arnold-Chiari Malformation

CHILD SYNDROME
See: Ichthyosis

CHOLESTATIS WITH PERIPHERAL PULMONARY STENOSIS
See: Alagille Syndrome

CHOLESTERYL ESTER STORAGE DISEASE
See: Tay-Sachs Disease

CHONDRODYSPLASIA PUNCTATA
See: Growth Disorders; Ichthyosis

CHONDRODYSTROPHY, HYPERPLASTIC
See: Dwarfism, Metatrophic

CHORIONIC VILLUS SAMPLING, RELATED DISABILITIES
See also: Limb Disorders
CVS Parent Network Support Group
15706 Reynolds Ln.
Oak Forest, IL 60452
(708) 535-2864
✉midsun@aol.com
1,2,3,4,7,9

CHOROIDEREMIA
See: Macular Diseases; Retinitis
Pigmentosa; Visual Impairments

CHRIST-SIEMENS-TOURAINE SYNDROME
See: Craniofacial Disorders;
Ectodermal Dysplasias

CHROMOSOME 13 & 18 DISORDERS
See also: Chromosome 18 Disorders
SOFT Canada: Support Organization for Trisomy 18, 13 and Related Disorders
760 Brant St., Ste. 420
Burlington, ON CAN L7R 4B8
(800) 668-0898 (Canada only)
(905) 632-7755
(905) 632-5997 (fax)
www.trisomy.org
✉barbsoft@aol.com
1,2,3,4,5,6,8,9; also covers other
rare trisomy disorders
SOFT: Support Organization for Trisomy 18, 13 and Related Disorders
2982 S Union St.
Rochester, NY 14624
(800) 716-7638
(716) 594-4621 (voice/fax)
www.trisomy.org
✉barbsoft@aol.com
1,2,3,5,6,9; also covers other
rare trisomy disorders

CHROMOSOME 17P-
See: Smith-Magenis Syndrome

CHROMOSOME 18 DISORDERS
See also: Chromosome 13 & 18 Disorders
Chromosome 18 Registry & Research Society
6302 Fox Head
San Antonio, TX 78247
(210) 657-4968 (voice/fax)
chr18.uthscsa.edu
✉CODY@UTHSCSA.EDU
1,3,6,8,9

CHROMOSOME 21 RING
See: Chromosome Deletions

CHROMOSOME 22 RING
See: Chromosome Deletions

CHROMOSOME 3, MONOSOMY 3P2
See: Chromosome Deletions

CHROMOSOME 4 RING
See: Chromosome Deletions; Wolf-
Hirschhorn Syndrome

CHROMOSOME 45, X
See: Turner Syndrome

CHROMOSOME 45, X/46, XX
See: Turner Syndrome

CHROMOSOME 46XY/47, XXY
See: Klinefelter Syndrome

CHROMOSOME 47, XXY
See: Klinefelter Syndrome

CHROMOSOME 47, XYY
See: Klinefelter Syndrome

CHROMOSOME 48, XXXY
See: Klinefelter Syndrome

CHROMOSOME 48, XXYY
See: Klinefelter Syndrome

CHROMOSOME 49,XXXXY
See: Klinefelter Syndrome

CHROMOSOME 4P-
See: Wolf-Hirschhorn Syndrome

CHROMOSOME 5P-
See: Cri Du Chat Syndrome

CHROMOSOME 8P DISORDERS
8p Duplication Support Group
Genetics Ctr.
Children's Medical Ctr.
1 Children's Plaza
Dayton, OH 45404
(937) 226-8408
(937) 463-5325 (fax)
✉genemail@aol.com
3,4,9

CHROMOSOME 9 DISORDERS
Support Group for Monosomy 9p
43304 Kipton Nickle Plate Rd.
La Grange, OH 44050
(440) 775-4255
3
Trisomy 9 International Parent Support
Children's Hospital of Michigan
3901 Beaubien Blvd.
Detroit, MI 48201-2196
(313) 745-4513
(313) 745-4827 (fax)
2,3

CHROMOSOME 9 RING
See: Chromosome Deletions;
Craniofacial Disorders

CHROMOSOME DELETIONS
Chromosome Deletion Outreach
Box 724
Boca Raton, FL 33429-0724
(561) 391-5098
(561) 395-4252 (fax)
✉cdo@worldnet.att.net
1,3,4,9; also deals with
chromosome translocations

CHROMOSOME DISORDERS
See also: Chromosome 13 & 18 Disorders
International 11; 22 Translocation Network; Chromosome 22 Central
22 Kent Ave.
Timmin, ON CAN P4N 3C3
(705) 268-3099 (voice/fax)
www.nt.net/~a815/chr22.htm
✉mum2_1@hotmail.com

CHROMOSOME INVERSIONS
National Center on Chromosome Inversions
1029 Johnson St.
Des Moines, IA 50315
(515) 287-6798 (voice/fax)
✉ncfci@msn.com
3,9

CHROMOSOME TRANSLOCATIONS
See: Chromosome Deletions

CHROMOSOME TRISOMY DISORDERS
See: Chromosome 13 & 18 Disorders

CHRONIC ENCEPHALITIS & EPILEPSY
See: Rasmussen Syndrome

CHRONIC FATIGUE SYNDROME
CIFDS Association of America
CIFDS Youth Alliance
PO Box 220398
Charlotte, NC 28222-0398
(800) 442-3437
(704) 365-9755 (fax)
www.cfids.org
✉info@cfdis.org
1,2,4,7,8

CHRONIC INFLAMMATORY DEMYELINATING POLYNEUROPATHY
See: Autoimmune Disorders

CHRONIC INFLAMMATORY DEMYELINATING POLYRADICULONEUROPATHY
See: Guillain-Barré Syndrome

CHRONIC LOCALIZED ENCEPHALITIS
See: Rasmussen Syndrome

CITRULLINEMIA
See: Urea Cycle Disorders

CLEFT PALATE
See also: Craniofacial Disorders
Cleft Palate Foundation
1829 E. Franklin St., Ste. 1022
Chapel Hill, NC 27514
(800) 242-5338
(919) 933-9044
(919) 933-9604 (fax)
www.cleft.com
✉cleftline@aol.com
2,4; Spanish materials

CMV, CONGENITAL
See: Cytomegalovirus (CMV), Congenital

COBALAMIN (B12) DEFIENCY
See also: Metabolic Disorders
Cobalamin Network
PO Box 174
Thetford Center, VT 05075-0174
(802) 785-4029
✉suebee18@valley.net
3

COCKAYNE SYNDROME
See also: Growth Disorders;
Xeroderma Pigmentosum
Share and Care Cockayne Syndrome Network
c/o Teresa Wall
PO Box 552
Stanleytown, VA 24168-0552
(540) 629-2369
(540) 647-3739 (fax)
✉cockayne@kimbanet.com
1,2,3,9; Spanish and
Japanese materials

COFFIM-SIRIS'S SYNDROME
See: Ectodermal Dysplasias

COFFIN-LOWRY SYNDROME
Coffin-Lowry Syndrome Foundation
13827 196th Ave. SE
Renton, WA 98059
(425) 204-9176
www.freeyellow.com/members
/clsf/index.html
✉clsfoundation@yahoo.com
1,2,3,9

COGAN'S SYNDROME
See: Autoimmune Disorders

COLITIS
See: Crohn Disease & Colitis

COLOBOMA
See: Visual Impairments

COMPLEX REGIONAL PAIN SYNDROME
See: Reflex Sympathetic
Dystrophy Syndrome

CONGENITAL SENSORY NEUROPATHY WITH ANHIDROSIS
See: Familial Dysautonomia

CONNECTIVE TISSUE DISORDERS
See also: Ehlers-Danlos Syndrome;
Epidermolysis Bullosa, Dystrophic;
Marfan Syndrome; Pseudoxanthoma
Elasticum (PXE)
Coalition for Heritable Disorders of Connective Tissue
382 Main St.
Port Washington, NY 11050
(800) 862-7326
(516) 883-8712
(516) 883-8040 (fax)
www.marfan.org
✉staff@marfan.org
2,7

CONRADI-HÜNERMANN SYNDROME
See: Growth Disorders; Ichthyosis

COOLEY ANEMIA
See also: Autoimmune Disorders
Cooley's Anemia Foundation
12909 26th Ave., #203
Flushing, NY 11354
(800) 522-7222
(718) 321-2873
(718) 321-3340 (fax)
www.thalassemia.org
✉nacf@aol.com
1,2,3,4,5,6,7,8,9; Italian/Greek/
Chinese materials
Thalassemia Action Group
12909 26th Ave., Ste. 203
Flushing, NY 11354
(800) 522-7222
(718) 321-2873
(718) 321-3340 (fax)
✉ncaf@aol.com
1,2,3,4,5,6,7,8,9
Thalassemia Foundation
32 Fern Ave.
Weston, Ontario CAN M9N 1M2
(416) 242-8425
✉josie.sirna@utoronto.ca
1,2,3,4,5,6,8,9

COPPER DEFICIENCY, X-LINKED
See: Menkes Disease

COPPER MALABSORPTION, X-LINKED
See: Menkes Disease

CORI DISEASE
See: Glycogen Storage Diseases;
Muscular Dystrophy

CORNELIA DE LANGE SYNDROME
Cornelia de Lange Syndrome Foundation
302 W. Main St. #100
Avon, CT 06001-3681
(800) 223-8355
(860) 676-8166
(860) 676-8337 (fax)
www.cdlsusa.org
✉cdlsintl@iconn.net
1,2,3,4,6,9; professional network

CORPUS CALLOSUM DISORDERS
See: Agenesis of the Corpus
Callosum; Aicardi Syndrome

COX DEFICIENCY
See: Leigh Disease

CRANIOCARPOTARSAL DYSTROPHY
See: Freeman-Sheldon Syndrome

CRANIOECTODERMAL SYNDROME
See: Ectodermal Dysplasias

CRANIOFACIAL DISORDERS

See also: Apert Syndrome;
Blepharophimosis, Ptosis, Epicanthus
Inversus Syndrome (BPES);
Carpenter Syndrome; Cleft Palate;
Dubowitz Syndrome; Freeman-
Sheldon Syndrome; Goldenhar
Syndrome; Holoprosencephaly;
Microtia, Moebius Syndrome; Nager
& Miller Syndromes; Nevi, Giant
Congenital; Robinow Syndrome;
Rubinstein-Taybi Syndrome; Sturge-
Weber Syndrome; Treacher Collins
Syndrome; Velo-Cardio-Facial Syndrome

AboutFace International
99 Crowns Ln., 4th Fl.
Toronto, ON CAN M5R 3P4
(800) 665-3223
(416) 944-3223
(416) 944-2488 (fax)
www.interlog.com/abtface
✉abtface@interlog.com
1,2,3,4,5,6,7

Children's Craniofacial Association
PO Box 280297
Dallas, TX 75228
(800) 535-3643
(972) 994-9902
(972) 240-7607(fax)
www.masterlink.com\children
✉dnkm90@prodigy.com
1,2,3,4,5,6,9; Spanish materials,
financial assistance for related
expenses, annual family retreat

Craniofacial Foundation of America
c/o Terri Farmer
975 E. Third St.
Chattanooga, TN 37403
(800) 418-3223
(423) 778-9192
(423) 778-8172 (fax)
pages.prodigy.com/cranio/facial.htm
✉dnkm90@prodigy.com
1,2,3,4,7

**FACES–National Association for
the Craniofacially Handicapped**
PO Box 11082
Chattanooga, TN 37401
(800) 332-2373
(423) 267-3124
1,2,3,4,7,9; financial assistance
for medical-related travel

**Forward Face: The Charity
for Children with
Craniofacial Conditions**
Inst. of Reconstructive Plastic Surgery
317 34th St., Rm. 901A
New York, NY 10016
(800) 393-3223
(212) 684-5860
(212) 684-5864 (fax)
1,2,3,4

Let's Face It
PO Box 29972
Bellingham, WA 98228-1972
(360) 676-7325
www.faceit.org/~faceit/
✉letsfaceit@faceit.org
1,3,7; publishes annual
resource guide

**National Foundation for
Facial Reconstruction**
317 E. 34th St., Rm. 901
New York, NY 10016
(800) 422-3233
(212) 263-6656
(212) 263-7534 (fax)
2,3,4,8,9

CRANIOSYNOSTOSIS

See: Craniofacial Disorders

CRI DU CHAT SYNDROME

5p- Society
7108 Katella #502
Stanton, CA 90680
(888) 970-0777
(714) 901-1544
(714) 890-9850
www.fivepminus.org
✉fivepminus@aol.com
1,2,3,6,7,9

CRIB DEATH

See: Sudden Infant Death
Syndrome (SIDS)

CRIGLER-NAJJAR

See: Liver Disease and Transplant

CROHN DISEASE & COLITIS

**CCFA: Crohn's & Colitis
Foundation of America**
386 Park Ave. S., 17th Fl.
New York, NY 10016-8804
(800) 932-2423
(212) 685-3440
(212) 779-4098 (fax)
www.ccfa.org
✉info@ccfa.org
1,2,4,5,7,8; Spanish materials

**Crohn's and Colitis Foundation
of Canada**
21 St. Clair Ave. E., Ste. 301
Toronto, ON CAN M4T 1L9
(800) 387-1479 (CAN only)
(416) 920-5035
(416) 929-0364 (fax)
www.ccfc.ca
✉ccfc@netcom.ca
1,2,5,6,8,9; French materials

**Pediatric Crohn's &
Colitis Association**
PO Box 188
Newton, MA 02168
(617) 489-5854 (voice/fax)
1,2,3,4,7,8

CURLY HAIR-
ANKYLOBLEPHARON-NAIL
DYSPLASIA (CHANDS)

See: Ectodermal Dysplasias

CUSHING SYNDROME

See: Adrenal Disorders

CUTIS HYPERELASTICA

See: Ehlers-Danlos Syndrome

CUTIS LAXA

See: Connective Tissue Disorders

CYCLIC VOMITING SYNDROME

**Cyclic Vomiting
Syndrome Association**
13180 Caroline Ct.
Elm Grove, WI 53122
(414) 784-6842
(414) 821-5494 (fax)
ezinfo.ucs.indiana.edu/~jdbickel/
cus.html
✉kadams@mcw.edu
1,2,3,4,5,6,8,9

CYSTIC FIBROSIS

Canadian Cystic Fibrosis Foundation
2221 Yonge St., Ste. 601
Toronto, ON CAN M4S 2B4
(800) 378-2233 (Canada only)
(416) 485-9149
(416) 485-0960 (fax)
www.ccff.ca/~cfwww/index.html
1,2,5,6,7,8,9; French materials

CYSTINOSIS

See also: Kidney Disorders

Cystinosis Foundation
2516 Stockbridge Dr.
Oakland, CA 94611
(800) 392-8458
(510) 482-8119
www.cystinosisfoundation.ucsd.edu
✉jd2jptz@qmis.net
1,2,3,6,7,8, Italian and
French materials

CYSTINURIA

See also: Kidney Disorders

Cystinuria Support Network
21001 NE 36th St.
Redmond, WA 98053
(425) 868-2996
✉cystinuria@aol.com
1,3,9

CYTOCHROME C OXIDASE
(COX) DEFICIENCY

See: Leigh Disease,
Mitochondrial Disorders

CYTOMEGALOVIRUS (CMV),
CONGENITAL

Clinical Care Center
CMV Registry, Ste. 1150
1102 Bates St.
Houston, TX 77030-2399
(713) 770-4387
(713) 770-4347 (fax)
✉cmv@bcm.tmc.edu
1,2,3,4

DARIER DISEASE

See: Ichthyosis

DE BARSEY SYNDROME

See: Connective Tissue Disorders

DE BARSEY-MOENS-
DIERCKS SYNDROME

See: Connective Tissue Disorders

DE MORSIER SYNDROME

See: Septo-Optic Dysplasia

DEAF-BLIND

See also: Hearing Impairments;
Visual Impairments

**American Association of the
Deaf-Blind**
814 Thayer Ave., Ste. 302
Silver Spring, MD 20910
(301) 588-6545 (TTY only)
(301) 588-8705 (fax)
1,2,6,7

**The Canadian Deafblind and
Rubella Association**
c/o The W Ross Macdonald School
350 Brant Ave.
Brantford, ON CAN N3T 3J9
(519) 754-0729
(519) 754-5400 (fax)
1,2,7

**National Family Association for
Deaf-Blind**
111 Middle Neck Rd.
Sands Point, NY 11050
(800) 255-0411, ext. 275
(516) 944-8637 (TTY)
(516) 944-7302 (fax)
www.helenkeller.org
✉hkncdir@aol.com
1,3,4,7

DEAFNESS

See: Hearing Impairments

DEATH

See: Bereavement Support

DEBRANCHER ENZYME
DEFICIENCY

See: Glycogen Storage Diseases;
Muscular Dystrophy

DECARBOXYLICACIDURIA

See: Fatty Oxidation Disorder

DECEREBRATE DEMENTIA

See: Subacute Sclerosing Panencephalitis

DEJERINE SOTTAS DISEASE

See: Muscular Dystrophy

DEJERINE-LANDOUZY

See: Muscular Dystrophy; Facio-
Scapulo-Humeral

DELTA STORAGE POOL DISEASE

See: Hermansky-Pudlak Syndrome

DENTOOCULOCUTANEOUS
SYNDROME

See: Ectodermal Dysplasias

DERMATITIS HERPETIFORMIS

See: Celiac Disease; Celiac Sprue;
Gluten Intolerance

DERMATOCHALASIA

See: Connective Tissue Disorders

DERMATOLYSIS

See: Connective Tissue Disorders

DERMATOMEGALY

See: Connective Tissue Disorders

DERMATOMYOSITIS

See: Arthritis; Muscular
Dystrophy; Myositis

DERMOODONTODYSPLASIA

See: Ectodermal Dysplasias

DERMOTRICHIC SYNDROME

See: Ectodermal Dysplasias

DEVELOPMENTAL DISABILITIES

See: Mental Retardation

DIABETES INSIPIDUS

See also: Autoimmune Disorders

**The Diabetes Insipidus
Foundation Inc.**
4533 Ridge Dr.
Baltimore, MD 21229
(410) 247-3953

DIABETES MELLITUS

See also: Autoimmune Disorders;
Kidney Disorders

American Diabetes Association
National Service Ctr.
1660 Duke St.
Alexandria, VA 22314
(800) 342-2383
(703) 549-1500
(703) 549-6995 (fax)
www.diabetes.org
1,2,4,5,6,7,8

DIABETES MELLITUS

See also: Kidney Disorders

Canadian Diabetes Association
15 Toronto St., Ste. 1001
Toronto, ON CAN M5C 2E3
(416) 363-3373
(416) 363-3393 (fax)
www.diabetes.ca
✉info@eda-nat.org
1,2,4,6,7,8; French materials

DIAPHYSEAL ACLASIS

See: Exostoses, Multiple Hereditary

DIGESTIVE DISORDERS

See: Celiac Disease; Celiac Sprue;
Crohn Disease & Colitis; Gluten
Intolerance; Intestinal Pseudo-
Obstruction Syndrome; Ostomy

DIGESTIVE DYSMOTILITY

See: Intestinal Pseudo-
Obstruction Syndrome

DIMORSIER SYNDROME

See: Growth Disorders

DISCOID LUPUS

See: Autoimmune Disorders

DOWN SYNDROME

**Association for Children with
Down Syndrome**
2616 Martin Ave.
Bellmore, NY 11710
(516) 221-4700
(516) 221-5867 (fax)
1,2,3,4, bilingual services

Canadian Down Syndrome Society
811 14th St. NW
Calgary, AB CAN T2N 2A4
(403) 270-8500
(403) 270-8291 (fax)
www.home./ican.net/cdss/index.html
✉cdss@ican.net
1,2,4,5,6,7; French materials

**Foundation for Children with
Down Syndrome**
17646 N. Cave Creek Rd., Ste. 152
Phoenix, AZ 85032
(602) 493-7688
(602) 265-8216 (fax)
www.ffcwds.org

**Foundation for Children with
Down Syndrome (NJ office)**
355 Bennetts Mills Rd.
Jackson, NJ 08527
(732) 833-1331

National Down Syndrome Congress
1605 Chantilly Dr., Ste. 250
Atlanta, GA 30324
(800) 232-6372
(404) 633-1555
(404) 633-2817 (fax)
www.carol.net/~ndsc/
✉ndsscenter@aol.com
1,2,3,4,6,7

**National Down Syndrome
Society**
666 Broadway, 8th Fl.
New York, NY 10012-2317
(800) 221-4602
(212) 460-9330
(212) 979-2873 (fax)
www.ndss.org
✉info@ndss.org
1,2,4,5,6,7,8; Spanish materials

KEY TO SERVICES

1 Periodical/newsletter
2 Informational materials
3 Networking/matching
4 Referrals to local resources
5 Local chapters
6 National conferences
7 National advocacy efforts
8 Fund research
9 Maintain research registry

International Foundation for Genetic Research
500A Garden City Dr.
Pittsburgh, PA 15146
(412) 823-6380
(412) 373-7713 (fax)
www.pennet.com/chuckdet/
index.html
✉tmf@pennet.com
1,2,4,7,8

DUAL SENSORY IMPAIRMENTS
See: Deaf-Blind

DUBOWITZ SYNDROME
See also: Craniofacial Disorders; Growth Disorders

Dubowitz Syndrome Parent Support Network
PO Box 2441
Vincennes, IN 47591
(812) 886-0575
(812) 886-1128 (fax)
✉INATTIC1@aol.com

DUCHENNE MUSCULAR DYSTROPHY
See: Muscular Dystrophy

DWARFISM
See also: Dwarfism, Metatrophic; Growth Disorders; Short Stature

Billy Barty Foundation
3393 Geneva Dr.
Santa Clara, CA 95051
(408) 244-6354
(408) 296-6317
✉figone@netgate.net
1,2,3,4,5,6,7; emergency financial assistance, scholarships

DYGENESIS OF THE CORPUS CALLOSUM
See: Agenesis of the Corpus Callosum

DYSAUTONOMIA, FAMILIAL
See: Familial Dysautonomia

DYSKERATOSIS, CONGENITAL
See: Ectodermal Dysplasias

DYSLEXIA
See also: Attention Deficit Disorder; Learning Disabilities

Dyslexia Research Institute
4745 Centerville Rd.
Tallahassee, FL 32308
(850) 893-2216
(850) 893-2440 (fax)
www.dyslexia-add.org
✉pathard@aol.com
1,2,4,7; teacher training, workshops

The Orton Dyslexia Society
8600 La Salle Rd.
Chester Bldg., Ste. 382
Baltimore, MD 21286-2044
(800) 222-3123
(410) 296-0232
(410) 321-5069 (fax)
www.pie.org/ods
✉info@interdys.org
1,2,3,4,5,6,7,8,9; Spanish materials

Recording for the Blind & Dyslexic
20 Roszel Rd.
Princeton, NJ 08540
(609) 452-0606
(609) 520-7990 (fax)
2; extensive lending library of academic textbooks on audiocassette (all levels)

DYSOSTOSIS, ACROFACIAL, NAGER TYPE
See: Nager & Miller Syndromes

DYSOSTOSIS, MANDIBULOFACIAL
See: Nager & Miller Syndromes; Treacher Collins Syndrome

DYSOSTOSIS, METAPHYSEAL, TYPE B IV
See: Shwachman Syndrome

DYSOSTOSIS, POSTAXIAL ACROFACIAL
See: Nager & Miller Syndromes

DYSPLASTIC ANGIECTASIA, CONGENITAL
See: Klippel-Trenaunay Syndrome

DYSTONIA

Dystonia Medical Research Foundation
One E Wacker Dr., Ste. 2430
Chicago, IL 60601-1905
(312) 755-0198
(312) 803-0138 (fax)
www.dystonia-foundation.org/
✉dystonia@dystonia-foundation.org/
1,2,3,4,5,6,7,8,9

Dystonia Medical Research Foundation—Canada
116-230 Heath St. W.
Toronto, ON CAN M5P 1N8
(800) 361-8061 (Canada only)
(416) 487-8326
✉dystfdtn@aol.com
1,2,3,4,5,7,8,9

DYSTROPHIC EPIDERMOLYSIS BULLOSA
See: Epidermolysis Bullosa, Dystrophic

EATON-LAMBERT SYNDROME
See: Muscular Dystrophy

ECTODERMAL DYSPLASIAS

Canadian Society for Ectodermal Dysplasia (Eastern Canada)
232 MacIntosh Dr.
Stoney Creek, ON CAN L8E 4C2
2,3,4,9

Canadian Society for Ectodermal Dysplasia (Western Canada)
304 Hawkwood Blvd., NW
Calgary, AB CAN T3G 2Y5
(416) 664-6121
2,3,4

ECTRODACTYLY-ECTODERMAL DYSPLASIA-CLEFT LIP/PALATE (EEC) SYNDROME
See: Cleft Palate; Craniofacial Disorders; Ectodermal Dysplasias

EEC SYNDROME
See: Cleft Palate; Craniofacial Disorders; Ectodermal Dysplasias

EHLERS-DANLOS SYNDROME
See also: Connective Tissue Disorders; Glaucoma; Visual Impairments

Ehlers-Danlos National Foundation
6399 Wilshire Blvd. #510
Los Angeles, CA 90048
(213) 651-3038
(213) 651-1366 (fax)
www.phoenix.net/~leigh/eds
✉LooseJoint@aol.com
1,2,3,4,5,6,8,9

EINSTEIN SYNDROME
See: Hearing Impairments; Kidney Diseases, Hereditary; Vision Impairments

ELASTORRHEXIS
See: Connective Tissue Disorders

ELASTOSIS DYSTROPHICA SYNDROME
See: Pseudoxanthoma Elasticum (PXE)

ELEPHANTITIS
See: Lymphedema

ELLIS-VAN CREVELD SYNDROME
See: Ectodermal Dysplasias

EMERY-DREIFUSS MUSCULAR DYSTROPHY
See: Muscular Dystrophy

EMG SYNDROME
See: Beckwith-Wiedemann Syndrome

ENCEPHALITIS, CHRONIC LOCALIZED
See: Rasmussen Syndrome

ENCEPHALITIS & EPILEPSY, CHRONIC
See: Rasmussen Syndrome

ENCEPHALITIS, RASMUSSEN
See: Rasmussen Syndrome

ENCEPHALOFACIAL ANGIOMATOSIS
See: Sturge-Weber Syndrome

ENCEPHALOMYELOPATHY
See: Leigh Disease

ENCEPHALOMYELORADICUL-OPATHY, ACUTE ISSEMINATED
See: Guillain-Barré Syndrome

ENCEPHALOTRIGEMINAL ANGIOMATOSIS
See: Sturge-Weber Syndrome

ENCHONDROMATOSIS
See: Ollier Disease

ENDOCARDIAL FIBROSLASTOSIS
See: Heart Disorders

ENTEROPATHY, GLUTEN-SENSITIVE
See: Celiac Disease; Celiac Sprue; Gluten Intolerance

EOSINOPHILIC GRANULOMA
See: Histiocytosis

EPICANTHUS INVERSUS
See: Blepharophimosis, Ptosis, Epicanthus Inversus Syndrome (BPES)

EPIDERMOLYSIS BULLOSA, DYSTROPHIC
See also: Connective Tissue Disorders

DEBRA: Dystrophic Epidermolysis Bullosa Research Association
40 Rector St.
New York, NY 10006
(212) 513-4090
(212) 513-4099
www.debra.org
1,2,3,4,5,6,7,8,9; Spanish materials

EPIDERMOLYTIC HYPERKERATOSIS
See: Ichthyosis

EPILEPSY
See also: Seizure Disorders

American Epilepsy Society
638 Prospect Ave.
Hartford, CT 06105-4240
(860) 586-7505
(860) 586-7550 (fax)
www.aesnet.org
✉info@aesnet.org
1,2,6

Epilepsy Canada
1470 Peel St., Ste. 745
Montreal, PQ CAN H3A 1T1
(514) 845-7855
(514) 845-7866 (fax)
generation.net/~epilepsy
✉epilepsy@epilepsy.ca
1,2,4,5,7,8; French materials

Epilepsy Foundation of America
4351 Garden City Dr.
Landover, MD 20785-2267
(800) 332-4050
(301) 459-3700
(301) 577-2684 (fax)
www.efa.org
✉postmaster@efa.org
1,2,4,5,6,7; Spanish materials

EPILOIA
See: Tuberous Sclerosis

ERB PALSY

Brachial Plexus/Erb's Palsy Support and Informational Network, Inc.
PO Box 23
Larsen, WI 54947
(920) 836-9955
(920) 836-9587
www.customforum.com/nationalbpi
✉nationalbpi@powernetonline.com
1,2,3,4,5,6

ERB/DUCHENNE PALSY
See: Erb Palsy

ERDHEIM-CHESTER DISEASE
See: Histiocytosis

ERYTHROBLASTOPHTHISIS
See: Anemia, Aplastic

ERYTHROBLASTOTIC ANEMIA OF CHILDHOOD
See: Cooley Anemia

ERYTHROHEPATIC PROTOPORPHYRIA
See: Liver Disorders; Porphyria

ERYTHROKERATODERMIAS
See: Ichthyosis

ERYTHROPHAGOCYTIC LYMPHOHISTIOCYTOSIS, FAMILIAL
See: Histiocytosis

ESOPHAGEAL ATRESIA
See: VATERL Association

EVANS SYNDROME
See also: Autoimmune Disorders; Neutropenia

Evans Syndrome Support and Research Group
c/o Lou Addington
5630 Devon St.
Port Orange, FL 32127
(904) 760-3031
(904) 760-5583 (fax)
73142.1315@compuserve.com
3,4,9

EXOMPHALOS-MACROGLOSSIA-GIGANTISM (EMG) SYNDROME
See: Beckwith-Wiedemann Syndrome

EXTRACORPOREAL MEMBRANE OXYGENATION

ECMO Moms and Dads International Parent Support
PO Box 53848
Lubbock, TX 79453
(806) 794-0259
(806) 792-1289 (fax)
1,2,3,4,5,9

FABRY DISEASE
See also: Tay-Sachs Disease

International Center for Fabry Disease
Dept of Human Genetics
Mt Sinai School of Medicine
5th Ave. at 100th St.
PO Box 1497
New York, NY 10029
(212) 241-6944
(212) 348-5811 (fax)
www.mssm.edu/crc/fabry
1,2,3,7,9

FACIAL DISFIGUREMENT
See: Craniofacial Disorders

FACIAL PARALYSIS
See: Bell Palsy

FACIO-AURICULO-VERTEBRAL ANOMALY
See: Goldenhar Syndrome

FACIO-CARDIO-CUTANEOUS SYNDROME
See: Cardio-Facio-Cutaneous Syndrome

FACIO-SCAPULO-HUMERAL MUSCULAR DYSTROPHY

Muscular Dystrophy Facio-Scapulo-Humeral Society
3 Westwood Rd.
Lexington, MA 02420
(617) 860-0501
(617) 860-0599 (fax)
www.disability.ucdavis.edu
✉carol.perez@fishsociety
1,2,3,4,6,7,9

FAMILIAL ATAXIA
See: Ataxia; Friedreich Ataxia

FAMILIAL DYSAUTONOMIA

Dysautonomia Foundation
20 E. 46th St., 3rd Fl.
New York, NY 10017
(212) 949-6644
(212) 682-7625 (fax)
1,2,3,9

Dysautonomia Foundation
343 Clarke Ave. W., Ste. 1103
Thornhill, ON CAN L4J 7K5
(905) 882-7725
(905) 764-7752 (fax)
1,2,3,4,5,6,8,9

FAMILIAL PEMPHIGUS
See: Ichthyosis

FAMILIAL SPLENIC ANEMIA
See: Gaucher Disease

FANCONI ANEMIA
See: Anemia, Fanconi

FANCONI II
See: Cystinosis

FANCONI PANMYELOPATHY
See: Anemia, Fanconi

FARBER DISEASE
See: Tay-Sachs Disease

FAS/FAE
See: Fetal Alcohol Syndrome/Effect

FATTY OXIDATION DISORDER
See also: Metabolic Disorders

Support Group for FOD Families
805 Montrose Dr.
Greensboro, NC 27410
(336) 547-8682
(336) 547-0196 (fax)
www.cinternet.net/FOD
✉goulddan@aol.com
1,3,4,7

FEMALE SEX CHROMOSOME DISORDERS
See: Turner Syndrome

FETAL ALCOHOL SYNDROME/EFFECT

Family Empowerment Network: Supporting Families Affected by FAS/FAE
519 Lowell Hall
610 Langdon St.
Madison, WI 53703
(800) 462-5254
(608) 262-6590
(608) 265-3352 (fax)
✉fen@mail.dcs.wisc.edu
1,2,3,4,6,7; Spanish materials

Fetal Alcohol Education Program
1975 Main St.
Concord, MA 01742
(508) 369 -7713
2,3,4,9

Fetal Alcohol Support Network
2266 Homeland Dr.
Mississauga, ON CAN L5K 1G6
(905) 822-0733 (voice/fax)
1,2,3,4,9

The Fetal Alcohol Syndrome Family Resource Institute
PO Box 2525
Lynnwood, WA 98036
(800) 999-3429 (WA only)
(253) 531-2878
(253) 531-2668 (fax)
www.accessone.com/~delindam/
✉vicfas@hotmail.com
1,2,3,4,9

National Organization on Fetal Alcohol Syndrome
418 C St. NE
Washington, DC 20002
(202) 785-4585
(202) 466-6456 (fax)
www.nofas.org
✉nofas@erols.com
1,2,4

Support and Education Network for FAS Parents and Caregivers
c/o Bergen County Council on Alcoholism & Drug Abuse, Inc.
PO Box 626
Paramus, NJ 07653
(201) 261-2183
(201) 261-0807 (fax)
✉jpmulhern@aol.com
2,3,4

FETAL FACE SYNDROME
See: Robinow Syndrome

FETAL IRITIS SYNDROME
See: Norrie Disease

FIBROMYALGIA
See: Arthritis

FIBROUS ANKYLOSIS OF MULTIPLE JOINTS
See: Arthrogryposis Multiplex Congenita

FIBROUS DYSPLASIA, MONOSTOTIC
See: McCune-Albright Syndrome

FIBROUS DYSPLASIA, POLYOSTOTIC
See: McCune-Albright Syndrome

FIBULAR HEMIMELIA
See: Limb Disorders

FIRST AND SECOND BRANCHIAL ARCH SYNDROME
See: Goldenhar Syndrome

FISCHER SYNDROME
See: Guillain-Barré Syndrome

FISCHER-JACOBSEN-CLOUSTON SYNDROME
See: Ectodermal Dysplasias

FOCAL DERMAL HYPOPLASIA (FDH) SYNDROME
See: Craniofacial Disorders; Ectodermal Dysplasias; Hearing Impairments

FOLATE METABOLISM; INBORN ERROR OF
See: Cobalamin (B12) Deficiency

FOOD ALLERGY
See also: Asthma & Allergy

The Food Allergy Network
10400 Eaton Pl., Ste. 107
Fairfax, VA 22030-2208
(703) 691-3179
(703) 691-2713 (fax)
www.foodallergy.org
✉fan@worldweb.net
1,2,4,6,7,9

FORBES DISEASE
See: Glycogen Storage Diseases; Muscular Dystrophy

FRAGILE X SYNDROME
See also: Attention Deficit Disorder; Autism; Learning Disabilities

FraXa Research Foundation
PO Box 935
West Newbury, MA 01985-0935
(978) 462-1990
(978) 463-9985 (fax)
www.qorx.net/fraxa
✉info@fraxa.org
1,2,3,5,7,8,9; Internet mailing list

National Fragile X Foundation
1441 York St., Ste. 303
Denver, CO 80206
(800) 688-8765
(303) 333-6155
(303) 333-4369 (fax)
www.infxf.org
✉natfragx@ix.netcom.com
1,2,3,4,5,6,7,8,9

FRANCHESCHETTI-KLEIN SYNDROME
See: Treacher Collins Syndrome

FRAXA
See: Fragile X Syndrome

FREDREICH DISEASE
See: Ataxia; Friedreich Ataxia

FREDREICH TABES
See: Ataxia; Friedreich Ataxia

FREEMAN-SHELDON SYNDROME
See also: Craniofacial Disorders

Freeman-Sheldon Parent Support Group
509 E. Northmont Wy.
Salt Lake City, UT 84103
(801) 364-7060
www.fspsg.org
✉fspsg@aol.com
1,2,3,4,7,9

FRIEDREICH ATAXIA
See also: Ataxia; Muscular Dystrophy

Canadian Association of Friedreich's Ataxia
5620 C A Jobin Rd.
St. Leonard, PQ CAN H1P 1H8
514) 321-8684
(514) 321-9257 (fax)
1,2,8,9; French materials

FUCOSIDOSIS
See: Tay-Sachs Disease

FULLER-ALBRIGHT SYNDROME
See: McCune-Albright Syndrome

FULMINATING HYPERPYREXIA
See: Malignant Hyperthermia

G SYNDROME
See: Opitz Syndrome

GALACTOSE-1-PHOSPHATE URIDYL TRANSFERASE DEFICIENCY
See: Galactosemia

GALACTOSEMIA
See also: Metabolic Disorders, Liver Disease

Parents of Galactosemic Children Inc.
2148 Bryton Dr.
Powell, OH 95252
(614)840-0473
www.galactosemia.org
✉gayled3@aol.com
1,2,3,6,9

GARDNER SYNDROME
See: Peutz-Jeghers Syndrome; Polyposis

GASTROESOPHAGEAL REFLUX
See also: Intestinal Pseudo-Obstruction Syndrome

Pediatric/Adolescent Gastroesophageal Reflux Association Inc. (PAGER)
PO Box 1153
Germantown, MD 20875-1153
(301) 601-9541
✉gergroup@aol.com
1,2,3,5,6,9

GASTROINTESTINAL CANCER
See: Peutz-Jeghers Syndrome; Polyposis

GASTROINTESTINAL DISORDERS

The Oley Foundation
214 Hun Memorial
Albany Medical Center, A-23
Albany, NY 12208-3478
(800) 776-OLEY (6539)
(518) 262-5079
(518) 262-5528 (fax)
www.wizvax.net/oleyfdn
✉joan_bishop@ccgateway.amc.edu
Information and support on home nutrition support including enteral and parental nutrition.

GAUCHER DISEASE
See: Tay-Sachs Disease

National Gaucher Foundation
11140 Rockville Pike, Ste. 350
Rockville, MD 20852-3106
(800) 925-8885
(301) 816-1515
(301) 816-1516 (fax)
www.gaucherdisease.org
✉ngf@gaucherdisease.org
1,2,3,4,5,6,7,8,9

GENEE-WIEDEMANN SYNDROME
See: Nager & Miller Syndromes

GENETIC DISORDERS

Alliance of Genetic Support Groups
4301 Conneticut Ave. NW, Ste. 404
Washington, DC 20008
(202)966-5557
(202) 966-8553 (fax)
www.geneticalliance.org
✉info@geneticalliance.org

Association of Genetic Support/Australia
66 Albion St.
Surrey Hills, Australia NSW 2010
(02) 9211 1462
(02) 9211 8077 (fax)
1,2,3,4,6,9

Northeast VCFS Support Group
2 Lansing Dr.
Salem, NH 03079
(603) 898-6332
(603) 898-0705
✉MLADJA@aol.com
1,2,3,6,9

GENITALIA, AMBIGUOUS
See also: Hermaphroditism

Ambiguous Genitalia Support Network (AGSN)
PO Box 313
Clements, CA 95227-0313
(209) 727-0313 (voice/fax)
✉agsn@jps.net
1,2,3,4,5,7,9

GILFORD SYNDROME
See: Progeria

GINGIVAL FIBROMATOSIS AND HYPERTRICHOSIS
See: Ectodermal Dysplasias

GIROUX-BARBEAU SYNDROME
See: Ichthyosis

GLAUCOMA
See also: Visual Impairments

Glaucoma Research Foundation
490 Post St., Ste. 830
San Francisco, CA 94102
(800) 826-6693
(415) 986-3162
www.glaucoma.org
✉info@glaucoma.org
1,2,3,4,8; Spanish materials

GLUCOSYL CEREBROSIDE LIPIDOSIS
See: Gaucher Disease

GLUTARIC ACIDURIA, TYPE I
See also: Acidemia, Organic; Lactic Acidosis

International Organization for Glutaric Aciduria, Type I
c/o Mike Metil and Cay Welch
RD 3, Box 167A
Jersey Shore, PA 17740
(717) 321-6487
1,2,3,4,6,8

GLUTARICACIDURIA I
See: Glutaric Aciduria, Type I

GLUTARICACIDURIA II
See: Acidemia, Organic; Lactic Acidosis

GLUTEN INTOLERANCE
See also: Celiac Disease; Celiac Sprue

Gluten Intolerance Group of North America
PO Box 23053
Seattle, WA 98102-0353
(206) 325-6980
(206) 320-1172 (fax)
✉gig@accessone.com
1,2,3,4,6,7; Spanish materials

GLUTEN-SENSITIVE ENTEROPATHY
See: Celiac Disease; Celiac Sprue; Gluten Intolerance

GLYCOGEN STORAGE DISEASES
See also: Hypoglycemia

Association for Glycogen Storage Disease
PO Box 896
Durant, IA 52747
(319) 785-6038 (voice/fax)
1,2,3,6,8,9

GLYCOGENOSES
See: Glycogen Storage Diseases

GLYCOSPHINGOLIPIDOSES
See: Tay-Sachs Disease

GOLDENHAR SYNDROME
See also: Craniofacial Disorders

Goldenhar Syndrome Research & Information Fund
PO Box 61643
St. Petersburg, FL 33714
(813) 522-5772
(813) 522-5885 (fax)
www.GOLDENHAR.com
✉btorman@pbsnet.com
2

GOLDENHAR-GORLIN SYNDROME
See: Goldenhar Syndrome

GOLDFLAM DISEASE
See: Myasthenia Gravis

KEY TO SERVICES
1 Periodical/newsletter
2 Informational materials
3 Networking/matching
4 Referrals to local resources
5 Local chapters
6 National conferences
7 National advocacy efforts
8 Fund research
9 Maintain research registry

GONADAL DYGENESIS (45, X)
See: Turner Syndrome

GORLIN-CHAUDHRY-MOSS SYNDROME
See: Ectodermal Dysplasias

GRANULOMA, EOSINOPHILIC
See: Histiocytosis

GRANULOMATOUS DISEASE, CHRONIC
See also: Immune Disorders
Chronic Granulomatous Disease Association Inc.
c/o Mary Hurley
2616 Monterey Rd.
San Marino, CA 91108
(626) 441-4118
www.pacific.net.net/amhurley
✉amhurlley@pacific.net
1,2,3,4,7,9

GRAVES DISEASE
See: Thyroid Disorders

GROENBLAD-STRANDBERG SYNDROME
See: Pseudoxanthoma Elasticum (PXE)

GROUP B STREP
Group B Strep Association
PO Box 16515
Chapel Hill, NC 27516
(919) 932-5344
(919) 932-3657 (fax)
www.groupbstrep.org
1,2,3,4,7,8,9

GROWTH DISORDERS
See also: Dwarfism; Short Stature
Human Growth Foundation
7777 Leesburg Pike, Ste. 202 S
Falls Church, VA 22043
(800) 451-6434
(703) 883-1773
(703) 883-1776 (fax)
www.genetic.org/hgf
✉hgfound@erols.com
1,2,3,4,5,6,8,9; Spanish materials
Little People's Research Fund
80 Sister Pierre Dr.
Towson, MD 21204
(800) 232-5773
(410) 494-0055
(410) 494-0062 (fax)
1,2,8
MAGIC Foundation for Children's Growth
1327 N. Harlem Ave.
Oak Park, IL 60302
(800) 362-4423
(708) 383-0808 (fax)
(708) 383-0899
www.magicfoundation.org
✉mary@magicfoundation.org
1,2,3,4,5,6,9; Spanish materials, pen pal program for children

GROWTH HORMONE DEFICIENCY
See: Growth Disorders

GROWTH RETARDATION, INTRAUTERINE
See: Growth Disorders

GROWTH RETARDATION-ALOPECIA-PSEUDOANODONTIA-OPTIC ATROPHY
See: Ectodermal Dysplasias

GUERIN-STERN SYNDROME
See: Arthrogryposis Multiplex Congenita

GUILLAIN-BARRÉ SYNDROME
See also: Autoimmune Disorders
Guillain-Barre Syndrome Foundation International
PO Box 262
Wynewood, PA 19096
(610) 667-0131
(610) 667-7036
www.webmast.com/gbs/
✉GBINT@ix.netcom.com
Guillain-Barré Syndrome Support Group of Ontario
2345 Yonge St., Ste. 901
Toronto, ON CAN M4P 2E5
(800) 567-2873
(519) 747-5777
(519) 747-5987 (fax)
✉info@brenfile.com
1,5,6,8,9

GÜNTHER PORPHYRIA
See: Porphyria

GUY-PATIN SYNDROME
See: Fibrodysplasia Ossificans Progressiva

HADDAD SYNDROME
See: Central Hypoventilation Syndrome, Congenital

HAILEY-HAILEY DISEASE
See: Ichthyosis

HAIRY ELBOWS DYSPLASIA
See: Ectodermal Dysplasias

HALLERMAN-STREIFF SYNDROME
See: Craniofacial Disorders; Ectodermal Dysplasias; Short Stature

HALLOPEAU-SIEMENS DISEASE
See: Epidermolysis Bullosa, Dystrophic

HAND-SCHÜLLER-CHRISTIAN SYNDROME
See: Histiocytosis

HAND-SHOULDER SYNDROME
See: Reflex Sympathetic Dystrophy Syndrome

HARLEQUIN ICHTHYOSIS
See: Ichthyosis

HAY-WELLS SYNDROME
See: Cleft Palate; Craniofacial Disorders; Deaf-Blind; Ectodermal Dysplasias; Hearing Impairments; Visual Impairments

HAYDEN SYNDROME
See: Ectodermal Dysplasias

HEAD INJURY
See: Brain Injury

HEARING IMPAIRMENT/VISUAL IMPAIRMENT
See: Deaf-Blind

HEARING IMPAIRMENTS
Alexander Graham Bell Association for the Deaf
3417 Volta Pl. NW
Washington, DC 20007-2778
(202) 337-5220 (voice/TTY)
(202) 337-8314 (fax)
www.agbell.org
✉agbell2@aol.com
1,2,3,4,5,6,7; Spanish materials, scholarship program

American Society for Deaf Children
1820 Tribute Rd., Ste. A
Sacramento, CA 95815
(800) 942-2732 (voice/TTY)
(916) 641-6084
(916) 641-6085 (fax)
www.deafchildren.org
✉asdc1@aol.com
1,2,3,4,5,6,7
American Speech, Language, Hearing Association
10801 Rockville Pike
Rockville, MD 20852
(301) 897-5700
Auditory-Verbal International
2121 Eisenhower, Ste. 402
Alexandria, VA 22314
(703) 739-1049
(703) 739-0874 (TTY)
(703) 739-0395 (fax)
www.digitalnation.com/avi
✉avi@csgi.com
1,2,3,4,6,7
Better Hearing Institute—U.S. and Canada
5021 Blacklick Rd.
Annandale, VA 22003
(800) 327-9355 (voice/TTY)
(703) 642-0580
(703) 750-9302 (fax)
1,2,4
The Canadian Hearing Society
271 Spadina Rd.
Toronto, ON CAN M5R 2V3
(416) 964-9595
(416) 964-0023 (TTY)
(416) 928-2525 (fax)
www.chs.ca
✉info@chs.ca
1,2,4,5,6,7; French/Italian/Portuguese/Chinese materials
Cochlear Implant Club International
5335 Wisconsin Ave. NW
Washington, DC 20015
(202) 895-2781
(202) 895-2782 (fax)
✉76207.3114@compuserve.com
1,2,3,4,5,6,7
Deafness Research Foundation
15 W. 39th St.
New York, NY 10018
(212) 768-1181
(800) 535-3323
(212) 768-1782 (fax)
www.drf.org
✉drf@DRF.org
1,2,4,7,8
HEAR Now
9745 E. Hampden Ave., Ste. 300
Denver, CO 80231-4923
(800) 648-4327 (voice/TTY)
(303) 695-7797 (voice/TTY)
(303) 695-7789 (fax)
www.leisurelan.com~hearnow/
✉jostetter@aol.com
1,2,7; accepts tax-deductible donations of used hearing aids
John Tracy Clinic for Preschool Deaf Children
806 W. Adams Blvd.
Los Angeles, CA 90007
(800) 522-4582 (voice/TTY)
(213) 748-5481
(213) 747-2924 (TTY)
(213) 749-1651 (fax)
www.jogntracyclinic.org
✉jtclinic@aol.com
2,3,4; free correspondence course for preschoolers, Spanish materials

Lead Line
House Ear Institute
2100 W. Third St., 5th Flr.
Los Angeles, CA 90057
(800) 352-8888 (voice/TTY)
(800) 287-4763 (voice/TTY, CA only)
(213) 483-8789 (fax)
www.hei.org
✉blincoln@hei.org
2,3,4
The Learning to Listen Foundation
Phillips House
North York General Hospital
10 Buchan Ct.
Toronto, ON CAN M2J IV2
(416) 491-4648
1,2,3,4,7
National Association of the Deaf
814 Thayer Ave.
Silver Spring, MD 20910-4500
(301) 587-1788
(301) 587-1789 (TTY)
(301) 587-1791 (fax)
www.nad.com
✉NADHQ@juno.com
1,2,4,5,6,7; youth program i
(SEE) Center for the Advancement of Deaf Children
PO Box 1181
Los Alamitos, CA 90720
(562) 430-1467 (voice/TTY)
(562) 795-6614 (fax)
2,4
SHHH: Self Help for Hard of Hearing People
7910 Woodmont Ave., Ste. 1200
Bethesda, MD 20814
(301) 657-2248
(301) 657-2249 (TTY)
(301) 913-9413 (fax)
ourworld.compuserve.com/homepages/shhh
✉71162.634@compuserve.com
1,2,4,5,6,7
Telecommunications for the Deaf, Inc.
8630 Fenton St., Ste. 604
Silver Spring, MD 20910-3803
(301) 589-3786
(301) 589-3006 (TTY)
(301) 589-3797 (fax)
1,2,4,6,7

HEARING IMPAIRMENTS
See also: Learning Disabilities,
National Cued Speech Association (NCSA)
4245 East Ave.
Rochester, NY 14618
(800) 459-3529
(716) 586-2456 (fax)
www.cuedspeech.org
✉cuedspdisc@aol.com
1,2,3,4,5,6,7

HEART DISORDERS
American Heart Association
7272 Greenville Ave
Dallas, TX 75231-4596
(800) 242-8721
(214) 706-1176
(214) 706-2139 (fax)
www.amhrt.org/
✉inquire@amhrt,org
2,3,4,5,6,7,8,9; Spanish materials

CHASER: Congenital Heart Anomalies—Support, Education, & Resources, Inc.
2112 N. Wilkins Rd.
Swanton, OH 43558
(419) 825-5575
(419) 825-2880 (fax)
www.csun.edu/~hfrmth006/chaser/chaser-news/html
✉chaser@compuserve.com
✉myer106w@cclc.gov
1,2,3,4,7,9
Children's Heart Association for Support and Education
c/o Cardiac Clinic
Hosp for Sick Children
555 University Ave.
Toronto, ON CAN M5G 1X8
(416) 813-5848
(416) 813-5582
1,2,3,4,8,9

HEMIDYSPLASIA, UNILATERAL
See: Ichthyosis

HEMIFACIAL MICROSOMIA
See: Goldenhar Syndrome

HEMIHYPERTROPHY
See: Beckwith-Wiedeman Syndrome

HEMIPLEGIA, ALTERNATING
See also: Epilepsy; Seizure Disorders
International Foundation for Alternating Hemiplegia of Childhood
239 Nevada St.
Redwood City, CA 06460
(650) 365-5798
✉laegan@aol.com
1,2,3,8,9

HEMISPERECTOMY
See: Rasmussen Syndrome

HEMOLYTIC ANEMIA
See: Cooley Anemia

HEMOLYTIC-UREMIC SYNDROME
See: Kidney Disorders

HEMOPHAGOCYTIC LYMPHOHISTIOCYTOSIS
See: Histiocytosis

HEMOPHAGOCYTIC RETICULOSIS
See: Histiocytosis

HEMOPHILIA
National Hemophilia Foundation
116 W. 32nd St., 11th Fl.
New York, NY 10001-3212
(800) 424-2634
(212) 328-3700
(212) 328-3777 (fax)
www.hemophilia.org
✉info@hemophilia.org
1,2,3,4,5,6,7,8; Spanish materials
World Federation of Hemophilia
1310 Green Ave., Ste. 500
Montreal, PQ CAN H3Z 2B2
(514) 933-7944
(514) 933-8916 (fax)
www.wfh.org
✉wsh@wfh.org
1,2,4,6,8; worldwide referrals, guide for travelers

HEMORRHAGIC NODULAR PURPURA
See: Fabry Disease

HEPATIC DUCTULAR HYPOPLASIA, SYNDROMATIC
See: Alagille Syndrome

HEPATOLENTICULAR DEGENERATION
See: Wilson Disease

HEPATOPHOSPHORYLASE DEFICIENCY GLYCOGENOSIS
See: Glycogen Storage Diseases; Muscular Dystrophy

HEREDITARY KIDNEY DISEASES
See: Kidney Diseases, Hereditary

HEREDITARY LEPTOCYTOSIS
See: Cooley Anemia

HERMANSKY-PUDLAK SYNDROME
See also: Albinism & Hypopigmentation; Visual Impairments

Hermansky-Pudlak Syndrome Network Inc.
1 South Rd.
Oyster Bay, NY 11771
(800) 789-9477
(516) 922-3440
(516) 922-4022 (fax)
www.medhelp.org/web/hspn.htm
✉hpsnw@juno.com
1,2,3,6,8,9

HERMAPHRODITISM
See also: Genitalia, Ambiguous

Intersex Society of North America
PO Box 31791
San Francisco, CA 94131
(415) 575-3885
(415) 252-8202
www.isna.org
✉info@isna.org
1,2,3,5,7

HERNIA, DIAPHRAGMATIC

CHERUBS
PO Box 1150
Creedmoor, NC 27522
(919) 693-8158
www.gloryroad.net/~cherubs
✉Cherubs@gloryroad
1,2,3,4,7,9

HERS DISEASE
See: Glycogen Storage Diseases; Muscular Dystrophy

HIRSCHSPRUNG DISEASE
See: Intestinal Pseudo-Obstruction Syndrome

HISTIOCYTOSIS
See also: Growth Disorders; Liver Disorders; Lung Disorders; Pituitary Disorders

Histiocytosis Association of America
302 N. Broadway
Pitman, NJ 08071
(800) 548-2758 (US and Canada)
(609) 589-6606
(609) 589-6614 (fax)
www.histio.org
✉hisiocyte@aol.com
1,2,3,4,8; Spanish materials

Histiocytosis Association of Canada
2316 Glastonbury Rd.
Burlington, ON CAN L7P 3Y3
(905) 335-2172
✉aprile.duda@sympatico.ca
1,2,3,4,6,8

HIV
See: AIDS

HODGKIN DISEASE
See: Leukemia

HOLOPROSENCEPHALY
See also: Brain Malformations; Chromosomal Abnormalities; Craniofacial Disorders

The Carter Centers for Brain Research in Holoprosencephaly and Related Malformations
Texas Scottish Rite Hospital for Children, Dept. of Neurology
2222 Welborn St.
Dallas, TX 75219
(800) 421-1121
(214) 559-8411
(214) 559-7835 (fax)
✉nclegg@tsrh.org
✉hpe@tsrh.org
1,2,3,4,8,9

HOSPITALITY HOUSING

Children's Hospital International
2202 Mt. Vernon Ave., Ste. 3C
Alexandria, VA 22301
(800) 2-4-CHILD (242-4453)
(703) 684-0330
(703) 684-0226 (fax)
www.chionline.org
✉chiorg@aol.com

National Association of Hospital Hospitality Houses
4915 Auburn Ave., Ste. 303
Bethesda, MD 20814
(800) 542-9730
(301) 961-5264
(301)961-3094
www.visit_usa.com/hhh
✉nahhhcom@aol.com

HUMAN IMMUNODEFICIENCY VIRUS
See: AIDS

HUNTER SYNDROME
See: Mucopolysaccharidosis; Tay-Sachs Disease

HURLER SYNDROME
See: Mucopolysaccharidosis; Tay-Sachs Disease

HURLER/SCHEIE SYNDROME
See: Mucopolysaccharidosis; Tay-Sachs Disease

HUTCHINSON-GILFORD SYNDROME
See: Progeria

HUTCHINSON-WEBER-PEUTZ SYNDROME
See: Peutz-Jeghers Syndrome; Polyposis

HYDROCEPHALUS

Guardians of Hydrocephalus Research Foundation
2618 Ave. Z
Brooklyn, NY 11235
(800) 458-8655
(718) 743-4473
(718) 743-1171 (fax)
1,2,3; Spanish materials

Hydrocephalus Association
870 Market St., Ste. 955
San Francisco, CA 94102
(415) 732-7040 (voice/fax)
www.heurosurgery.mgh.harvard.edu/ha/
✉hydroassoc@aol.com
1,2,3,6,7,8,9; Spanish materials

Hydrocephalus Support Group, Inc.
PO Box 4236
Chesterfield, MO 63006-4236
(314) 532-8228
(314) 995-4108 (fax)
✉hydro@inlink.com
1,2,3,4,6,7,9

National Hydrocephalus Foundation
12413 Centralia Rd.
Lakewood, CA 90715-1623
(562) 402-3523
(562) 924-6666 (fax)
www.geocities.com/HOTSPRINGS/villa/2300
✉hydrobrat@earthlink.net
1,2,3,4,5,6,7,8,9; Have videos and cassettes available

HYDROCEPHALUS, OBSTRUCTIVE
See: Dandy-Walker Syndrome

HYPERAMMONEMIA
See: Urea Cycle Disorders

HYPERCALCEMIA SYNDROME, INFANTILE, IDIOPATHIC
See: Williams Syndrome

HYPERCALCEMIA-SUPRAVALVAR AORTIC STENOSIS
See: Williams Syndrome

HYPERCYSTINURIA
See: Cystinuria

HYPERGLYCINEMIA WITH KETOACIDOSIS AND LEUKOPENIA
See: Acidemia, Organic

HYPERLEXIA
See: Autism

Canadian Hyperlexia Association
300 John St.
PO Box 87673
Thornhill,ON CAN L3T 7R3
(905) 886-9163
(905) 886-4624 (fax)
www.ican-net/~cha
✉cha@ican.net
1,2,3,4,5,6,9

HYPERLIPODEMA
See. Autoimmune Disorders

HYPEROXALURIA
See: Oxalosis & Hyperoxaluria

HYPERTELORISM/HYPOSPADIUS SYNDROMES
See: Opitz Syndrome

HYPERTHERMIA OF ANESTHESIA
See: Malignant Hyperthermia

HYPERTHYROID MYOPATHY
See: Muscular Dystrophy; Thyroid Disorder

HYPERURICEMIA–CHOREOATHETOSIS–SELF-MUTILATION SYNDROME
See: Lesch-Nyhan Disease

HYPERURICEMIA, HEREDITARY
See: Lesch-Nyhan Disease

HYPODONTIA AND NAIL DYSGENESIS
See: Ectodermal Dysplasias

HYPOERYTHEMIA, PROGRESSIVE
See: Anemia, Aplastic

HYPOGAMMAGLOBULINEMIA
See: Immune Disorders

HYPOMELANOSIS OF ITO
See: Ectodermal Dysplasias; Epilepsy; Incontinentia Pigmenti; Vitiligo

HYPOMYELINATION
See: Myelin Disorders; Myelin, Insufficient

HYPOPARATHYROIDISM
See also: Thyroid Disorders

Hypoparathyroidism Newsletter
2835 Salmon St.
Idaho Fall, ID 83406
(208)524-3857
✉hpth@june.com
1,3

HYPOPIGMENTATION
See: Albinism & Hypopigmentation; Vitiligo

HYPOPLASIA OF THE CORPUS CALLOSUM
See: Agenesis of the Corpus Callosum

HYPOPLASTIC ANEMIA
See: Anemia, Aplastic

HYPOPLASTIC LEFT HEART SYNDROME
See: Heart Disorders

HYPOSPADIUS/HYPERTELORISM SYNDROMES
See: Opitz Syndrome

HYPOTHYROID MYOPATHY
See: Muscular Dystrophy; Thyroid Disorders

HYPOTHYROIDISM, CONGENITAL
See: Growth Disorders; Thyroid Disorders

HYPOTONIA, BENIGN CONGENITAL
See: Spinal Muscular Atrophy

I-CELL DISEASE
See: Mucopolysaccharidosis; Tay-Sachs Disease

ICHTHYOSIFORM ERYTHRODERMA-DEAFNESS-KERATITS
See: Ectodermal Dysplasias

ICHTHYOSIS

FIRST: Foundation for Ichthyosis and Related Skin Types
PO Box 669
Ardmore, PA 19003
(800) 545-3286
(610) 789-3995
(610) 789-4366 (fax)
✉ichthyosis@aol.com
1,2,3,4,6,7,9; Spanish materials

IDIOPATHIC THROMBOCYTOPENIA PURPURA (ITP)
See: Purpura, Idiopathic Thrombocytopenia (ITP)

IDIOSYNCRATIC PORPHYRIA
See: Porphyria

ILLIOSTOMY
See: Ostomy

ILLNESS, TERMINAL
See also: Bereavement Support

Children's Hospice International
2202 Mt. Vernon Ave., Ste. 3C
Alexandria, VA 22301
(800) 2-4-CHILD (242-4453)
(703) 684-0330
(703) 684-0226 (fax)
1,2,4,6,7

IMMUNE DEFICIENCY
See: Immune Disorders

IMMUNE DISORDERS
See also: Autoimmune Disorders

Immune Deficiency Foundation
25 W. Chesapeake Ave., Ste. 206
Towson, MD 21204
(800) 296-4433
(410) 321-6647
(410) 321-9165 (fax)
www.primaryimmune.org
✉idf@clark.net
1,2,4,5,6,7,8,9; Spanish materials

IMPERFORATE ANUS
See: Anorectal Malformations

INCLUSION BODY MYOSTISIS
See: Immune Disorders

INCONTINENCE

National Association For Continence
PO Box 8310
Spartanburg, SC 29305
(800) 252-3337
(864) 579-7900
(864) 579-7902 (fax)
www.nafc.org
✉sbrewer@nafc.org
1,2,7; Spanish materials

Simon Foundation for Continence
PO Box 815
Wilmette, IL 60091
(800) 237-4666
(847) 864-3913
(847) 864-9758 (fax)
1,2,4,7; French material

INCONTINENTIA PIGMENTI
See also: Ectodermal Dysplasias

National Incontinentia Pigmenti Foundation
30 E. 72th St., 16th Fl.
New York, NY 10021
(212) 452-1231
(212) 452-1406 (fax)
www.medhelp.org/www/nipf.html
✉nipf@pipeline.com
1,2,3,4,5,6,9

INCONTINENTIA PIGMENTI ACHROMIANS
See: Ectodermal Dysplasias; Epilepsy; Incontinentia Pigmenti

INDIA RUBBER SKIN
See: Ehlers-Danlos Syndrome

INFANTILE FACIO-SCAPULO-HUMERAL MUSCULAR DYSTROPHY
See: Facio-Scapulo-Humeral Muscular Dystrophy

INFANTILE HYPERCALCEMIA SYNDROME, IDIOPATHIC
See: Williams Syndrome

INFANTILE SPASMS
See: Epilepsy

INTESTINAL NEURONAL DYSPLASIA
See: Intestinal Pseudo-
Obstruction Syndrome

INTESTINAL POLYPOSIS
See: Peutz-Jeghers Syndrome; Polyposis

**INTESTINAL POLYPOSIS-
CUTANEOUS PIGMENTATION
SYNDROME**
See: Peutz-Jeghers Syndrome; Polyposi

**INTESTINAL PSEUDO-
OBSTRUCTION SYNDROME**

**ASAP: American Society of
Adults with Pseudo-Obstruction**
Young Adults Network
19 Carroll Rd.
Woburn, MA 01801-6161
(781) 935-9776
(781) 933-4151 (fax)
✉asapgi@sprynet.com
1,2,3,4,7,8,9

**INTRAHEPATIC BILE
DUCT PAUCITY**
See: Alagille Syndrome

**INTRAUTERINE GROWTH
RETARDATION**
See: Growth Disorders

ISOVALERIC ACIDEMIA (IVA)
See: Acidemia, Organic

**ISOVALERYL-COA
CARBOXYLASE DEFICIENCY**
See: Acidemia, Organic

**JANSKY-BIELSCHOWSKY
DISEASE**
See: Batten Disease; Tay-Sachs Disease

JEGHERS SYNDROME
See: Peutz-Jeghers Syndrome; Polyposis

**JERVELL & LANGE-
NIELSEN SYNDROME**
See: Hearing Impairments; Long
Q-T Syndrome

JEUNE SYNDROME
See: Growth Disorders

JOHANSON-BLIZZARD SYNDROME
See: Craniofacial Disorders;
Ectodermal Dysplasias; Growth
Disorders; Hearing Impairments;
Short Stature

JORGENSON SYNDROME
See: Ectodermal Dysplasias

JOUBERT SYNDROME
See also: Apnea, Sleep

Joubert Syndrome Foundation
12348 Summer Meadow Rd.
Rock, MI 49880-9552
(906) 359-4707
(906) 359-4707 (fax)
www.erols.com/joubert
✉joubert@match.org
1,2,3,4,5,6,9

**JUVENILE GOUT-
CHOREOATHETOSIS-MENTAL
RETARDATION SYNDROME**
See: Lesch-Nyhan Disease

KALLMAN SYNDROME
See: Cleft Palate; Growth Disorders;
Hearing Impairments; Kidney Disorders

KAST SYNDROME
See: Cancer; Hemangioma;
Ollier Disease

KEARNS-SAYRE SYNDROME
See: Heart Disorders; Mitochondrial
Disorders; Retinitis Pigmentosa;
Visual Impairments

**KERATITIS FOLLICULARIS
SPINULOSA DECALVANS**
See: Ectodermal Dysplasias; Ichthyosis

**KERATITIS-ICHTHYOSIS-
DEAFNESS (KID) SYNDROME**
See: Ectodermal Dysplasias;
Ichthyosis; Hearing Impairments

KETOACIDURIA
See: Maple Syrup Urine Disease

KETOTIC HYPERGLYCINEMIA
See: Acidemia, Organic

KID SYNDROME
See: Ectodermal Dysplasias;
Ichthyosis; Hearing Impairments

KIDNEY DISEASES, HEREDITARY
See also: Cystinosis; Kidney
Diseases, Hereditary;
Oxalosis & Hyperoxaluria

Hereditary Nephritis Foundation
PO Box 57294
Murray, UT 84157-0294
(801) 262-1465
1,3,4

KIDNEY DISORDERS
See also: Cystinosis; Kidney
Diseases, Hereditary;
Oxalosis & Hyperoxaluria

**American Association of
Kidney Patients**
100 S. Ashley Dr., Ste. 280
Tampa, FL 33602
(800) 749-2257
(813) 223-7099
(813) 223-0001 (fax)
✉aakpnat@aol.com
1,2,3,6,7,

American Kidney Fund
6110 Executive Blvd., Ste. 1010
Rockville, MD 20852
(800) 638-8299
(301) 881-0898 (fax)
www.arbon.com/kidney
✉helpline@akfinc.org
1,2,6,8; Spanish materials, financial assistance for treatment-
related expenses

**Canadian Pediatric Kidney
Disease Research Center**
401 Smith Rd.
Ottawa, ON CAN K1H 8L1
(613) 737-4098
(613) 738-4800 (fax)
www.cpkdrc.org
2,4

Kidney Foundation of Canada
300-5165 Sherbrooke St. W.
Montreal, PQ CAN H4A IT6
(514) 369-4806
(514) 369-2472 (fax)
✉comm-mktg@kidney.ca
2,3,4,5,8; French/Chinese/
Punjabi materials

National Kidney Foundation
30 E. 33rd St., 11th Fl.
New York, NY 10016
(800) 622-9010
(212) 889-2210
(212) 689-9261 (fax)
www.kidney.org
1,2,4,5,7,8

**Polycystic Kidney
Research Foundation**
4901 Main St., Ste. 200
Kansas City, MO 64112-2674
(800) 753-2873
(816) 931-2600
(816) 931-8655 (fax)
www.kumc.edu/pkrf/
✉pkdcure@pkfoundation.org
1,2,5,6,8;Spanish/French/German/
Italian/Japanese materials

KIDNEY STONES
See: Cystinuria

KINKY HAIR DISEASE
See: Menkes Disease

KIRGHIZIAN DERMATOOSTEOLYSIS
See: Ectodermal Dysplasias

KLINEFELTER SYNDROME

49 XXXXY Syndrome Association
10001 NE 74th St.
Vancouver, WA 98662-3801
(360) 892-7547
✉kimbj@juno.com
1,3

**Klinefelter Syndrome
and Associates**
PO Box 119
Roseville, CA 95661-0119
(916) 773-2999
www.medhelp.org/web/ks.htm
✉ks47xxy@ix.netcom.com
1,2,3,4,6,7,9; Spanish materials

**Klinefelter's Syndrome
Association of America**
N5879 30th Rd.
Pine River, WI 54965
(920) 987-5782
1,2,3,5

KLIPPEL-TRENAUNAY SYNDROME
See also: Nevi, Giant Congenital;
Sturge-Weber Syndrome;
Vascular Malformations

Klippel-Trenaunay Support Group
c/o Judy Vessey
4610 Wooddale Ave.
Edina, MN 55424
(612) 925-2596
(612) 333-8685 (fax)
www.umn.edu/vesse001
✉vesse001@maroon.fc.umn.edu
1,2,3,6

**KLIPPEL-TRENAUNAY-
WEBER SYNDROME**
See: Klippel-Trenaunay Syndrome

KRABBE DISEASE
See: Leukodystrophy, Tay-Sachs Disease

KUFS DISEASE
See: Batten Disease; Tay-Sachs Disease

KUGELBERG-WELANDER DISEASE
See: Spinal Muscular Atrophy

KUSSMAUL-LANDRY PARALYSIS
See: Guillain-Barré Syndrome

KYPHOSIS
See: Scoliosis

**LACTATE DEHYDROGENASE
DEFICIENCY**
See: Muscular Dystrophy

LACTIC ACIDOSIS
See also: Glutaric Aciduria, Type I;
Leigh Disease; Metabolic Disorders

Lactic Acidosis Support Group
1620 Mable Ave.
Denver, CO 80229
(303) 287-4953
2,3,4,9

LAMBERT-EATON SYNDROME
See: Muscular Dystrophy

**LANDOUZY-DEJERINE
MUSCULAR DYSTROPHY**
See: Facio-Scapulo-Humeral
Muscular Dystrophy

LANDRY ASCENDING PARALYSIS
See: Guillain-Barré Syndrome

LANGERHANS CELL HISTIOCYTOSIS
See: Histiocytosis

LATEX ALLERGY

Latex Allergy Information Service
176 Roosevelt Ave.
Torrington, CT 06790
(860) 482-6869
(860) 482-2294 (fax)
www.latexallergyhelp.com
✉76500.1452@compuserve.com
1,2,4,6

LAURENCE-MOON SYNDROME
See: Laurence-Moon-Bardet-
Biedl Syndrome

**LAURENCE-MOON-BARDET-
BIEDL SYNDROME (LMBBS)**
See also: Kidney Disorders;
Retinitis Pigmentosa

**Laurence-Moon-Bardet-Biedl
Syndrome Network**
18 Strawberry Hill
Windsor, CT 06095
(203) 688-7880
1,2,8

LE JEUNE SYNDROME
See: Cri Du Chat Syndrome

LEARNING DISABILITIES
See also: Attention Deficit
Disorder; Dyslexia

**Learning Disabilities
Association of America**
4156 Library Rd.
Pittsburgh, PA 15234
(412) 341-1515
(412) 341-8077
(412) 344-0224 (fax)
www.ldanatl.org
✉ldanatl@usaor.org
1,2,4,5,7; Spanish Materials

**Learning Disabilities
Association of Canada**
323 Chapel St., Ste. 200
Ottawa, ON CAN K1N 7Z2
(613) 238-5721
(613) 235-5391 (fax)
www.educ.queensu.ca/~ida
✉ldactaac@fox.nstn.ca
1,2,4,5,6,7; French materials

**National Center for
Learning Disabilities**
381 Park Ave. S., Ste. 1401
New York, NY 10016
(888) 575-7373 (inform)
(212) 545-7510
(212) 545-9665 (fax)
www.ncld.org
1,2,4,7

Parents of Gifted/LD Students
2420 Eccleston St.
Silver Spring, MD 20902-4925
(301) 986-1422
(301) 681-4884 (fax)
www.geocities.com/athens/1105/
gtld.htm
✉jilmeyers@aol.com
1,2,3,4,5

**Resource for Children with
Special Needs, Inc.**
200 Park Ave. S., Ste. 816
New York, NY 10003
(212) 677-4650
(212) 254-4040 (fax)
✉resourcenyc@prodigy.net
2,4

LEIGH'S DISEASE
See also: Lactic Acidosis;
Mitochondrial Disorders

**National Leigh's
Disease Foundation**
608 E. Waldron St., PO Box 2222
Corinth, MS 38834
(800) 819-2551
(601) 286-2551 (fax)
1,2,3,4,7,8,9

**LENTICULAR DEGENERATION,
PROGRESSIVE**
See: Wilson Disease

LENZ-PASSARGE DYSPLASIA
See: Ectodermal Dysplasias

LEPTOCYTOSIS, HEREDITARY
See: Cooley Anemia

LEPTOMENINGEAL ANGIOMATOSIS
See: Sturge-Weber Syndrome

LESCH-NYHAN DISEASE

**International Lesch-Nyhan
Disease Association**
11042 Ferndale St.
Philadelphia, PA 19116
(215) 677-4206
2,3

Lesch-Nyhan Registry
Dept of Psychiatry
New York Univ., School of Medicine
550 First Ave.
New York, NY 10016
(212) 263-6458
(212) 629-9523 (fax)
✉andersnl@is2.nyu.edu

LETTERER-SIWE DISEASE
See: Histiocytosis

LEUKEMIA
See also: Bone Marrow
Transplant; Cancer

**Leukemia Research Fund
of Canada**
Attn: Chris Thomas
1110 Finch Ave. W., Ste. 220
Toronto, ON CAN M3J 2T2
(800) 268-2144 (Canada only)
(416) 661-9541
(416) 661-7799 (fax)
1,2,4,6

Leukemia Society of America
600 Third Ave., 4th Fl.
New York, NY 10016
(800) 955-4572
(212) 573-8484
(212) 450-8844
(212) 856-9686 (fax)
www.leukemia.org
1,2,3,4,5,7,8; Spanish materials

LEUKODYSTROPHY
See also: Myelin Disorders, Tay-Sachs Disease

United Leukodystrophy Foundation
2304 Highland Dr.
Sycamore, IL 60178
(800) 728-5483
(815) 895-3211
(815) 895-2432 (fax)
⊠ulf@ceet.niu.edu
1,2,3,6,8,9; Spanish/French materials

LEUKODYSTROPHY, METACHROMATIC
See: Leukodystrophy, Tay-Sachs Disease

LIMB DISORDERS
See also: Amputation; Chorionic Villus Sampling, Related Disabilities

Superkids: A Newsletter for Families and Friends of Children with Limb Differences
60 Clyde St.
Newton, MA 02460-2250
1,3

LIMB-GIRDLE MUSCULAR DYSTROPHY
See: Muscular Dystrophy

LIMIT DEXTRINOSIS
See: Glycogen Storage Diseases; Muscular Dystrophy

LIPID HISTIOCYTOSIS
See: Niemann-Pick Disease

LIPIDOSIS, CEREBROSIDE
See: Gaucher Disease

LIPOFUSCINOSES, NEURONAL CEROID
See: Batten Disease

LIPOMYELOMENINGOCELE

Lipomyelomeningocele Family Support Network
321 Hopewell St.
Birdsboro, PA 19508
(610)582-5937
www.home.ptd.net/~ifsn
⊠gmcafee@ptd.net

LISCH-NYHAN DISEASE

International Lesch-Nyhan Disease Registry
Institute of Applied Research
PO Box 339
Peapack, NJ 07977
(908) 234-0618
(908) 234-0963
www.Mathenynj.com
⊠registry@mathenynj.com
2,3,9

LISSENCEPHALY
See also: Epilepsy

Lissencephaly Network
716 Autumn Ridge Ln.
Fort Wayne, IN 46804
(219) 432-4310 (voice/fax)
www.lissencephaly.org
⊠lta1@is2.nyu.edu
1,2,3,4,9

The Lissencephaly Network, Inc.—Canada Division
1549 Regent St.
Regina, SK CAN S4N 1S1
(306) 569-0146
www.lissencephaly.org
1,2,3,4,6,8,9; toy-lending library

LIVER DISEASE AND TRANSPLANT (PEDIATRICS)
See also: Liver Disorders

Children's Liver Alliance (formerly the Biliary Atresia & Liver Transplant Network BALT)
3835 Richmond Ave., Box 190
Staten Island, NY 10312-3828
(718) 987-6200 (voice/fax)
www.livertx.org
⊠Livers4Kids@earthlink.net
1,2,3,4,5,6,7,9; Spanish materials

LIVER DISEASES
See: Liver Disorders

LIVER DISORDERS
See also: Biliary Atresia

American Liver Foundation
1425 Pompton Ave.
Cedar Grove, NJ 07009
(800) 223-0179
(800) GO-LIVER (465-4837)
(888) 4-HEP-ABC (443-7222)
(201) 256-2550
(201) 256-3214 (fax)
www.liverfoundation.org
⊠webmail@liverfoundation.org
1,2,4,5,7,8,9; Spanish materials

Canadian Liver Foundation
365 Bloor St. E, Ste. 200
Toronto, ON CAN M4W 3L4
(800) 563-5483 (Canada only)
(416) 964-1953
(416) 964-0024 (fax)
www.liver.ca/
⊠clf@liver.ca
2,5,6,8; French materials

United Liver Association
3021 Airport Ave.
Santa Monica, CA 90064-2987
(310) 313-0707
(310) 575-5595 (fax)
1,2,6,8

LIVER PHOSPHORYLASE DEFICIENCY
See: Glycogen Storage Diseases; Muscular Dystrophy

LOBSTEIN DISEASE, TYPE I
See: Osteogenesis Imperfecta

LONG Q-T SYNDROME
See also: Heart Disorders

International Long QT Syndrome Registry
PO Box 653
University of Rochester Medical Ctr.
Rochester, NY 14642-8653
(716) 275-5391
(716) 473-2751 (fax)
4,9

Sudden Arrhythmia Death Syndromes Foundation
508 E. South Temple, Ste. 20
Salt Lake City, UT 84102
(800) 786-7723
(801) 531-0945 (fax)
www.sads.org
⊠sads@mail.aros.net
1,2,3,4,5,7,8,9; Spanish materials

LORDOSIS
See: Scoliosis

LOWE SYNDROME
See also: Arthritis; Cystinuria, Glaucoma; Growth Disorders; Kidney Disorders; Metabolic Disorders; Visual Impairments

Lowe Syndrome Association
222 Lincoln St.
W. Lafayette, IN 47906
(765)743-3634
www.medhelp.org/lowesyndrome
⊠lsa@medhelp.org
1,2,3,6,8,9; Japanese/French/ Norwegian materials

LOWE-BICKEL SYNDROME
See: Lowe Syndrome

LOWE-TERRY-MACHLACHLAN SYNDROME
See: Lowe Syndrome

LUNG DISEASES

American Lung Association
1740 Broadway, 14th Fl.
New York, NY 10019
(800) LUNG-USA (586-4872)
(212) 265-5642 (fax)
(212) 315-8872
www.lung.usa.org
⊠info@lungusa.org
2,4,5,6,7,8; Spanish materials

Canadian Lung Association
Attn: Alana Fox
1900 City Park Dr., Ste. 508
Gloucester, ON CAN K1J 1A3
(613) 747-6776
(613) 747-7430 (fax)
www.lung.ca
⊠info@lung.ca
2,4,5,6,7

LUPUS ERYTHEMATOSIS

American Lupus Society
260 Maple Ct., Ste. 123
Ventura, CA 93003
(800) 331-1802 (info line)
(805) 339-0443
(805) 339-0467 (fax)
1,2,4,5,8

Lupus Canada
PO Box 64034
5512 4th NW
Calgary, AB CAN T2K 6J1
(800) 661-1468
(403) 274-5599(fax)
www.lupuscanada.org
⊠lupuscan@cadvision.com
2,4,5,6,7,8; French materials

Lupus Foundation of America
1300 Picard Dr., Ste. 200
Rockville, MD 20850
(800) 558-0121
(800) 558-0231 (Spanish)
(301) 670-9292
(301) 670-9486 (fax)
www.lupus.org/lupus
1,2,4,5,6,7,8; Spanish materials

SLE Foundation
149 Madison Ave., Ste. 205
New York, NY 10016
(212) 685-4118
(212) 545-1843 (fax)
www.holausa.org/lupustemp
⊠lupus@lupus.ny
1,2,3,4,5,6,7,8; Spanish materials

LYME DISEASE

Lyme Disease Foundation
1 Financial Plaza, Gold Bldg., 18th Fl.
Hartford, CT 06103-2610
(800) 886-5953 (info line)
(860) 525-2000
(860) 525-8425 (voice/fax)
www.lyme.org
⊠lymefnd@aol.com
1,2,4,6,7; Spanish materials

Lyme Disease Resource Center
PO Box 1423
Santa Rosa, CA 95482
(707) 468-8460
⊠pcm@pacific.net
1,2,4,6,7

LYMPHANGIOMA
See: Vascular Malformations

LYMPHANGIOMA, CAVERNOUS
See: Lymphatic Malformations

LYMPHATIC MALFORMATIONS
See also: Vascular Malformations

CALM: Children Anguished with Lymphatic Malformations
16 River Bend Rd.
Montgomery, IL 60538
(708) 906-9028
1,2,3,4,9

LYMPHOHISTIOCYTOSIS, FAMILIAL ERYTHROPHAGOCYTIC
See: Histiocytosis

LYMPHOHISTIOCYTOSIS, HEMOPHAGOCYTIC
See: Histiocytosis

LYMPHOHISTIOCYTOSIS, MALIGNANT
See: Cancer; Histiocytosis

LYMPHOMA
See: Leukemia

MACULAR DISEASES
See also: Retinitis Pigmentosa; Usher Syndrome; Visual Impairments

Association for Macular Diseases
210 E. 64th St.
New York, NY 10021
(212) 605-3719
(212) 605-3795 (fax)
www.macula@macula.org
⊠macula@macula.org
1,2,4

Macular Degeneration Foundation
PO Box 9752
San Jose, CA 95157
(888) 633-3937
(408) 260-1335
(408) 260-1336
www.eyesight.org
⊠eyesight@eyesight.org
1,2,4,9

Stargardt Macular Dystrophy and Other Juvenile Macular Dystrophies Self Help Network
c/o Macular Degeneration International
2968 West Oma Rd. #106
Tucson, AZ 85741
(800) 393-7634
(520) 797-2525
(520) 797-8018 (fax)
⊠Perski@aol.com

MACULAR DYSTROPHIES, JUVENILE
See: Macular Diseases; Stargardt Disease

MAFFUCCI SYNDROME
See: Cancer; Hemangioma; Ollier Disease

MALE SEX CHROMOSOME DISORDERS
See Klinefelter Syndrome

MALIGNANT HYPERTHERMIA

Malignant Hyperthermia Association
200 Elizabeth St.
CCRW, Rm. 2-834
Toronto, ON CAN M5G 2C4
(416) 340-3238
(416) 340-4960 (fax)
www.mhassn.com
⊠mha@mhassn.com
1,2,8

Malignant Hyperthermia Association of United States
32 S. Main St., PO Box 1069
Sherburne, NY 13460
(800) 986-4287
(607) 674-7901
(800) 674-7910 (fax)
gasnet.med.yale.edu/homepage.html
⊠mhaus@norwich.net
1,2,9; Spanish/Italian materials

North American Malignant Hyperthermia Registry of the Hyperthermia Association of the United States (MHAUS)
Dept of Anesthesia
Penn State Univ.
PO Box 850 Hershey, PA 17033
(717) 531-6936
(717) 531-6221 (fax)
www.mhaus.org
⊠mhaus@norwich.net
9; provides physicians with summaries of consenting, registered patients' anesthesia histories

MANDIBULOFACIAL DYSOSTOSIS
See also Nager & Miller Syndromes; Treacher Collins Syndrome

MANNOSIDOSIS
See also Tay-Sachs Disease

MAPLE SYRUP URINE DISEASE
See also: Acidemia, Organic; Metabolic Disorders

Maple Syrup Urine Disease Family Support Group
24806 State Rd. 119
Goshen, IN 46526
(219) 862-2992
(219) 862-2012 (fax)
www.msud-support.org/
⊠jbrubacher@juno.com
1,2,3,4,6,8

MARDEN-WALKER SYNDROME
See: Cleft Palate; Connective Tissue Disorders; Growth Disorders

MARFAN SYNDROME
See also: Connective Tissue Disorders; Heart Disorders; Scoliosis

KEY TO SERVICES

1 Periodical/newsletter
2 Informational materials
3 Networking/matching
4 Referrals to local resources
5 Local chapters
6 National conferences
7 National advocacy efforts
8 Fund research
9 Maintain research registry

Canadian Marfan Association
Central Plaza PO
128 Queen St. S., PO Box 42257
Mississauga,ON CAN L5M 4Z0
(905) 826-3223
(905) 826-2125 (fax)
✉marfan@istar.ca
1,2,4,5,8,9

National Marfan Foundation
382 Main St.
Port Washington, NY 11050
(516) 883-8712
(516) 883-8040 (fax)
www.marfan.ca
✉staff@marfan.ca
1,2,3,4,5,6,7,8

MARKER X SYNDROME
See: Fragile X Syndrome

MAROTEAUX-LAMY SYNDROME
See: Mucopolysaccharidosis: Tay-Sachs Disease

MARSHALL SYNDROME, TYPE I
See: Ectodermal Dysplasia

MARTIN-BELL SYNDROME
See: Fragile X Syndrome

MAST CELL DISEASE, SYSTEMIC

Mastocytosis Society
4771 Waynes Trace Rd.
Hamilton, OH 45011
(513) 726-4642
(513) 726-4601 (fax)
www.gil.com.au/comm/mast/
✉masto@dmv.com
1,2,3

MCARDLE DISEASE
See: Glycogen Storage Diseases; Muscular Dystrophy

MEDITERRANEAN ANEMIA
See: Cooley Anemia

MEDIUM-CHAIN ACYL -COA DEHYDROGENASE DEFICIENCY (MCAD)
See: Fatty Oxidation Disorder

MEDULLOBLASTOMA, HEREDITARY
See: Brain Tumors

MEERKEREN-EHLERS-DANLOS SYNDROME
See: Ehlers-Danlos Syndrome

MEIGE DISEASE
See: Lymphedema

MELANOLEUCODERMA ECTODERMAL DYSPLASIAS
See: Peutz-Jeghers Syndrome; Polyposis

MELAS SYNDROME
See: Growth Disorders, Lactic Acidosis, Mitochondrial Disorders

MELNICK NEEDLES SYNDROME
See: Growth Disorders

MEN SYNDROME I
See: Multiple Endocrine Neoplasia I

MENIERE SYNDROME
See: Crouzon Disease

MENINGEAL CAPILLARY ANGIOMATOSIS
See: Sturge-Weber Syndrome

MENKES DISEASE
See: Liver Disorders; Metabolic Disorders

Corporation for Menkes Disease
5720 Buckfield Ct.
Fort Wayne, IN 46804
(219) 436-0137
1,2,3,6,9; parent-professional network

MENTAL ILLNESS

Canadian Mental Health Association
2160 Yonge St.
Toronto, ON CAN M4S 2Z3
(416) 484-7750
(416) 484-4617 (fax)
www.icomm.ca/cmhacan
✉cmhanat@interlog.com
1,2,4,5,6,7; French materials

Federation of Families for Children's Mental Health
1021 Prince St.
Alexandria, VA 22314-2971
(703) 684-7710
(703) 836-1040 (fax)
www.cals.com/vikings/nami/index.html
✉ffcmh@crosslink.net
1,2,3,4,5,6,7; Spanish materials

National Alliance for the Mentally Ill
200 N. Glebe Rd., Ste. 1015
Arlington, VA 22203-3754
(703) 524-7600
(703) 524-9094 (fax)
www.nami.org
✉NAMIOFFC@aol.com
1,2,3,4,5,6,7,8

National Mental Health Association
1021 Prince St.
Alexandria, VA 22314-2971
(800) 969-6642 (info line)
(703) 684-5968
www.cais.com/vikings/nami/index.html
✉namiofc@aol.com
1,2,3,4,5,6,9

MENTAL RETARDATION
See also: Mental Illness; Mental Retardation/Mental Illness

The Arc
500 E. Border St., Ste. 300
PO Box 1047
Arlington, TX 76010
(800) 433-5255
(817) 261-6003
(817) 277-0553 (TTY)
(817) 277-3491 (fax)
www.TheArc.org/welcome.html
✉thearc@metronet.com
1,2,4,5,6,7,8; Spanish materials

Bethpage
2245 Midway Rd.
Carrolton,TX 75006
(972) 866-9989
(972) 991-0834
✉psanchez@bethpage.org
1,2

Bethphage Mission, Inc.
Lind Center, Ste. A
4980 S. 118th St.
Omaha, NE 68137-2220
(402) 896-3884
(402) 896-1511 (fax)
www.bethphage.org
✉psanchez@bcthphage.org

Canadian Association for Community Living & The Roeher Institute
4700 Keele St.
Kinsman Bldg. York University
North York, ON CAN M3J 1P3
(416) 661-9611
(416) 661-2023 (TTY)
(416) 661-5701 (FAX)
www.roeher.ca
www.cacl.ca
✉info@roeher.ca
✉info@cacl.ca
1,2,3,4,5,6,7,8,9; French materials

People First International
PO Box 12642
Salem, OR 97309
(503) 362-0336
(503) 585-0287 (fax)
www.open.org/people1/people1/:htm
✉heathd@open.org
1,2,4,5,6,7; leadership/self-advocacy training

Voice of the Retarded
5005 Newport Dr., Ste. 108
Rolling Meadows, IL 60008
(847) 253-6020
(847) 253-6054 (fax)
✉vor@compuserve.com
1,2,3,4,7

MENTAL RETARDATION/ MENTAL ILLNESS
See also: Mental Illness; Mental Retardation

(AAMR) American Association on Mental Resources
44 N. Capitol St., Ste. 846
Washington, DC 20001
(800) 424-3688
(202) 387-1968
(202) 387-2193 (fax)
www.aamr.org
✉aamr@access.digex.net
1,2,4,5,6

Developmental Disabilities Nurses Association (DDNA)
Attn: Randy Bryson
1720 Willow Creek Circle, Ste. 515
Eugene, OR 97402
(800) 888-6733
(541) 485-7372 (fax)
✉ddnahq@aol.com
1,2,5,6

National Association of the Dually Diagnosed (NADD)
132 Fair St.
Kingston, NY 12401
(800) 331-5362
(914) 331-4336
(914) 331-4569 (fax)
✉nadd@ulster.net
1,2,3,4,5,6,7; regional conferences

MERRF SYNDROME
See: Myoclonus; Mitochondrial Disorders

METABOLIC DISORDERS
See also: Acidemia, Organic; Galactosemia; Lactic Acidosis; Maple Syrup Urine Disease; Niemann-Pick Disease; Phenylketonuria (PKU)

Association for Neurometabolic Disorders
5223 Brookfield Ln.
Sylvania, OH 43560-1809
(419) 885-1497
1,3,6

Canadian Society for Metabolic Disease
3738 Sunset St.
Barnaby, BC CAN V5G 1T2
(604) 435-0085 (voice/fax)
1,2,3,4,6,8,9

Metabolic Information Network
PO Box 670847
Dallas, TX 75367-0847
(800) 945-2188 (USA/Canada)
(214) 696-2188
(800) 955-3258 (fax, USA/Canada)
(214) 696-3258 (fax)
✉mizesg@ix.netcom.com
1

The Research Trust for Metabolic Diseases in Children (RTMDC)
Golden Gates Lodge
Weston Road, Crewe
Cheshire, England CW25XN
00441270 250221
00441270 250244 (fax)
1,2,3,4,5,6,7,8,9; English, French, German, Spanish materials Metabolic Disorders

The World Life Foundation
PO Box 571
Bedford, TX 76095-5433
(800) 289-5433
1,4

METACHROMATIC LEUKODYSTROPHY
See: Leukodystrophy, Tay-Sachs Disease

METAPHYSEAL DYSOSTOSIS, TYPE B IV
See: Shwachman Syndrome

METATROPHIC DYSPLASIA
See: Dwarfism, Metatrophic

METHYLMALONIC ACIDEMIA
See: Acidemia, Organic

MICROCEPHALY

Microcephaly Network
362 Jean Talon
St. Vanier, ON CAN K1L 6T9
(613) 742-5936
www.microcephaly.org
✉amanda@inetdirect.com

MICROPHTHALMIA
See: Anophthalmia; Visual Impairments

MICROSOMIA, HEMIFACIAL
See: Craniofacial Disorders; Goldenhar Syndrome

MICROTIA
See also: Craniofacial Disorders

Microtia-Atresia Support Group
c/o Jack Gross
330 7th Ave., #1203
New York, NY 10001
(212) 947-0770
(212) 714-1224 (fax)
✉grossinsco@aol.com

MIKAELIAN SYNDROME
See: Ectodermal Dysplasias

MILLER SYNDROME
See: Nager & Miller Syndromes

MILLER-DIEKER SYNDROME
See: Lissencephaly

MILLER-FISCHER SYNDROME
See: Guillain-Barré Syndrome

MILROY DISEASE
See: Lymphatic Malformations; Lymphedema

MITOCHONDRIAL DISORDERS

COX Foundation for All Mitochondrial Diseases
PO Box 1151
Monroeville, PA 15146-1151
(412) 856-1297
(412) 856-7072 (fax)
biochemgen.ucsd.edu/umdf/
1,2,3,5,6,7,8,9

MITOCHONDRIAL MYOPATHY
See: Mitochondrial Disorders; Muscular Dystrophy

MOEBIUS SYNDROME
See: Craniofacial Disorders; Limb Disorders

Moebius Syndrome Support Group
38883 FoxHolm Dr.
Palmdale, CA 93551
(805) 267-2570 (voice/fax)
www.wincom.net/moebius/
✉1orit@netport.com
1,2,3,6,8,9

MONOSOMY X
See: Turner Syndrome

MORQUIO SYNDROME
Mucopolysaccharidosis; Tay-Sachs Disease

MORVAN DISEASE
See: Syringomyelia

MOTOR-SENSORY NEUROPATHY, HEREDITARY
See: Charcot-Marie-Tooth Disease

MOYAMOYA DISEASE
See: Stroke; Vascular Malformations

Families with Moyamoya Network
c/o Dawn Gruettner
4900 McGowan St. SE
Cedar Rapids, IA 52403
(800) 261-6692
2,3

MUCOLIPIDOSES
See: Mucopolysaccharidosis; Mucolipidosis Type IV; Tay-Sachs Disease

MUCOLIPIDOSIS TYPE IV
See: Mucopolysaccharidosis; Tay-Sachs Disease; Visual Impairments

ML4 Foundation
719 E. 17th St.
Brooklyn, NY 11230
(718) 434-5067
(718) 859-7371
www.ml4.org
✉ml4@aol.com
1,2,3,4,5,7,8,9

MUCOPOLYSACCHARIDOSIS
See: Metabolic Disorders; Tay-Sachs Disease

National Mucopolysaccharidosis Society (MPS)
17 Kraemer St.
Hicksville, NY 11801
(516) 931-6338
(516) 822-2041
www.members.aol.com/mpssociety/index.html
✉cohenzec@aol.com
1,2,3,4,5,6,8,9; Spanish materials

MUCOSULFATIDOSIS
See: Hearing Impairments; Ichthyosis; Leukodystrophy; Tay-Sachs Disease

MULTIPLE CARBOXYLASE DEFICIENCY
See: Metabolic Disorders

MULTIPLE CARTILAGNOUS ENCHONDROSES
See: Ollier Disease

MULTIPLE ENDOCRINE NEOPLASIA I
See also: Adrenal Disorders;
Diabetes Mellitus; Thyroid Disorders.

Multiple Endocrine Neoplasia I
c/o Mrs. Cathy McMillan-Fitch
Box 100
Meota, SK CAN S0M 1X0
(306) 892-2080
3,9

MULTIPLE SCLEROSIS

Multiple Sclerosis Society of Canada
250 Bloor St. E., Ste. 1000
Toronto, ON CAN M4W 3P9
(800) 361-2985 (Canada only)
(416) 922-6065
(416) 922-7238 (fax)
www.mssoc.ca
✉info@mssoc.ca
1,2,4,6,7,8,9

National Multiple Sclerosis Society
733 3rd Ave., 6th Fl.
New York, NY 10017-3288
(800) 344-4867
(212) 986-3240
(212) 986-7981 (fax)
www.nmss.org
✉nat@nmss.org
1,2,4,5,8; Spanish materials

MULTIPLE SULFATASE DEFICIENCY
See: Hearing Impairments;
Ichthyosis; Leukodystrophy; Tay-
Sachs Disease

MUSCLE PHOSPHOFRUCTOKINASE DEFICIENCY
See: Glycogen Storage Diseases;
Muscular Dystrophy

MUSCLE PHOSPHORYLASE DEFICIENCY
See: Glycogen Storage Diseases;
Muscular Dystrophy

MUSCULAR ATROPHY, PERONEAL
See: Charcot-Marie-Tooth Disease

MUSCULAR DYSTROPHY
See also: Facio-Scapulo-Humeral
Muscular Dystrophy; Ventilator Use

Duchenne Parent Project
125 Marymount Ct.
Middletown, OH 45042-3755
(800) 714-KIDS (5437)
(513) 424-7452
(513) 425-9907
www.parentdmd.org
✉patfurlong@aol.com

MUSCULAR DYSTROPHY DEJERINE-LANDOUZY
See: Facio-Scapulo-Humeral
Muscular Dystrophy; Ventilator Use

Muscular Dystrophy Association
3300 E. Sunrise Dr.
Tucson, AZ 85718-3208
(800) 572-1717
(520) 529-2000
(520) 529-5300 (fax)
www.mdausa.org
✉74431.2513@compuserve.com
1,2,3,4,5,8; Spanish materials,
local clinics, financial assistance
for wheelchair purchases,

Muscular Dystrophy Association of Canada
2345 Yonge St., Ste. 901
Toronto, ON CAN M4P 2E5
(800) 567-2873 (Canada only)
(416) 488-0030
(416) 488-7523(voice/fax)
www.mdac.ca
✉ragbar@mdac.ca
1,2,3,4,5,6,8,9; French materials

Society for Muscular Dystrophy Information International
PO Box 479
Bridgewater, NS CAN B4V 2X6
(902) 685-3961
(902) 685-3962 (fax)
✉smdi@aura.com.com
1,4

MYASTHENIA GRAVIS

Myasthenia Gravis Association
25 Caravan Dr.
North York, ON CAN M3B 1M9
(416) 444-8357
1,2,4,5,8,9

Myasthenia Gravis Foundation of America
222 S. Riverside Plaza, Ste. 1540
Chicago, IL 60606
(800) 541-5454
(312) 258-0461 (fax)
www.med.unc.edu/mgfa/
✉myastheniagravis@msn.com
1,2,4,5,6,7,8,9; Spanish materials

MYASTHENIC SYNDROME OF LAMBERT-EATON
See: Muscular Dystrophy

MYELIN DISORDERS
See also: Leukodystrophy;
Myelin, Insufficient

The Myelin Project
1747 Pennsylvania Ave. NW, Ste. 950
Washington DC 20006
(202) 452-8994
(202) 785-9578 (fax)
www.myelin.org/
✉myelin@erols.com
1,2,8; Italian/French/German/
Danish/Spanish materials

The Myelin Project of Canada
c/o Julie and Wayne Simmons
4330 Spinningdale Ct.
Mississauga, ON CAN L5M 3J8
(905) 567-8843
(905) 567-9189 (fax)
2,6,7,8,9

MYELODYSPLASIA
See: Anemia, Aplastic

MYELOMA
See: Cancer; Leukemia

International Myeloma Foundation
2129 Stanley Hills Dr.
Los Angeles, CA 90046
(800) 452-2873
(213) 654-3023
(213) 656-1182 (fax)
www.comed.com/imf/imf.html
✉theimf@aol.com
1,2,3,4,6,7,8

MYELOMA, MULTIPLE
See: Myeloma

MYELOSYRINGOSIS
See: Syringomyelia

MYOADENYLATE DEAMINASE DEFICIENCY
See: Muscular Dystrophy

MYOCLONUS
See also: Epilepsy; Opsoclonus-
Myoclonus Syndrome

Moving Forward
2934 Glenmore Ave.
Kettering, OH 45409
(513) 293-0409
www.acor.org/diseases/
hematology/mpd
✉editormdp@aol.com
2

MYODENYLATE DEAMINASE DEFICIENCY
See: Muscualr Dystrophy

MYOPATHIES, CONGENITAL
See: Myotubular Myopathy, X-Linked

MYOPATHY, CENTRONUCLEAR
See: Myotubular Myopathy, X-
Linked; Muscular Dystrophy

MYOPATHY, HYPOTHYROID
See: Muscular Dystrophy;
Thyroid Disorders

MYOPHOSPHORYLASE DEFICIENCY
See: Glycogen Storage Diseases

MYOSITIS AUTOIMMUNE DISORDERS

National Myositis Association
7720B El Camino Real, Ste. 367
Rancho La Costa, CA 92009
(800) 230-0441
(619) 436-2185
1,2,3,4,5,9

MYOSITIS OSSIFICANS
See: Fibrodysplasia Ossificans Progressiva

MYOTONIA, CONGENITA
See: Muscular Dystrophy

MYOTUBULAR MYOPATHY, X-LINKED
See also: Muscular Dystrophy

X-Linked Myotubular Myopathy Resource Group
2602 Quaker Dr.
Texas City, TX 77590
(409) 945-8569
www.mtmrg.org
✉gscoggin@aol.com
1,2,3,9

MYXEDEMA
See: Thyroid Disorders

N-ACETYL GLUTAMATE SYNTHETASE (NAGS) DEFICIENCY
See: Urea Cycle Disorders

NAEFELI-FRANCESCHETTI-JADASSOHN DYSPLASIA
See: Ectodermal Dysplasias

NAEGELI-FRANCESCHETTI-JADASSOHN SYNDROME
See: Incontinentia Pigmenti

NAGER & MILLER SYNDROMES
See also: Craniofacial Disorders;
Hearing Impairments; Limb Disorders

Foundation for Nager and Miller Syndromes (FNMS)
1827 Grove St. #2
Glenview, IL 60025-2913
(800) 507-3667
(847) 724-6449 (fax)
www.nagerormillersynd.com
✉fnms@interaccess.com
1,2,3,4,5,6,8,9

NASAL ENCEPHALOCELE
See: Craniofacial Disorders

NEMALINE MYOPATHY
See: Muscular Dystrophy

NEPHRITIS
See: Kidney Diseases, Hereditary
Neurodevelopmental Abnormalities,
Fetal Alcohol Syndrome

NEUROFIBROMATOSIS
See also: Acoustic Neuroma; Hearing
Impairments; Visual Impairments

National Neurofibromatosis Foundation
95 Pine St., 16th Fl.
New York, NY 10005
(800) 323-7938 (voice/TTY)
(212) 344-6633
(212) 747-0004 (fax)
www.nf.org
✉nnff@aol.com
1,2,4,5,8

Neurofibromatosis, Inc.
8855 Annapolis, Ste. 110
Lanham, MD 20706-2924
(800) 942-6825
(301) 577-8984
(301) 577-0016 (fax)
members.gnn.com/nfic/page1.htm
✉nfinc@gnn.com
1,2,3,4,5,7,8

Neurofibromatosis Society of Ontario
923 Annes St.
Whitby, ON CAN L1N 5K7
(905) 430-6141 (voice/fax)
1,2,4,6,8

NEUROLOGICAL DISORDERS

Association for Comprehensive Neurotherapy
1128 Royal Palm Beach Blvd. # 283
Royal Palm Beach, FL 33411
(561) 798-0472
(561) 798-9820 (fax)
www.latitudes.org
Ωacn@latitudes.org

Making Headway Foundation, Inc.
115 King St.
Chappaqua, NY 10514-3460
(914) 238-8384
(914) 238-1693 (fax)
1,2,4,8

NEUROMETABOLIC DISORDERS
See: Metabolic Disorders

NEURONAL CEROID LIPOFUSCINOSES
See: Batten Disease

NEUROPATHY, HEREDITARY, SENSORY MOTOR
See: Charcot-Marie-Tooth Disease

NEUROPATHY, PERIPHERAL
See: Charcot-Marie-Tooth Disease

NEUTROPENIA

Neutropenia Support Association
PO Box 243
905 Corydon Ave.
Winnipeg, MB CAN R3M 3S7
(800) 663-8876
(204) 489-8454
www.neutropenia.ca
✉stevensl@neutropenia.ca
1,2,3,4,5,6,7,8,9; French materials

Neutropenia SCN International Registry
Puget Sound Plaza
1325 4th Ave., Ste. 620
Seattle, WA 98101-2509
(800) 726-4463
(206) 543-9749
(206) 543-3668 (fax)
www.scnir.medicine.washington.edu/
✉registry@u.washington.edu
1,2

NEUTROPENIA-PANCREATIC INSUFFICIENCY
See: Shwachman Syndrome

NEVI, GIANT CONGENITAL
See also: Craniofacial Disorders;
Ichthyosis; Klippel-Trenaunay
Syndrome; Sturge-Weber Syndrome;
Vascular Malformations

Nevus Network
PO Box 1981
Woodbridge, VA 22193
(703) 492-0253
www.nevusnetwork.org
✉nevusnet@bigfoot.com
1,2,3,9; French/Spanish materials

NEVILLE DISEASE
See: Niemann-Pick Disease

NEVO SYNDROME
See: Sotos Syndrome

NIEMANN-PICK DISEASE
See also: Ataxia; Metabolic
Disorders; Tay-Sachs Disease

Ara Parseghian Medical Research Foundation
1760 E. River Rd., Ste. 115
Tucson, AZ 85718
(520) 577-5106
(520) 577-5212 (fax)
www.parseghian.org
✉victory@axstarnet.com

NONKETOTIC HYPERGLYCINEMIA
See: Acidemia, Organic

NONNE-MILROY-MEIGE SYNDROME
See: Lymphatic Malformations;

NOONAN SYNDROME
See: Cardio-Facio-Cutaneous
Syndrome; Growth Disorders; Heart
Disorders; Malignant Hyperthermia;
Williams Syndrome

(TNSSG) Noonan Syndrome Support Group, Inc.
PO Box 145
Upperco, MD 21155
(888) 686-2224
(410) 374-5245
www.noonansyndrome.org
✉wandar@bellatlantic.net

NORMAN-ROBERTS SYNDROME
See: Lissencephaly

NORRIE DISEASE
See also: Hearing Impairments;
Visual Impairments

Norrie Disease Foundation
Developmental Neurogenetics Unit
Mass General Hospital
CNY #6217 149 13 St.
Charlestown,MA 02129
(617) 726-5718
(617) 724-9620 (fax)
www.neuro-www.mgh.harvard.edu
✉ sinis@helix.mgh.harvard.edu
2,3,4

NUTRITION

The Oley Foundation
214 Hun Memorial A-23
Albany Medical Center
Albany, NY 12208
(800) 776-OLEY (6539)
(578) 262-5079
(518) 262-5528
www.wizvax.net/oleyfdn
✉ ljoan_bishop@ccgateway.amc.edu

NYHAN SYNDROME
See: Lesch-Nyhan Syndrome

OAV SYNDROME
See: Goldenhar Syndrome

OBSESSIVE-COMPULSIVE
DISORDER

OC Foundation
PO Box 70
Milford, CT 06460
(203) 878-5669
(203) 874-2826 (fax)
pages.prodigy.com/alwillen/ocf.html
✉ jjphs28a@prodigy.com
1,2,3,4,5,6,7,8

OBSTRUCTIVE HYDROCEPHALUS
See: Dandy-Walker Syndrome

OCULO-AURICULO-
VERTEBRAL SPECTUM
See: Goldenhar Syndrome

OCULOCEREBRORENAL
SYNDROME
See: Lowe Syndrome

OCULODENTODIGITAL
SYNDROME; TYPE I & II
See: Ectodermal Dysplasias

OCULOOSTEOCUTANEOUS
SYNDROME
See: Ectodermal Dysplasias

ODONTOONYCHODERMAL
DYSPLASIA
See: Ectodermal Dysplasias

ODONTOONYCHOHYPOHIDROTI
C DYSPLASIA
See: Ectodermal Dysplasias

ODONTOTRICHODYSPLASIA
WITH NEUTROPENIA
See: Ectodermal Dysplasias; Neutropenia

ODONTOTRICHOMELIC
SYNDROME
See: Ectodermal Dysplasias

OLDFIELD SYNDROME
See: Peutz-Jeghers Syndrome; Polyposis

OLIGOPHRENIA-
MICROPHTHALMOS
See: Norrie Disease

OLIGOSACCHARIDOSES
See: Tay-Sachs Disease

OLLIER DISEASE
See also: Growth Disorders

Ollier's/Maffuci Self-Help Group
c/o Bonnie Hatch-schmid Founder
c/o Hermann Schmid Secretary
Newletters Offices
1824 Millwood Rd.
Sumter, SC 29150
(803) 775-1757
(803) 469-9749
www.uhsweb.edu.olliers/olliers.htm
✉ olliers@aol.com
1,3,4,9

ONDINE'S CURSE
See: Central Hypoventilation
Syndrome, Congenital

OPHTHALMOARTHROPATHY
See: Stickler Syndrome

OPITZ FG SYNDROME
See: Opitz Syndrome

OPITZ HYPERTELORISM-
HYPOSPADIUS SYNDROME
See: Opitz Syndrome

OPITZ OCULOGENITOLARYNGEAL
SYNDROME
See: Opitz Syndrome

OPITZ SYNDROME

Opitz G/BBB Family Network
PO Box 516
Grand Lake, CO 80447
(970) 627-8935 (voice/fax)
www.rkymtnhi.com/opitz
✉ opitznet@rkymtnhi.com
1,2,3,9

OPITZ-BBBG
COMPOUND SYNDROME
See: Opitz Syndrome

OPITZ-FRIAS SYNDROME
See: Opitz Syndrome

OPSOCLONUS-MYOCLONUS
SYNDROME
See also: Epilepsy; Myoclonus

Opsoclonus-Myoclonus Parent-
Talk Support Network
c/o Connie Quinn
725 North St.
Jim Thorpe, PA 18229
(717) 325-3302
www.geocities.com/hotsprings/spa/2
✉ clquinn@ptd.net
3

OPTIC NERVE HYPOPLASIA
See: Septo-Optic Dysplasia

ORBITAL HYPERTELORISM
See: Craniofacial Disorders

ORGANIC ACIDEMIA
See: Acidemia, Organic

ORNITHINE TRANSCARBAMYLASE
(OTC) DEFICIENCY
See: Urea Cycle Disorders

OROFACIODIGITAL SYNDROME,
TYPE I
See: Ectodermal Dysplasias

OSLER-WEBER-
RENDU SYNDROME
See: Hemorrhagic Telangiectasis,
Hereditary

OSTEOGENESIS IMPERFECTA
See also: Growth Disorders

Canadian Osteogenesis
Imperfecta Society
128 Thornhill Crescent
Chatham, ON CAN N7L 4M3
(519) 436-0025
(519) 351-4043 (fax)
✉ mkearney@kent.net
1,2,3,6

Osteogenesis Imperfecta Foundation
804 West Diamond Ave., Ste. 210
Gaithersburg, MD 20878
(800) 981-2663
(301) 947-0083
(301) 947-0456 (fax)
members.aol.com/bonelink/
✉ bonelink@aol.com
1,2,3,4,5,6,7,8,9; Spanish materials

OSTOMY

United Ostomy Association, Inc.
19722 MacArthur Blvd., Ste. 200
Irvine, CA 19772
(800) 826-0826
(949) 660-8624
(949) 660-9262 (fax)
www.uoa.org
✉ uoa@deltanet.com
1,2,4,5,6,7

United Ostomy Association of
Canada, Inc.
PO Box 46057, College Park PO
444 Yonge St.
Toronto, ON CAN M5B 2L8
(416) 595-5452
(416) 595-9924 (fax)
business.atcon.com/voacanada/
✉ uoacan@magic.com
1,2,3,4,5,6,7,9; youth network

OXALOSIS & HYPEROXALURIA
See also: Kidney Disorders

Oxalosis & Hyperoxaluria
Foundation
12 Pleasant St.
Maynard, MA 01754
(888) 721-2432
(978) 461-0614
www.ohf.org
✉ ohf@ohf.ultranet.com
1,2,3,8,9

OXOPROLINURIA
See: Acidemia, Organic

PACHYGYRIA
See: Lissencephaly

PACHYONYCHIA, CONGENITAL
See: Ectodermal Dysplasias

PAGON SYNDROME
See: Hydrocephalus; Lissencephaly

PALLISTER-HALL SYNDROME
See also: Anorectal Malformations;
Pituitary Disorders

Pallister-Hall Foundation
RFD Box 3000, Fairground Rd.
Bradford, VT 05033
(802) 222-9683
✉ lmesser@sover.net
2,3,4,9

PALLISTER-KILLIAN SYNDROME
See also: Epilepsy

Pallister-Killian Family
Support Network
3700 Wyndale Ct.
Ft Worth, TX 76109
(817) 927-8854
(817) 927-2073 (fax)
3

PALMOPLANTAR HYPERKERATOSIS
AND ALOPECIA
See: Ectodermal Dysplasias

PANCREATIC INSUFFICIENCY
WITH NEUTROPENIA
See: Shwachman Syndrome

PANCYTOPENIA, CONGENITAL
See: Anemia, Fanconi

PANHYPOPITUITARISM
See: Growth Disorders

PANMYELOPATHY
See: Anemia, Aplastic

PANMYELOPHTHISIS
See: Anemia, Aplastic

PAPILLOMAS
See: Respiratory Papillomatosis, Recurrent

PAPILLON-LEFEVRE SYNDROME
See: Ectodermal Dysplasias

PARALYSIS, PERIODIC
See: Muscular Dystrophy

PARALYTIC POLIO
See: Polio

PARAMYOTONIA CONGENITA
See: Muscular Dystrophy

PARKES-WEBER SYNDROME
See: Klippel-Trenaunay Syndrome

PARRY-ROMBERG SYNDROME
See: Craniofacial Disorders

PATIN SYNDROME
See: Fibrodysplasia Ossificans Progressiva

PDD
See: Autism

PELIZAEUS-MERZBACHER
DISEASE
See: Leukodystrophy

PEMPHIGUS, FAMILIAL
See: Ichthyosis

PEPCK DEFICIENCY
See: Lactic Acidosis;
Mitochondrial Disorders

PERIPHERAL NEUROPATHY
See: Charcot-Marie-Tooth Disease

PERONEAL MUSCULAR ATROPHY
See: Charcot-Marie-Tooth Disease

PERVASIVE DEVELOPMENTAL
DISORDER (PDD)
See: Autism

PEUTZ-JEGHERS SYNDROME
See also: Polyposis

Hereditary Colon Cancer Registry
c/o Jill D. Brensinger
Johns Hopkins Hospital
550 N. Broadway, Ste. 108
Baltimore, MD 21205
(410) 614-4038
(410) 614-9544 (fax)
✉ hccregistry@jhmi.edu
2,3,4,8,9

PEUTZ-TOURAINE SYNDROME
See: Peutz-Jeghers Syndrome; Polyposis

PFEIFFER SYNDROME
See: Craniofacial Disorders

PHAKOMATOSIS
See: Tuberous Sclerosis

PHENYLKETONURIA (PKU)

Metabolic Disorders Children's
PKU Network
1520 State St., Ste. 111
San Diego, CA 92101
(619) 233-3202
(619) 233-0838 (fax)
✉ pkunetwork@aol.com
1,2,3,4,9; Spanish materials

Metabolic Disorders
National PKU News
c/o Virginia Schuett
6869 Woodlawn Ave. NE, Ste. 116
Seattle, WA 98115-5469
(206) 525-8140
(206) 525-5023 (fax)
www.wolfenet.com/~kronmal
✉ schuett@pkunews.org
1,2

PHOSPHOENOLPYRUVATE
CARBOXYKINASE DEFICIENCY
See: Lactic Acidosis;
Mitochondrial Disorders

PHOSPHOFRUCTOKINASE
DEFICIENCY
See: Glycogen Storage Diseases;
Muscular Dystrophy

PHOSPHOGLYCERATE KINASE
DEFICIENCY
See: Muscular Dystrophy

PHOSPHOGLYCERATE MUTASE
DEFICIENCY
See: Muscular Dystrophy

PHOSPHORYLASE B
KINASE DEFICIENCY
See: Glycogen Storage Diseases;
Muscular Dystrophy

PHOSPHORYLASE DEFICIENCY
See: Glycogen Storage Diseases;
Muscular Dystrophy

PIERRE ROBIN SYNDROME
See: Craniofacial Disorders;
Growth Disorders

PIGMENT DISORDERS
See: Albinism & Hypopigmentation; Vitiligo

PILI TORTI AND
ENAMEL HYPOPLASIA
See: Ectodermal Dysplasias

PILI TORTI AND
ONYCHODYSPLASIA
See: Ectodermal Dysplasias

PITUITARY DISORDERS

Pituitary Network Association
16350 Ventura Blvd., Ste. 231
Encino, CA 91436
(805) 499-9973
(805) 499-1523 (fax)
www.pituitary.com
✉ ptna@pituitary.com
1,2,3,4,6,7,9

PITUITARY TUMORS
See also: Pituitary Disorders
Pituitary Tumor Support
Network of Canada
61 Markbrook Ln.
Etiboke, ONT CAN M9V 5E7
(416) 749-1997
1,2,3,4,6,8

PITYRIASIS RUBRA PILARIS
See: Ichthyosis

POLIO

Informed Parents Against VAPP (Vaccine Associated Paralytic Polio)
PO Box 53212
Washington, DC 20009
(888) 363-8277
(703) 319-8277 (fax)
www.ipav.org
✉NOVAPP@aol.com
2,3,7,8,9

International Polio Network
4207 Lindell Blvd., #110
Saint Louis, MO 63108-2915
(314) 534-0475
(314) 534-5070 (fax)
✉gini_intl@msn.com
1,2,3,4,5,6,7

POLYCYSTIC KIDNEY DISEASE
See: Kidney Disorders

POLYENDOCRINE ADENOMATOSIS
See: Multiple Endocrine Neoplasia I

POLYMYOSITIS
See: Muscular Dystrophy; Myositis

POLYNEURITIS, ACUTE IDIOPATHIC
See: Guillain-Barré Syndrome

POLYNEUROPATHY, CHRONIC RELAPSING
See: Guillain-Barré Syndrome

POLYPOSIS
See also: Cancer; Peutz-Jeghers Syndrome

Familial Gastrointestinal Cancer Registry
Mount Sinai Hospital
600 University Ave., Ste. 1157
Toronto, ON CAN M5G 1X5
(416) 586-8334
(416) 586-8644 (fax)
✉tburke@mtsinai.on.ca
1,2,3,4,9; French materials

POLYRADICULONEUROPATHY
See: Guillain-Barré Syndrome

POMPE DISEASE
See: Glycogen Storage Diseases; Muscular Dystrophy; Tay-Sachs Disease

PORPHYRIA

Metabolic Disorders American Porphyria Foundation
PO Box 22712
Houston, TX 77227
(713) 266-9617
(713) 871-1788
www.enterprise.het/2pf/
✉porphyrus@juno.com
1,2,3,4,7,8,9

Metabolic Disorders Canadian Porphyria Foundation
Box 1206
Neepawa, MB CAN R0J 1H0
(204) 476-2800
1,2,3,9; French materials

PORT WINE STAINS
See: Sturge-Weber Sydrome

POSTAXIAL ACROFACIAL DYSOSTOSIS
See: Nager & Miller Syndromes

PRADER-WILLI SYNDROME

Ontario Prader-Willi Syndrome Association
1920 Yonge St. c104
Toronto, ON CAN M4S 3B2
(800) 563-1123
(416) 481-8657 (voice/fax)
www3.sympatico.ca/prader-willi/
✉prader-willi@sympatico.ca
1,2,3,4,5,8,9; French materials

Prader-Willi Foundation
223 Main St.
Port Washington, NY 11050
(800) 253-7993
(516) 944-3173 (fax)
willi.inter.net
prader_willi.inter.net
✉foundation@prader-
2,3,4,7,8

The Prader-Willi Syndrome Association (USA)
5700 Midnight Pass Rd., Ste. 6
Sarasota, FL 34242
(800) 926-4797
(941) 312-0400
(941) 312-0142
www.alhenet.net/~pwsausa/index.html
✉pwsausa@aol.com
1,2,3,4,5,6,7,8,9 English, Spanish and French materials

PROGERIA

International Progeria Registry
c/o W. Ted Brown, MD, PhD
NY State Inst. for Basic Research
in Developmental Disabilities
1050 Forest Hill Rd.
Staten Island, NY 10314
(718) 494-5333
(718) 494-1026 (fax)
✉wtbibr@aol.com
3,9

PROGRESSIVE HYPOERYTHEMIA
See: Anemia, Aplastic

PROGRESSIVE OSSEOUS HETEROPLASIA
See: Connective Tissue Disorders

PROPINONYL-COA CARBOXYLASE (PCC)
See: Deficiency Acidemia, Organic

PROPIONIC ACIDEMIA
See: Acidemia, Organic

PROTEUS SYNDROME
See: Neurofibromatosis

PROTOCOPROPORPHYRIA
See: Liver Disorders; Porphyria

PROTOPORPHYRIA
See: Liver Disorders; Porphyria

PRUNE BELLY SYNDROME

Prune Belly Syndrome Network
100 UCLA Medical Plaza, Ste. 690
Los Angeles, CA 90095
(310) 825-6865
(310) 794-9962 (fax)
3,4,9

PSEUDO-HURLER POLYDYSTROPHY
See: Mucopolysaccharidosis; Tay-Sachs Disease

PSEUDOCHOLINESTERASE DEFICIENCY
See: Malignant Hyperthermia

PSEUDOXANTHOMA ELASTICUM (PXE)
See also: Connective Tissue Disorders; Heart Disorders; Macular Diseases; Visual Impairments

National Association for Pseudoxanthoma Elasticum
3500 E. 12th Ave.
Denver, CO 80218-1910
(800) 832-3765
(303) 355-3866
(303)355-3859
www.ttuhsc.edu
✉derckd@ttuhsc.edu
1,2,3,4,6,9

PSORIASIS

Canadian Psoriasis Foundation
1306 Wellington St., Ste. 500A
Ottawa, ON CAN K1Y 3B2
(800) 265-0926 (Canada only)
(613) 728-4000
(613) 728-8913 (fax)
1,2,4,5,6,8; French materials

National Psoriasis Foundation
92nd Ave.
Portland, OR 97223
(503) 244-7404
(503) 245-0626 (fax)
www.psoriasis.org
✉getinfo@npsusa.org
1,2,3,4,6,7,8,9; Spanish materials

PTOSIS
See: Blepharophimosis, Ptosis, Epicanthus Inversus Syndrome (BPES)

PULMONARY VALVULAR STENOSIS
See: Heart Disorders

PURINE METABOLIC DISORDERS

Purine Research Society
5424 Beech Ave.
Bethesda, MD 20814-1730
(301) 530-0354
(301) 564-9597
www.2.dgsys.com/~purine/
✉purine@erols.com
1,2,3,4,8

PURPURA HEMORRHAGICA
See: Purpura, Idiopathic Thrombocytopenia (ITP)

PURPURA, IDIOPATHIC THROMBOCYTOPENIA (ITP)

ITP Society
Children's Blood Foundation
333 E. 38th St.
New York, NY 10016-2745
(800) 487-7010
(212) 297-4340
(212) 297-4366 (fax)
www.ultranet.com/~itpsoc
1,2,3,4,7,8,9

PYRIMIDINE METABOLIC DISORDERS
See: Purine Metabolic Disorders

PYROGLUTAMICACIDURIA
See: Acidemia, Organic

PYRROLORPHYRIA
See: Porphyria

PYRUVATE CARBOXYLASE DEFICIENCY
See: Acidemia, Organic; Lactic Acidosis; Leigh Disease

PYRUVATE DEHYDROGENASE DEFICIENCY
See: Acidemia, Organic; Lactic Acidosis; Leigh Disease

PYRUVATE DEHYDROGENASE PHOSPHATASE
See: Lactic Acidosis; Leigh Disease

Q-T PROLONGATION
See: Long Q-T Syndrome

RAPP-HODGKINS SYNDROME
See: Cleft Palate; Craniofacial Disorders; Deaf-Blind; Ectodermal Dysplasias; Hearing Impairments; Visual Impairments

RASMUSSEN ENCEPHALITIS
See: Rasmussen Syndrome

RASMUSSEN SYNDROME
See also: Epilepsy; Seizure Disorders

Rasmussen Syndrome Support Group
c/o Al and Lynn Miller
8235 Lethbridge Rd.
Millersville, MD 21108
(410) 987-5221 (voice/fax)
www.medhlp.netusa.net/www/rasm.htm
✉rssnlynn@aol.com
1,2,3,5,6,9; Spanish/French/Russian/Greek materials

RECKLINGHAUSEN DISEASE
See: Neurofibromatosis

REFLEX SYMPATHETIC DYSTROPHY SYNDROME

Reflex Sympathetic Dystrophy Syndrome Association of America
116 Haddon Ave., Ste. D
Haddonfield, NJ 08033
(609) 795-8845 (voice/fax)
www.rsds.org
1,2,3,4,6,8,9

REFRACTORY ANEMIA
See: Anemia, Aplastic

REFSUM DISEASE
See: Ichthyosis; Leukodystrophy; Tay-Sachs Disease

RENAL DISORDERS
See: Kidney Disorders

RENDU-OSLER-WEBER SYNDROME
See: Hemorrhagic Telangiectasis, Hereditary

RESPIRATORY PAPILLOMATOSIS, RECURRENT

Recurrent Respiratory Papillomatosis Foundation
PO Box 6643
Lawrenceville, NJ 08648-0643
(609) 530-1443
(609) 258-3943 (fax)
www.members.aol.com/rrpf/rrpf.html
✉mstern@pucc.princeton.edu
1,2,3,4,7,8,9

RETINITIS PIGMENTOSA (RP)
See also: Macular Diseases; Usher Syndrome; Visual Impairments

The Foundation Fighting Blindness
Executive Plz. 1, Ste. 800
11350 McCormick Rd.
Hunt Valley, MD 21031
(888) 394-3937
(410) 771-9470 (fax)
www.blindness.org
1,2,3,4,5,6,8,9; young adult program, retina donor program

Retinitis Pigmentosa International
23241 Ventura Blvd.
Woodland Hills, CA 91364
(800) 344-4877
(818) 992-0500
(818) 992-3265 (fax)
www.rpinternational.org
✉RPINT@pacbell.net
1,2,4,7,8,9; Spanish materials

RP Research Foundation Fighting Blindness
c/o Sharon Cole or Margot Alward
36 Toronto St., Ste. 910
Toronto, ON CAN M5C 2C5
(800) 461-3331 (Canada only)
(416) 360-4200
(416) 360-0060
1,2,3,5,7,8; French materials

RETINOBLASTOMA
See also: Cancer; Visual Impairments

National Retinoblastoma Parent Group
PO Box 317
Watertown, MA 02272
(800) 562-6265
1,2,3,4,6,9

RETINOCEREBRAL ANGIOMATOSIS
See: Von Hippel-Lindau Syndrome

RETINOPATHY OF PREMATURITY (ROP) DH
See: Neonatal Illness/Prematurity; Visual Impairments

Prevent Blindness in Premature Babies
PO Box 44792
Madison, WI 53744-4792
2,3,4,9

RETT SYNDROME

International Rett Syndrome Association
9121 Piscataway Rd., Ste. 2B
Clinton, MD 20735
(800) 818-7388
(301) 856-3334
(301) 856-3336 (fax)
www.paltech.com/irsa/irsa.htm
✉irsa@paltech.com
1,2,3,4,6,7,8,9; Spanish/French/Russian/German materials

Ontario Rett Syndrome Association
147 Westdale Rd.
Oakville, ON CAN L6L 4Z7
(905) 844-7673
1,2,3,4,5,6,7,8,9

REYE SYNDROME
See: Fatty Oxidation Disorder

RILEY-DAY SYNDROME
See: Familial Dysautonomia

RING CHROMOSOME 4
See: Chromosome Deletions; Wolf-Hirschhorn Syndrome

RING CHROMOSOME 6
See: Chromosome 6 Disorders

RING CHROMOSOME 9
See: Chromosome Deletions; Craniofacial Disorders

RING CHROMOSOME 15
See: Chromosome 15 Disorders; Chromosome Deletions; Craniofacial Disorders; Epilepsy; Heart Disorders; Kidney Disorders; Limb Disorders; Scoliosis

RING CHROMOSOME 18
See: Chromosome 13 & 18 Disorders; Chromosome 18 Disorders; Chromosome Deletions; Craniofacial Disorders; Deaf-Blind; Hearing Impairments; Visual Impairments

RING CHROMOSOME 21
See: Chromosome Deletions

RING CHROMOSOME 22
See: Chromosome Deletions

ROBINOW SYNDROME
See also: Craniofacial Disorders; Short Stature

Robinow Syndrome Foundation
c/o Karla M. Kruger
15955 Uplander St. NW
Andover, MN 55304-2501
(612) 434-1152
(612) 778-2331 (fax)
1,2,3

ROMANO-WARD SYNDROME
See: Long Q-T Syndrome

ROSAI-DORFMAN DISEASE
See: Histiocytosis

ROSSELI-GULIENETTI SYNDROME
See: Ectodermal Dysplasias

ROTHMUND-THOMPSON'S SYNDROME
See: Ectodermal Dysplasias

RSH SYNDROME
See: Smith-Lemli-Opitz Syndrome

RUBINSTEIN SYNDROME
See: Rubinstein-Taybi Syndrome

RUBINSTEIN-TAYBI SYNDROME
See also: Craniofacial Disorders; Heart Disorders

Rubinstein-Taybi Parent Group
c/o Lorrie Baxter
PO Box 146
Smith Center, KS 66967
(785) 697-2984
(785) 697-2985 (fax)
www.tucson.com/rts
✉lbaxter@ruraltel.net
1,2,3,9

RUSSELL SYNDROME
See: Russell-Silver Syndrome

RUSSELL-SILVER SYNDROME
See also: Growth Disorders; Short Stature

Russell-Silver Support Group
1327 Harlem Dr.
Oak Park, IL 60302
(800) 3-Magic-3 (362-4433)
(313) 586-8038
www.nettap.com/~magic
✉lantana@awol.com
2,3,4,5,6

SAETHRE-CHOTZEN SYNDROME
See: Craniofacial Disorders

SALAMON SYNDROME
See: Ectodermal Dysplasias

SANDHOFF DISEASE
See:Tay-Sachs Disease

SANFILIPPO SYNDROME
See: Mucopolysaccharidosis; Tay-Sachs Disease

SCHEIE SYNDROME
See: Mucopolysaccharidosis; Tay-Sachs Disease

SCHINZEL-GIEDION SYNDROME
See: Apnea, Sleep; Deaf-Blind; Ectodermal Dysplasias; Epilepsy; Growth Disorders; Hearing Impairments; Visual Impairments

SCID
See: Immune Disorders

SCLERODERMA
See also: Arthritis; Autoimmune Disorders

Scleroderma Federation
Peabody Office Bldg.
89 Newbury St.
Panvers, MA 01923
(800) 722-HOPE (4673)
(978) 750-4499
(978) 750-9902 (fax)
www.scleroderma.org
✉sclerofed@aol.com
1,2,3,4,5,6,7,8,9

Scleroderma Research Foundation
PO Box 200
Columbus, NJ 08022
(800) 637-4005
(609) 723-7400
(609) 723-6700 (fax)
1,2,4

United Scleroderma Foundation, Inc.
89 Newbury St.
Peabody, MA 01960
(978) 750-4499
(978) 535-6696 (fax)
www.scleroderma.com
✉sclerofed@aol.com
1,2,4,5,6,7,8,9

SCOLIOSIS
National Scoliosis Foundation
5 Cabot Place
Stoughton, MA 02072
(781) 341-6333
(617) 341-8333
www.scoliosis.org
✉scoliosis@aol.com
1,2,3,4,5,6,7

SECKEL SYNDROME
See: Craniofacial Disorders; Growth Disorders

SEIZURE DISORDERS
See also: Aicardi Syndrome; Epilepsy

THRESHOLD—Intractable Seizure Disorder Support Group & Newsletter
2150 Highway 35, Ste. 207C
Sea Girt, NJ 08750
www.efnj.com
✉fsnj@aol.com
1

SENSORY MOTOR NEUROPATHY, HEREDITARY
See: Charcot-Marie-Tooth Disease

SENSORY NEUROPATHY WITH ANHIDROSIS, CONGENITAL
See: Familial Dysautonomia

SEPTO-OPTIC DYSPLASIA
See also: Pituitary Disorders; Visual Impairments

FOCUS: For Our Children's Unique Sight
2571 Pico Pl.
San Diego, CA 92109
(619) 273-1473 (voice/fax)
www.telepath.com/canance/focus/
✉daphari@adnc.com
1,2,3,9

SERUM PROTEASE INHIBITOR DEFICIENCY
See: Alpha-1-Antitrypsin (AAT) Deficiency

SEVERE COMBINED IMMUNODEFICIENCY (SCID)
See: Immune Disorders

SEX CHROMOSOME DISORDERS, FEMALE
See: Turner Syndrome

SEX CHROMOSOME DISORDERS, MALE
See: Klinefelter Syndrome

SHORT STATURE
See also: Dwarfism; Growth Disorders

Little People of America
PO Box 745
Lubbock, TX 79408
(888) 572-2001
www.lpaonline.org
1,2,3,5,6; Spanish materials

LPBC: A Society for Short Stature Awareness
Box 4280
Vancouver, BC CAN V6B 3Z7
(604) 688-4757
✉mmrlpbc@bc.sympatico.ca
1,2,3,4,6

SHPRINTZEN SYNDROME
See: DiGeorge Syndrome; Velo-Cardio-Facial Syndrome

SHWACHMAN SYNDROME
See also: Growth Disorders

Shwachman Syndrome Support Services
c/o Joan Mowery
4118 Quincy St
St. Louis, MO 63116
(314)352-1821 phone/fax
www.xmission.com/~4sskids
✉jjmowery@mo.net
1,2,3,4,7,9; French/Italian/Dutch materials

SHWACHMAN-DIAMOND SYNDROME
See: Shwachman Syndrome

SIALIDOSIS
See: Mucopolysaccharidosis; Tay-Sachs Disease

SIALOLIPIDOSIS
See: Mucolipidosis Type IV

SICKLE CELL ANEMIA
See: Sickle Cell Disease

SICKLE CELL DISEASE
Sickle Cell Disease Association of America
200 Corporate Pointe, Ste. 495
Culver City, CA 90203-7633
(800) 421-8453
(310) 216-6363
(310) 215-3722 (fax)
1,2,3,4,5,6,8,9

Sickle Cell Disease Association of the Piedmont
1102 E. Market St.
Greensboro, NC 27401-0964
(800) 733-8297
(336) 274-1507
(336) 275-7984 (fax)
✉scdap@aol.com
1,2,3,4,7

Sickle Cell Society
6999 Cote Des Neiges, Ste 33
Montreal, PQ CAN H3S 2B8
(514) 735-5109
(514) 735-5100 (fax)
2,3,4,8,9; French materials

SIDS
See: Sudden Infant Death Syndrome (SIDS)

SILVER SYNDROME
See: Russell-Silver Syndrome

SILVER-RUSSELL SYNDROME
See: Russell-Silver Syndrome

SIMPSON-GOLABI-BEHMEL SYNDROME
See: Beckwith-Wiedermann Syndrome

SKELETAL ANOMALIES
See: Ectodermal Dysplasias

SKELETAL DYSPLASIA
See: Dwarfism; Growth Disorders; Short Stature

SLEEP APNEA
See: Apnea, Sleep

SLO SYNDROME
See: Smith-Lemli-Opitz Syndrome

SLY SYNDROME
See: Mucopolysaccharidosis; Tay-Sachs Disease

SMITH-LEMLI-OPITZ SYNDROME
See also: Craniofacial Disorders

Smith-Lemli-Opitz Advocacy & Exchange
32 Ivy Ln.
Glen Mills, PA 19342
(610)361-9663
www.members.aol.com/slo97/index.htm
1,2,3,6,9

SMITH-MAGENIS SYNDROME
PRISMS: Parents & Researchers Interested in Smith-Magenis Syndrome
11875 Fawn Ridge Ln.
Reston, VA 20194
(703) 709-0568
✉acmsmith@nchgr.nih.gov
1,2,3,4,6,9

SOTOS SYNDROME
See also: Cerebral Palsy; Growth Disorders, Neurofibromatosis.

Sotos Syndrome USA Support Association
Three Danada Sq. E., #235
Wheaton, IL 60187
(888) 246-SSSA
(630) 682-8815 (international)
www.well.com/user/sssa/
✉sssa@well.com
1,2,3,6

SOUQUES-CHARCOT SYNDROME
See: Progeria

SOUTH AFRICAN GENETIC PORPHYRIA
See: Liver Disorders; Porphyria

SPASMODIC DYSPHONIA
See: Dystonia

SPASMODIC TORTICOLLIS
See: Dystonia

SPASMODIC WRYNECK
See: Dystonia

SPASTIC PARAPLEGIA, FAMILIAR
See: Ataxia

SPEECH DISORDERS
See: Aphasia; Apraxia; Stuttering

SPHINGOMYELIN LIPIDOSIS
See: Niemann-Pick Disease

SPIELMEYER-VOGT DISEASE
See: Batten Disease

SPIELMEYER-VOGT-BATTEN SYNDROME
See: Batten Disease

SPINA BIFIDA
See also: Arnold-Chiari Malformation; Hydrocephalus; Incontinence; Latex Allergy

Spina Bifida Association of America
4590 MacArthur Blvd. NW, Ste. 250
Washington, DC 20007-4226
(800) 621-3141
(202) 944-3285
(202) 944-3295 (fax)
www.sbaa.org
✉sbaa@abaa.org
1,2,4,5,6,8; Spanish materials, scholarship program

Spina Bifida Association of Canada
220-388 Donald St.
Winnipeg, MB CAN R3B 2J4
(800) 565-9488 (CAN only)
(204) 925-3650
(204) 925-3654 (fax)
✉spinab@mts.net
1,2,4,5,6,7,8; French materials

SPINAL CORD INJURIES
See also: Ventilator Use

American Paralysis Association
500 Morris Ave.
Springfield, NJ 07081
(800) 225-0292
(973) 379-2690
(973) 912-9433 (fax)
www.apa/paralysis
✉paralysis@aol.com
1,2,8

National Spinal Cord Injury Association
8300 Colesville Rd., Ste. 551
Silver Spring, MD 20910
(800) 962-9629 (hotline only)
(301) 588-6959
(301) 588-9414 (fax)
www.trader.com/users/5010/1020/nscia.html
✉NSCIA2@aol.com
1,2,3,4,5,8; Spanish materials

National Spinal Cord Injury Hotline
2200 Kernon Dr.
Baltimore, MD 21207
(800) 526-3456
(410) 448-6623 (local)
(410) 448-6627 (fax)
✉scihotline@aol.com
2,3,4

SPINAL MUSCULAR ATROPHY
See also: Muscular Dystrophy; Ventilator Use

Families of SMA
PO Box 196
Libertyville, IL 60048-0196
(800) 886-1762
(847) 367-7620
(847) 367-7623 (fax)
www.abacus96.com/fsma/
✉sma@interaccess.com
1,2,3,4,5,6,7,8,9; Spanish materials

SPINOCEREBELLAR ATAXIA
See: Ataxia; Friedreich Ataxia

SPLENIC ANEMIA, FAMILIAL
See: Gaucher Disease

SPONDYLOEPIPHYSEAL DYSPLASIA CONGENITA
See: Cleft Palate; Growth Disorders; Visual Impairments

SPONDYLOEPIPHYSEAL DYSPLASIA TARDA
See: Growth Disorders

SSPE
See: Subacute Sclerosing Panencephalitis

STAR PROTEIN DEFICIENCY
See: Adrenal Hyperplasia, Congenital

STEELY HAIR DISEASE
See: Menkes Disease

STENGEL SYNDROME
See: Batten Disease

STENGEL-BATTEN-MAYOU-SPIELMEYER-VOGT DISEASE
See: Batten Disease

STROKE

Heart and Stroke Foundation of Canada
222 Queens St., Ste. 1402
Ottawa, ON CAN K1P 5V9
(613) 569-4361
(613) 241-3278 (fax)

National Stroke Association
96 Inverness Dr. E., Ste. 1
Englewood, CO 80112-5112
(800) 787-6537
(303) 649-9299
(303) 649-1328 (fax)
www.stroke.org
✉info@stroke.org
1,2,5,6,7,8;Spanish/French materials

STURGE-KALISCHER-WEBER SYNDROME
See: Sturge-Weber Syndrome

STURGE-WEBER SYNDROME
See: Craniofacial Disorders; Epilepsy; Glaucoma; Klippel-Trenaunay Syndrome; Nevi, Giant Congenital; Neurofibramatosis; Tuberous Sclerosis; Vascular Malformations; Von Hippel-Lindau Syndrome

Sturge-Weber Foundation
PO Box 418
Mount Freedom, NJ 07970
(800) 627-5482
(201) 895-4445
(201) 895-4846 (fax)
www.inforamp.net/~crs0590/mission.html
✉swf@pobox.com
1,2,3,4,6,7,8,9

Sturge-Weber Foundation (Canada) Inc.
1960 Prairie Ave.
Port Coquitlam, BC CAN V3B 1V4
(604) 942-9209
(604) 942-6429 (fax)
www.inforamp.net/~cvs0590
✉kmoore@axionet.com
1,2,3,4,6,7,8,9

STURGE-WEBER-DIMITRI SYNDROME
See: Sturge-Weber Syndrome

STUTTERING

National Center for Stuttering
200 E. 33rd St.
New York, NY 10016
(800) 221-2483
(212) 683-1372 (fax)
www.stuttering.com
✉executivedirector@stuttering.com
2,4,5; Spanish materials

Speak Easy
c/o Mike Hughes
95 Evergreen Ave.
St. John, NB CAN E2N 1H4
(506) 696-6799 (voice/fax)
www.mi.net/poley/speakezy.htm
✉speakez@nbnwt.nb.ca
1,2,4,5,6,7

Stuttering Foundation of America
PO Box 11749
Memphis, TN 38111-0749
(800) 992-9392
(901) 452-7343
(901) 452-3931 (fax)
www.stuttersfa.org
✉stuttersfa@aol.com
1,2,4; Spanish materials

SUBACUTE NECROTIZING ENCEPHALOPATHY
See: Leigh Disease; Mitocondrial Disorders

SUBACUTE SCLEROSING PANENCEPHALITIS
See also: Epilepsy; Visual Impairments

National Subacute Sclerosing Panencephalitis Registry
c/o Paul Dyken, Director
Institute of Research in Childhood Neurodegenerative Disorders
PO Box 70191
Mobile, AL 36610-0191
(334) 478-6424
(334) 476-8277 (fax)
✉pdyken@awol.com
2,6,9

SUCCINYLCHOLINE SENSITIVITY
See: Malignant Hyperthermia

SUDDEN INFANT DEATH SYNDROME (SIDS)
See also: Bereavement Support

Canadian Foundation for the Study of Infant Deaths
586 Eglinton Ave. E., Ste. 308
Toronto, ON CA M4P1P2
(800) 363-7437
(416) 488-3260
(416) 488-3864 (fax)
www.sidscanada.org/sids
✉sidscanada@inforamp.net
1,2,3,4,5,6,8; French/Spanish materials

National Sudden Infant Death Syndrome Resource Center
8201 Greensboro Dr., Ste. 600
McLean, VA 22102
(703) 821-8955
(703) 821-2098 (fax)
www.ichp.ufl.edu/mch_netlink/sids/sids1.htm
1,2,4; Spanish materials

SUDECK ATROPHY
See: Reflex Sympathetic Dystrophy Syndrome

SULFATIDOSIS, JUVENILE, AUSTIN TYPE
See: Hearing Impairments; Ichthyosis; Leukodystrophy; Tay-Sachs Disease

SURDICARDIAC SYNDROME
See: Hearing Impairments; Long Q-T Syndrome

SWEDISH PORPHYRIA
See: Porphyria

SYNDACTYLIC OXYCEPHALY
See: Apert Syndrome

SYRINGOBULBIA
See: Syringomyelia

SYRINGOMYELIA
See also: Arnold-Chiari Malformation

ASAP: American Syringomyelia Alliance Project
PO Box 1586
300 Green St., Ste. 206
Longview, TX 75606-1586
(800) 272-7282
(903) 236-7079
(903) 757-7456 (fax)
www.dataprompt.com/syringo
✉102563.3507@compuserve.com
1,2,3,6,9

SYSTEMIC ELASTORRHEXIS OF TOURAINE
See: Pseudoxanthoma Elasticum (PXE)

SYSTEMIC MAST CELL DISEASE
See: Mastocytosis

TANGIER DISEASE
See: Tay-Sachs Disease

TARGET CELL ANEMIA
See: Cooley Anemia

TARUI DISEASE
See: Glycogen Storage Diseases; Muscular Dystroph

TAY SYNDROME
See: Ichthyosis

TAY-SACHS DISEASE

National Tay-Sachs and Allied Diseases Association
2001 Beacon St., Ste. 204
Brighton, MA 02135
(800) 90-NTSAD
(617) 277-4463
(617) 277-0134 (fax)
www.mcrcr2.med.nyu.edu/murph01/taysachs.htm
✉ntsad_boston@worldnet.att.net
1,2,3,4,5,6,7,8,9; Russian materials

TEF
See: VATERL Association

TESCHLER-NICOLA/KILLIAN SYNDROME
See: Pallister-Killian Syndrome

THALASSEMIA MAJOR
See: Cooley Anemia

THROMBOCYTOPENIA ABSENT RADIUS (TAR) SYNDROME
See also: Heart Disorders; Kidney Disorders; Short Stature

Thrombocytopenia Absent Radius Syndrome Association
212 Sherwood Dr.
Egg Harbor Twp, NJ 08234-7658
(609) 927-0418
✉tarsa@aol.com
1,2,3,4,9

THYROID DISORDERS

Hypoparathyroidism Thyroid Foundation of America
Ruth Sleeper Hall, RSL 350
40 Parkman St.
Boston, MA 02114-2698
(800) 832-8321
(617) 726-8500
(617) 726-4136 (fax)
www.tfawev.org/pub/tfa
✉tfa@clark.net
1,2,4,5,7

Hypoparathyroidism Thyroid Foundation of Canada
1040 Gardeners Rd., Ste. C
Kingston, ON CAN K7P 1R7
(613) 634-3426
(613) 634-3483 (fax)
www.home.ican.net/~!thyroid.Canada.html
✉thyroid@limestone.kosone.com
1,2,5,6,8

TOOTH AND NAIL SYNDROME
See: Ectodermal Dysplasias

TORSION DYSTONIA, IDIOPATHIC
See: Dystonia

TOURETTE SYNDROME
See also: Attention Deficit Disorder; Obsessive-Compulsive Disorder

Tourette Syndrome Association
42-40 Bell Blvd.
Bayside, NY 11361-2820
(718) 224-2999
(718) 279-9596 (fax)
neuro.www2.mgh.harvard.edu/tsa/tsamain.nclk
✉tourette@ix.netcom.com
1,2,4,5,6,7,8,9; Spanish materials

Tourette Syndrome Foundation of Canada
194 Jarvis St., Ste. 206
Toronto, ON CAN M5B 2B7
(800) 361-3120 (Canada only)
(416) 861-8398
(416) 861-2472 (fax)
www.tourette.ca
✉tffc.org@sympatico.ca
1,2,3,4,5,6,7,8,9; French materials

TOXIC PARALYTIC ANEMIA
See: Anemia, Aplastic

TOXOCARIASIS

National Toxicariasis Foundation Project Mustard Seed
815 Hillboro Rd.
Edwardsville, IL 62025
(618) 659-1212
(618) 656-3965
✉lmsjursen@hotmail.com
1,2,3,4,5,6,7,8,9

TRACHEOESOPHAGEAL FISTULA (TEF)
See: VATERL Association

TREACHER COLLINS SYNDROME
See also: Craniofacial Disorders; Hearing Impairments

Treacher Collins Foundation
PO Box 683
Norwich, VT 05055
(800) 823-2055
(802) 649-3050
1,2,3,4,6

TREMOR

International Tremor Foundation
7046 W. 105th St.
Overland Park, KS 60607
(913) 341-3880
(913) 341-1296 (fax)
✉inttremorfnd@worldnet.att.net
1,2,3,4,5,8,9

TRICHODENTOOSSEOUS SYNDROME; TYPES I, II & III
See: Ectodermal Dysplasias

TRICHODYSPLASIA-ONYCHOGRYPOSIS-HYPOHIDROSIS-CATARACT
See: Ectodermal Dysplasias

TRICHOFACIOHYPOHIDROTIC SYNDROME
See: Ectodermal Dysplasias

TRICHONYCHODENTAL DYSPLASIA
See: Ectodermal Dysplasias

TRICHONYCHODYSPLASIA WITH XERODERMA
See: Ectodermal Dysplasias

TRICHOOCULODERMOVERTEBRAL SYNDROME
See: Ectodermal Dysplasias

KEY TO SERVICES

1 Periodical/newsletter
2 Informational materials
3 Networking/matching
4 Referrals to local resources
5 Local chapters
6 National conferences
7 National advocacy efforts
8 Fund research
9 Maintain research registry

TRICHOODONTOONYCHIAL DYSPLASIA
See: Ectodermal Dysplasias

TRICHOODONTOONYCHO-HYPOHIDROTIC DYSPLASIA WITH CATARACT
See: Ectodermal Dysplasias

TRICHOODONTOONYCHO-DERMAL SYNDROME
See: Ectodermal Dysplasias

TRICHOODONTOONYCHO-DYSPLASIA WITH PILI TORTI
See: Ectodermal Dysplasias

TRICHOPOLIODYSTROPHY
See: Menkes Disease

TRICHORHINOPHA-LANGEAL SYNDROME (TRPS), TYPE 1
See: Ectodermal Dysplasias

TRICHOTILLOMANIA
See: Obsessive-Compulsive Disorder

TRIPHALANGEAL THUMBS-ONYCHODYSTROPHY-DEAFNESS
See: Ectodermal Dysplasias;
Hearing Impairments

TRP SYNDROME, TYPE I
See: Ectodermal Dysplasias

TRPS SYNDROME, TYPE II
See: Langer Gideon Syndrome

TUBEROUS SCLEROSIS
See also: Autism; Epilepsy;
Learning Disabilities

National Tuberous Sclerosis Association
8181 Professional Pl., Ste. 110
Landover, MD 20785-2226
(800) 225-6872
(301) 459-9888
(301) 459-0394 (fax)
www.ntsa.org
✉ntsa@ntsa.org
1,2,3,4,8,9

Tuberous Sclerosis Canada Sclérose Tubéreuse
2443 New Wood Dr.
Oakville, ON CA L6H 5Y3
(800) 347-0252
(905) 257-1997
www.sky.net/~adamse/
tuberous.htm
✉jillian.dasilva@ablelink.org
1,2,3,4,7,8,9; lending library
(books, videos)

TURCOT SYNDROME
See: Brain Tumors; Cancer

TURNER SYNDROME
See also: Growth Disorders

Turner's Syndrome Society of Canada
814 Glencairn Ave.
Toronto, ON CAN M6B 2A3
(800) 465-6744
(416) 781-2086
(416) 781-7245 (fax)
✉tssincan@web.net
1,2,3,4,5,6, French Materials

Turner's Syndrome Society of the US
1313 SE 5th St., Ste. 327
Minneapolis, MN 55414
(800) 365-9944
(612) 379-3607
(612) 379-3619 (fax)
www.turner-syndrome-us.org
✉Lampim@aol.com
1,2,3,5,6,9; Spanish materials

TWIN-RELATED DISEASES

Conjoined Twins International
PO Box 10895
Prescott, AZ 86304-0895
✉jmsjr@northlink.com

Twin Hope
2592 W. 14th St.
Cleveland, OH 44113
(216) 228-8887
www.twinhope.com
✉twinhope@mail.ohio.net
1,2,3,4,5,7,8,9

TWIN TO TWIN TRANSFUSION SYNDROME
See also: Twin-Related Diseases

Twin to Twin Transfusion Syndrome Foundation
411 Longbeach Pkwy.
Bay Village, OH 44140
(440) 899-8887
(440) 401-8887 (urgent calls only)
(440) 899-1184 (fax)
www.tttsfoundation.org
✉tttsfound@aol.com
1,2,3,4,5,7,8,9

TYROSINEMIA, HEREDITARY, HEPATORENAL TYPE
See: Tyrosinemia I

TYROSINEMIA I
See also: Kidney Disorders;
Liver Disorders

Groupe Aide aux Enfants Tyrosinemiques du Quebec
3162 rue Granville
Jonquiere, QC CAN G7S 2B9
(418) 548-1580
✉gerard.tremlay@sympatico.ca
1,2,4,5,9; French materials

TYROSYLURIA
See: Tyrosinemia I

UREA CYCLE DISORDERS
See: Metabolic Disorders

National Urea Cycle Disorders Foundation
4841 Hill St.
La Canada, CA 91011
(800) 386-8233
www.nucdf.org
1,2,3,4,6,7,8,9

UROLOGIC DISORDERS
See: Incontinence; Kidney Diseases;
Hereditary; Kidney Disorders

UROSTOMY
See: Ostomy

URTICARIA PIGMENTOSA
See: Mastocytosis

USHER SYNDROME
See also: Deaf-Blind; Hearing
Impairments; Retinitis Pigmentosa;
Visual Impairments

Usher Around The World
c/o Kathie Anderson
PO Box 17318
Minneapolis, MN 55417
(612) 729-4630 (voice/TTY)
1,3

VACTERL ASSOCIATION
See also: Anorectal Malformations;
CHARGE Association; Heart
Disorders; Kidney Disorders; Limb
Disorders; Spina Bifida

TEF/VATER International Support Network
c/o Greg and Terri Burke
15301 Grey Fox Rd.
Upper Marlboro, MD 20772
(301) 952-6837
1,2,3,7,8,9

VAN MEERKEREN I SYNDROME
See: Ehlers-Danlos Syndrome

VASCULAR MALFORMATIONS
See also: Arteriovenous
Malformations (AVMs); Hemangioma;
Hemorrhagic Telangiectasis,
Hereditary; Klippel-Trenaunay
Syndrome; Lymphatic Malformations;
Moyamoya Disease; Nevi, Giant
Congenital; Sturge-Weber Syndrome;
Von Hippel-Lindau Syndrome

National Vascular Malformations Foundation
8320 Nightingale
Dearborn Heights, MI 48127
(313) 274-1243
(313) 274-1393 (fax)
1,2,3,4,6

VATER ASSOCIATION
See: VACTERL Association

VELO-CARDIO-FACIAL SYNDROME
See also: CHARGE Association;
Craniofacial Disorders; Heart Disorders

Northeast VCFS Support Group
2 Lansing Dr.
Salem, NH 03079
(603) 898-6332
✉MLADJA@aol.com
1,2,3,6,9; International
educational foundation
for research

Velo-Cardio-Facial Syndrome Parent Support Group
110-45 Queens Blvd.
Forest Hills, NY 11375-5501
(718) 261-8049
(718) 261-7346 (fax)
2,3,4,9

VENOUS MALFORMATIONS
See: Vascular Malformations

VENTILATOR USE

Citizens for Independence in Living & Breathing
78 Golfwood Hights
Toronto, ON CAN M9P 3M2
(416) 244-2248 (voice/fax)
2,3,4,6,7,9

International Ventilator Users Networks
4207 Lindell Blvd., #110
St Louis, MO 63108-2915
(314) 534-0475
(314) 534-5070 (fax)
✉gini_intl@msn.com
✉jfisc48232@aol.com
1,2,3,4,6,7,9

VENTRICULAR DEFECTS
See: Heart Disorders

VERMIS CEREBELLAR AGENESIS
See: Joubert Syndrome

VESTIBULAR DISORDERS
See also: Balance Disorders & Dizziness

Vestibular Disorders Association
PO Box 4467
Portland, OR 97208-4467
(800) 837-8428
(503) 229-8604 (fax)
www.vestibular.org
✉veda@teleport.org
1,2,3,4,5; Spanish materials

VISUAL IMPAIRMENT/ HEARING IMPAIRMENT
See: Deaf-Blind

VISUAL IMPAIRMENT
See also: Albinism; Glaucoma;
Macular Diseases; Retinitis
Pigmentosa; Retinoblastoma;
Retinopathy of Prematurity; Septo-
Optic Dysplasia; Usher Syndrome

American Council of the Blind
1155 15th St. NW, Ste. 720
Washington, DC 20005
(800) 424-8666 (3–5:30 p.m. EST)
(202) 467-5081
(202) 467-5085 (fax)
www.acb.org
✉ncrabb@access.digex.net
1,2,4,5,6,7

American Foundation for the Blind
11 Penn Plz., Ste. 300
New York, NY 10001
(800) 232-5463
(212) 502-7600
(212) 502-7662 (TTY)
www.afb.org/afb
✉afbinfo@afb.org
1,2,4,5,8

Blind Childrens Center
4120 Marathon St.
Los Angeles, CA 90029
(800) 222-3566
(800) 222-3567 (CA only)
(213) 664-2153
(213) 665-3828 (fax)
www.blindcntr.org/bcc
✉info@blindcntr.org
1,2,3,4,8; Spanish materials

Blind Childrens Fund
4740 Okemos Rd.
Okemos, MI 48864
(517) 347-1357
(517) 347-1459 (fax)
www.blindchildrensfund.org
✉lblindschildrensfund@aol. com
1,2,4,6

Blind Children's Fund Resource Center
2971 53rd St. SE
Auburn, WA 98092
(206) 735-6350 (voice/fax)
✉blindchildrensfund@charitiesusa.com
1,2,4,6

Braille Institute of America
741 N. Vermont Ave.
Los Angeles, CA 90029
(213) 663-1111
www.brailleinstitute.org
✉julief@brailleinstitute.org

Canadian National Institute for the Blind
1929 Bayview Ave.
Toronto, ON CAN M4G 3E8
(416) 486-2500
(416) 480-7417 (TTY)
(416) 480-7699 (fax)
✉marjerb@east.cnib.ca
1,2,3,4,6,7,8; French materials

Council of Citizens with Low Vision International
6511 26th St. W.
Bradenton, FL 34207
(800) 317-2258
(941) 755-3846
1,2,3,4,7,8

Council of Families with Vision Impairment
6212 W. Franklin St.
Richmond, VA 23226
(804) 288-0395
1,2,3,4,6,7

The Lighthouse National Center for Vision and Child Development
111 E. 59th St.
New York, NY 10022
(800) 829-0500
(212) 821-9200
(212) 821-9713 (TTY)
(212) 821-9705 (fax)
✉mbeck@lighthouse.org
1,2,4,7; Spanish materials

National Association for Parents of the Visually Impaired
PO Box 317
Watertown, MA 02471
(800) 562-6265
(617) 972-7441
(617) 972-7444 (fax)
www.spedex.com/napvi
1,2,3,5,7; Spanish materials

National Association for Visually Handicapped
22 W 21st St., 6th Fl.
New York, NY 10010
(212) 889-3141
(212) 727-2931 (fax)
www.navh.org
✉staff@navh.org
1,2,4,7; Spanish materials, large-print lending library

National Braille Press
88 St. Stephen St.
Boston, MA 02115
(617) 266-6160
(617) 437-0456 (fax)
(800) 548-7323
www.npb.org
✉orders@nbp.org
2

National Organization of Parents of Blind Children
1800 Johnson St.
Baltimore, MD 21230
(410) 659-9314
(612) 696-1975 (BBS)
(410) 685-5653 (fax)
www.nfb.org
✉nfb@access.digex.net
1,2,3,4,5,6,7

Prevent Blindness America
500 E. Remington Rd.
Schaumburg, IL 60173-4557
(800) 331-2020
(847) 843-2020
(847) 843-8458 (fax)
www.prevent_blindness.org
✉74777.100@compuserve.com
1,2,5,6,7,8; Spanish materials

Recording for the Blind & Dyslexic
20 Roszel Rd.
Princeton, NJ 08540
(609) 520-8079
(609) 520-7990 (fax
www.rfbd.org
✉info2rfbd.org
2

Vision World Wide, Inc.
5707 Brockton Dr., Ste. 302
Indianapolis, IN 46220-5481
(800) 431-1739
(317) 254-1332
(317) 251-6588 (fax)
www.netdirect.net/vision-enhancement/
✉patprice@aol.com
1,2,4

**VITAMIN B12 METABOLISM;
INBORN ERROR OF**
See: Cobalamin (B12) Deficiency

VITILIGO
National Vitiligo Foundation
100 Independence Pl., Ste. 200
Tyler, TX 75703
(903) 534-2925
(903) 534-8075 (fax)
www.nvfi.org
✉373071.33@compuserve.com
1,2,5,8, Spanish materials

The Canadian Vitiligo Society
Dr. Danuta Pawlowski
Western General Hospital
8th Fl., Rm. 542
399 Bathurst St.
Toronto, ON CAN M5T 2S8
(416) 603-5721

VOGT CEPHALODACTYLY
See: Apert Syndrome

VON GIERKE DISEASE
See: Glycogen Storage Diseases

VON HIPPEL-LINDAU SYNDROME
*See also: Ataxia; Balance
Disorders & Dizziness; Brain
Tumors; Visual Impairments*
**Von Hippel-Lindau Syndrome
Family Alliance**
171 Clinton Rd.
Brookline, MA 02445-5815
(800) 767-4845
(617) 232-5946
(617) 734-8233
neurosurgery_mbh.harvard.edu/
vhl-fa/
✉vhl@pipeline.com
*1,2,3,4,5,7,8,9;
Spanish/French/German/Dutch/
Italian materials*

VON RECKLINGHAUSEN DISEASE
See: Neurofibromatosis

VON WILLEBRAND DISEASE
See: Hemophilia

VROLIK DISEASE, TYPE II
See: Osteogenesis Imperfecta

WAGNER SYNDROME
See: Stickler Syndrome

**WALBAUM-DEHEANE-
SCHLEMMER SYNDROME**
See: Ectodermal Dysplasias

WALKER-WARBURG SYNDROME
See: Hydrocephalus; Lissencephaly

WARBURG SYNDROME
See: Hydrocephalus; Lissencephaly

WEAVER-SMITH SYNDROME
See: Weaver Syndrome

WEBER SYNDROME
See: Sturge-Weber Syndrome

WEGENER GRANULOMATOSIS
See also: Immune Disorders
**Wegener's Granulomatosis
Support Group, Inc. (International)**
PO Box 28660
Kansas City, MO 64188-8660
(800) 277-9474
(816) 436-8211 (fax)
✉wgsg@wgsg.org
www.wgsg.org
1,2,3,5,6,9

WERDNIG-HOFFMAN DISEASE
See: Spinal Muscular Atrophy

WERLHOF DISEASE
*See: Purpura, Idiopathic
Thrombocytopenia (ITP)*

WERMER SYNDROME
See: Multiple Endocrine Neoplasia I

WERNER SYNDROME
See: Progeria

WHISTLING FACE SYNDROME
See: Freeman-Sheldon Syndrome

**WHISTLING FACE-WINDMILL
VEIN HAND SYNDROME**
See: Freeman-Sheldon Syndrome

WHITE MATTER DISORDERS
See: Leukodystrophy

WHITE SPOT DISEASE
See: Vitiligo

WHITNALL-NORMAN SYNDROME
See: Norrie Disease

WILLIAMS SYNDROME
*See also: Autism; Attention Deficit
Disorder; Growth Disorders; Heart
Disorders; Learning Disabilities;
Noonan Syndrome*
**Canadian Association for
Williams Syndrome**
PO Box 2115
Vancouver, BC CAN V6B 3T5
(604) 852-2662
(604) 855-0032 (fax)
www.bmts.com/~williams/
✉lsev@uniserve.com
1,2,3,4,5,7,8,9

Williams Syndrome Association
PO Box 297
Clawson, MI 48017-0297
(241) 541-3630
(241) 541-3631 (fax)
members.aol.com/BobHazard/
wsc.html
✉WSAoffice@aol.com
*1,2,3,4,5,6,8,9; DNA research
bank, annual music camp*

WILLIAMS-BEUREN SYNDROME
See: Williams Syndrome

WILMS TUMOR
See: Kidney Disorders

WISKOTT-ALDRICH SYNDROME
*See: Immune Disorders; Purpura,
Immune Thrombocytopenia*

WOLF SYNDROME
See: Wolf-Hirshhorn Syndrome

WOLF-HIRSCHHORN SYNDROME
4p- Parent Network
913 Herons Run Ln.
Woodbridge, VA 22191
(703) 497-2807
members.aol.com/lbent503/whs
✉tombecr@aol.com
1,2,3,6,9

**Wolf-Hirschhorn Syndrome
Support Group and Newsletter**
c/o Brenda Grimmett
5536 Virginia Ct.
Amherst, OH 44001
(440) 282-1460
members.aol.com/lbent503/whs
✉lbentely@orednet.org
1,2,3,6,9

X-LINKED COPPER DEFICIENCY
See: Menkes Disease

**X-LINKED COPPER
MALABSORPTION**
See: Menkes Disease

**X-LINKED MYOTUBULAR
MYOPATHY**
*See: Myotubular Myopathy, X-Linked;
Muscular Dystrophy*

XERODERMA PIGMENTOSUM
**Canadian Organization of Rare
Disorders (CORD)**
PO Box 814
Coaldale, AB CAN T1M 1M7
(403) 345-3948
(403) 345-4544
www.bulli.com/~cord
✉cord@bulli.com
1,4,5,6

Easter Seals Society
1185 Eglinton Ave., Ste. 800
Don Mills, ON CAN 3C 3P2
(416) 421-8377
(416)696-1035 (fax)
www.easterseals.org
✉info@easterseals.org

**XERODERMA-TALIPES-
ENAMEL DEFECT**
See: Ectodermal Dysplasias

ZANIER-ROUBICEK SYNDROME
See: Ectodermal Dysplasias

ZELLWEGER SYNDROME
See: Leukodystrophy

ZIEHEN-OPPENHEIM DISEASE
See: Dystonia

KEY TO SERVICES
1 Periodical/newsletter
2 Informational materials
3 Networking/matching
4 Referrals to local resources
5 Local chapters
6 National conferences
7 National advocacy efforts
8 Fund research
9 Maintain research registry

MATCHING RESOURCES

This directory of "Matching Resources"—both national and international—can help some parents who have children with extremely rare conditions or unique combinations of disabilities. Others may be dealing with unique family situations, such as single parenting, raising twins, or adoption. These networking organizations do parent-to-parent matching based on children's disabilities and, in some cases, other unique family situations. Most maintain ongoing contact with other groups worldwide.

Unless otherwise noted, all services are provided free of charge. This symbol, ✉, indicates an e-mail address. All international calls from the US or Canada require dialing 011 before the number. Please be aware of timezone differences when making any calls, particularly international ones. (Unless otherwise noted, telephone numbers are for voice only.)

Association of Birth Defect Children
930 Woodcock Rd., Ste. 225
Orlando, FL 32803
(800) 313-2232 (24-hour
registry line)
(407) 245-7035
(407) 895-0824 (fax)
www.birthdefects.org
✉abdc@birthdefects.org

**Association of Genetic
Support/ Australia**
740 66 Albion St.
Surry Hills, NSW 2010
Australia
(61) 2211 1462

**Canadian Organization for Rare
Disorders (CORD)**
PO Box 814
Coaldale, AB CAN T1M 1M7
(403)345-3948
(403)345-4544
www.bulli.com/~cord
✉cord@bulli.com

**The Centre for Rare Diseases
and Disabilities**
Copenhagen:
Bredgrade 25
Sct. Annae Passage,
opg F, 5th Fl.
DK-1260 Copenhagen K
Denmark
(45) 33 91 40 20
(45) 33 91 40 19 (fax)

Easter Seal Society
250 Ferrand Dr., Ste. 200
Don Mills, ON CAN M3C 3P2
(416) 421-8377
(416) 696-1035 (fax)
www.easterseals.org
✉info@easterseals.org

MUMS
Mothers United for Moral Support
c/o Julie Gordon
150 Cousta Ct.
Green Bay, WI 54301-1243
(920) 336-5333
(920) 339-0995 (fax)
www.waisman.wisc.edu/~rowley/
mums/home.htmlx
✉mums@netnet.net

**National Organization for Rare
Disorders (NORD)**
100 Rt. 37, PO Box 8923
New Fairfield, CT 06812-8923
(800) 999-6673 (voice)
(203) 746-6518 (voice)
(203) 746-6927 (TTY)
(203) 746-6481 (fax)
www.nord_rdb.com/~orphan
✉orphan@nord_rdb.com

NPSIS
**National Parent to Parent
Support and Information Service**
PO Box 907
Blue Ridge, GA 30513
(800) 651-1151
(706) 632-8830
www.npsis.org
✉jjudd103w@wonder.em.cdc.gov

Parent-to-Parent Link Program
The Easter Seal Society, Ontario
1185 Eglinton Ave., Ste. 800
Don Mills, ON CAN M3C 3P2
(416) 421-8377
(416) 696-1035 (fax)
www.easterseals.org
✉info@easterseals.org

Rare Chromosome Disorder Group
160 Locket Rd.
Harrow Weald
Middlesex
England HA3 7NZ
(44) 181-863-3557 (voice, evening)

**Research Trust for Metabolic
Diseases in Children**
Golden Gates Lodge
Weston Rd., Crewe
Cheshire, England CW2 5XN
(44) 1270 250221
(44) 1270 250244 (fax)

OTHER RESOURCES
Search and Respond
c/o Exceptional Parent Magazine
555 Kinderkamack Rd.
Oradell, NJ 07649-1517
(201) 634-6550
(201) 634-6570 (fax)
www.eparent.com
Exceptional Parent magazine accepts letters from parents and professionals searching for information, networking, or advice from others on a disability or related problem. Some are selected for publication in our monthly Search column. Anyone offering a suggestion may write a Respond letter, which will be forwarded and may also be published.

Information

To order more books, please check with your local bookstore. If not available, please send a check for $27.50 (includes $2.50 shipping and handling) to:

A Certain Kind of Love
P.O. Box 97
Westerly, Rhode Island 02891

To request information about speaking engagements by the authors please write to *A Certain Kind of Love* at the above address.

Visit our Web site at:
www.acertainkindoflove.com

Web site created by:
Erin Michelle Wright and Jeff Tucker

To comment about the book e-mail us at:
book@acertainkindoflove.com

A very special thanks
to our writers and their families
for opening their homes and hearts to our readers.